Green Volunteers

The World Guide to Voluntary Work in Nature Conservation

Green Volunteers
Publications

Green Volunteers

The World Guide to Voluntary Work in Nature Conservation

Editor:	Fabio Ausenda, assisted by Francesco Foresti
Cover design:	Roberta Romagnoni, Milano
Cover photos:	African Impact Lion Rehabilitation Programme, Zimbabwe
	Courtesy Umberto Pajarola, Switzerland (1st winner of the
	Green Volunteers Photo Contest, see page 254).
	Sea Turtle Summer Field Work, Greece
	Courtesy Erin McCloskey, Canada
	Gibbon Rehabilitation Program, Thailand
	Courtesy Rossella Rossi, Italy

This Guide is not an annual publication. Readers can keep it up to date and be constantly informed of new conservation volunteering opportunities through the *Green Volunteers Database* (see page 3 for access details) and its e-mail newsletter.

Published by: Green Volunteers di Fabio Ausenda
Via Canonica 72
I-20154 Milano, Italy
www.greenvolunteers.com - green@greenvolunteers.org

US & Canada distribution:	Universe Publishing
	A division of Rizzoli International Publications, Inc.
	300 Park Avenue South,
	New York, NY 10010
UK distribution:	Crimson Publishing
	A division of Crimson Business
	Westminster House, Kew Road,
	Richmond TW9 2ND, England
Australia and	
New Zealand distribution:	Woodslane Pty Ltd
	Unit 7/5 Vuko Place
	Warriewood NSW 2102

Printed in Jan. 2011 by: Consorzio Artigiano L.V.G. srl, Azzate (VA), Italy
ISBN: 978-88-89060-19-3
Library of Congress Control Number: 2010942355

The Editor wish to thank all the individuals and organisations who made this publication possible. In particular Debra Pevear and Debra Royal for their assistance and dedication. Special thanks also go to Nini Naegeli, Umberto Pajarola, Erin McCloskey and Rossella Rossi for their precious contribution for the cover photos.

To access the *Green Volunteers Database* for updates on the new conservation volunteering opportunties that are constantly submitted to *Green Volunteers* and to join our non-expiring e-mail newsletter, readers must send an e-mail to: **green@greenvolunteers.org**. Proof of ownership of this guide will be required to receive the UserID and password to access the *Green Volunteers Database* at **www.greenvolunteers.org** where the updates are listed.

Green Volunteers Hostel

Menaggio, Lake Como (Italy)

THE HEART OF LAKE COMO!

- Spectacular View
- Fine Dining
- Sailing School
- Excellent Hiking
- Bike Tours
- Kayaks
- Sailing boats
- Mountain Bikes

- Excellent rock climbing within walking distance.
- Affordable location for meetings, conferences and courses.
- Lake navigation, just minutes away.

For **Reservations** and **Group Programmes** see:

www.lakecomohostel.com

Just one hour away from main *Low Cost* Airports (Bergamo and Milan). No car needed!

TABLE OF CONTENTS

Before joining any project or organisation prospective volunteers should carefully read the Warning on page 3 and the Important Note on pages 15-16.

The Editors highly recommend the following introductory pages are read. These pages explain what conservation volunteering involves and will increase the volunteer's chances of being accepted to a project.

PREFACE

In the last 20 years there has been a growing demand for volunteers for nature conservation projects in general and for wildlife related projects in particular. Volunteering provides wildlife and nature enthusiasts with an opportunity to become involved in worldwide conservation efforts. Students can gain experience allowing them to pursue a career in nature conservation as well as ideas for a thesis. Until recently, large organisations were mostly responsible for offering this kind of opportunity, but usually the financial contributions required limited the number of people who could afford them and become volunteers. However, there are many smaller nature conservation and wildlife protection projects with a constant shortage of funding which greatly need volunteers for research assistance and financial resources. Often these contributions by volunteers can maintain projects for years. The Gibbon Rehabilitation Project in Thailand, for example, has been running successfully for over 15 years exclusively on the contributions and help of international volunteers. Until now many of these projects throughout the world did not have a worldwide forum. With this guide these valuable projects have the opportunity to connect with prospective volunteers and vice versa.

The objective of *Green Volunteers* is to provide information to fill the communication gap between people who are willing to join interesting and valuable projects worldwide, and the projects in need of volunteers. For this reason, the Geneva-based World Conservation Union's Species Survival Commission (the body which publishes the "Red Lists" of endangered species) considers the *Green Volunteers* guide a useful instrument for supporting conservation projects throughout the world.

HOW TO BE LISTED IN THE
Green Volunteers Guide and Database

If you are an organisation or project based anywhere in the world and you would like to be listed in the next edition of this guide and or on our website at **www.greenvounteers.org**, please contact *Green Volunteers* at the addresses on page 2. Should you require any information on how to recruit and organise volunteers as a valuable instrument to support a nature conservation project Green Volunteers is willing to assist you.

INTRODUCTION

Green Volunteers is a directory. There are 2 sections: one dedicated to organisations and one to specific projects.

Organisations play an important role in providing opportunities for volunteer work; listed are those offering projects on a wide range of species, habitats and geographic locations, at various costs to volunteers (from zero to a few thousand dollars). Organisations are listed in alphabetical order. Should an organisation have an acronym, as many do, the organisation is listed according to the alphabetical order of the acronym. For example, BTCV, CVA, WWF, are listed according to the acronym's alphabetical order. For some of the larger organisations, or for those offering interesting projects to prospective volunteers, a few projects have been described in greater detail in the second section. These projects are listed at the end of the organisations' descriptions under the heading: Selected Projects. For most of the organisations no projects have been described in the second section due to limited space in this guide. Prospective volunteers are therefore encouraged to contact the organisations directly (or visit their websites), and inquire for further information about available projects.

Projects are found in the second section of this guide. Greater detail about the projects offered by the organisations is provided, and many more independent projects, which are not part of major organisations, are listed.

MEANING OF ABBREVIATIONS

For each organisation and project the guide lists:

The **address** and the **telephone** and **fax** numbers with the international codes. Remember to change the local area code according to the country's telephone system. For example, to call The Monkey Sanctuary, (UK) phone number (listed as ++44 (1503) 262 532), people calling from the UK should not dial ++44 (the international code), but should add 0 (zero) before 1503 (the local area code). People calling from the Netherlands should add 00 before 44 to call the UK. Whereas people calling from the US should dial 011, then 44, the international access codes from the US to the UK. **E-mail** and World Wide Web (**www**) addresses are listed where available. A quick phone call or an e-mail will help you to communicate and get information much faster than through regular mail and will speed your selection of the right organisation for you. One project indicated its Skype ID, this very cheap (or even free) method of communication (voice via the internet) will be used more and more in the future.

Desc.: The main activity and objectives of the organisations or projects.

Spp.: The species or the group of species involved. The common name, and Latin name if necessary for clarification, is provided. For projects involving groups of species, families, classes or communities, these groupings are cited in more general terms such as marine mammals, tropical birds, African herbivores, etc. Abbreviations are occasionally used.

Hab.: Specific habitats or wider biogeographical areas an organisation is involved with, such as tropical seas and coasts, African savannah, Mediterranean islands, etc. Abbreviations are occasionally used.

Loc.: The countries, regions (such as south-east Asia) or continents where an organisation conducts its projects.

Travel: A basic summary of travel directions. Organisations and projects will give full details to the volunteers once accepted.

Dur.: The duration of the volunteering time, either a set period or a minimum and maximum duration.

Per.: The period of the year when a volunteer can join a project such as year round, the summer, July to August, etc.

L.term: Long-term volunteering is a longer stay than the set volunteer duration. Some projects do not allow long-term volunteering, others do, but they typically continue charging the volunteers the same contribution (per week, for example) without recognizing any discount for the additional experience acquired by the volunteer. Other organisations or projects encourage long-term volunteering for this benefit. The Ecovolunteer Network is one organisation that encourages a longer permanence on some of the projects by considerably decreasing the cost to the volunteer the longer a volunteer stays. Some projects or organisations require professionally qualified labour and staff and accept graduate students for their thesis work.

Age: Minimum and maximum age for joining a project. Elderly volunteers must always consider that most projects are located in remote areas and in developing countries where good quality health facilities are out of reach or non existing. The nature of the work expected from the volunteers, which can span from hard manual labor to data collection, and the climate conditions, must also be carefully considered.

Qualif.: The qualifications and skills required of a volunteer who wants to join a project. Most of the time no special qualifications are needed, other than a strong motivation and enthusiasm. Adaptation to harsh climates, long walks, hot or cold temperatures, basic accommodation and very little comfort is almost always required. Where possible, the Editor has specified particularly extreme working or lodging conditions present at a given project. However, specific information is to be obtained from the organisation or project. Other typical requirements include a strong flexibility to work with other people, a willingness to accept very little privacy (very rarely volunteers will be able to lodge in a single or even double rooms) and the ability to adapt to different cultures. These requirements apply to almost all projects but are not always stated. A volunteer may offer special skills, such as photography, good computer literacy, mechanical skills, etc. Never expect, nor impose these skills onto a project - there may already be very qualified people performing these duties with the accuracy required by the project.

For long-term volunteering, or for organisations or projects where little or no contribution is required, volunteers are often selected according to their qualifications or previous experience in related work. Contact the organisation directly for more information on the skills and qualifications required.

Work: The main activities performed by volunteers are listed for projects. Since most organisations manage several projects, the work performed by volunteers is not described in detail because it will vary with each project. Prospective volunteers can predict what kind of activities to expect from the description of an organisation and the projects it supports. Further details are given by the organisations directly.

Lang.: The languages that are required for a volunteer to work on a project. The importance of communicating with the project staff or with local or international researchers should not be overlooked. Prospective volunteers should never underestimate the importance of this aspect and never overestimate their ability to understand a foreign language in a working environment.

Accom.: (Not described within the organisation description.) The style of accommodation the volunteers will be lodged in. For most of the projects volunteers should be prepared for very basic accommodations such as bunk beds in research stations (rarely in houses) tents or hammocks. Bathroom facilities can also be very basic and hot showers, particularly in the tropics, can be quite rare. Chores such as housecleaning, cooking, washing dishes, etc., are often expected. Comfort and privacy is rare. The ability to do without these privileges must be considered for environmental volunteering.

Cost: Most of the projects require a contribution from the volunteers, which is often the major funding for a project. Projects are often conducted with the financial contribution and the work volunteers perform. The cost of projects may vary from a few hundred to a few thousands dollars US. The Editor has tried to list as many organisations as possible requiring little or no contributions. These organisations, however, are difficult to find; they are either small projects in developing countries that have no means for communication or until now did not perceive the importance of taking volunteers. It is fair, however, that even these small projects or organisations ask for a small contribution, especially in developing countries.

Usually, the volunteer's contribution covers food and accommodation or there may be a common kitty for food costs. Very rarely will the cost include the international airfare to reach a project site. Some projects have introduced a very useful 'progressively decreasing cost' policy, depending on the length of stay. The rationale is that the longer a volunteer stays with a project, the more useful he or she becomes because of the experience he or she gains. Long-term volunteers selected according to their skills are often reimbursed for their living expenses. This is typically the case for long-term volunteers with Government Agencies, such as the US National Park Service, the US Forest Service or The US Fish and Wildlife Service.

Part of the volunteer contribution likely pays for the project costs: marketing, reservation staff, rent, telephone, mail, etc. Money going towards an agency or larger organisation or overhead should not be considered money diverted from the conservation objective. Larger organisations perform a basic role in a world-wide conservation effort by providing volunteers and funding to projects that alone would not have been able to reach these important resources. However, when overhead costs are in excess of a reasonable percentage (max. 20-25%) an organisation should try to become more efficient by reducing costs, in order to devote a higher percentage of a volunteer's contribution to actual projects. It is perfectly in the right of a volunteer to know how much of his or her contribution goes into a project, and what is the organisation's overhead.

Agents: The agents or organisations where a prospective volunteer can or should apply. Many organisations have branches in other countries that act as agents for projects. Other organisations use outside agents such as travel agencies to recruit volunteers. Many organisations do not have agents and require direct application.

Applic.: This section briefly describes application procedures that may be required such as filling out an application form, sending a deposit or initial contribution, or becoming a member of a specific organisation.

Selected Projects are listed for some organisations. If detailed description of projects are not provided, volunteers should contact the organisation directly in order to receive further information.

TIPS FOR CONTACTING
AN ORGANISATION OR PROJECT

1) Have clear in mind what you want to do, the species or habitats you prefer, the geographical location, the duration of your volunteering period and the costs you can afford. This will help you in selecting and reducing the number of organisations or projects you want to apply to. Select a list of both organisations and projects and divide them into your first and second priority. The first priority should include not only those organisations or projects that are of primary interest to you, but also those which are more remote and harder to contact.

2) Use the fastest possible method to contact an organisation. Remember that interesting projects or organisations also have many applicants, and they usually fill their available positions on a first come, first serve basis. Therefore, you want to be as fast as possible in letting them know that you are interested in taking a position with them. You may send via e-mail the *Green Volunteers Standard Application Form* found at page 255. Should you not receive a reply within 3-5 days, be prepared to send reminders or telephone them to confirm their e-mail address. These addresses often change, particularly when an organisation finds a cheaper internet server.

3) Inform as much as possible the organisation or project you would like to work for about yourself. With your request for information, send a description of your skills and interests and possibly a CV. You can find at page 255 the *Green Volunteers Standard Application Form*, modeled on the application forms of many organisations. This form may be sufficient for applying and it may help you to save time. The form (which is not an official application form but just a tool to help in the application process) is also available from the *Green Volunteers Database* at www.greenvolunteers.org (the Database is accessible with your User ID and password, see page 3 for details). Always enclose a cover letter (preferably typed and not handwritten) and ask if the organisation accepts the *Green Volunteers Standard Application Form*.

4) Do exactly what is required by an organisation for being accepted. If they do not accept the *Green Volunteers Standard Application Form*, fill in the proper application form, pay the required deposit or membership fee and comply with other requirements. Once accepted, don't miss an opportunity by not paying a deposit on time. Inquire about the fastest method to transfer funds: by international telegraph money order, credit card, money wire from bank to bank, etc.

5) **Contact many projects and organisations.** Select the projects well in advance. Properly plan your vacation or time off, find the best air fares and select the best research period. Get detailed information on what to expect: the type of work, accommodation, food, climate, clothing and equipment necessary, etc. Owing to a lack of space this information is not included in the *Green Volunteers* guide. This guide aims to give a general overview of a given project or organisation. Do not show up at a project location without having applied first and having been accepted and confirmed. Most projects have limited positions, lodging and personnel. Very rarely are they equipped to take on an unexpected volunteer. If you want to do so, because you were already travelling in a certain area, do not be disappointed if you are rejected.

WILDLIFE REHABILITATION CENTRES

To volunteer with wildlife you don't necessarily need to cross an ocean or stay away for weeks or months. You may indeed be able to volunteer and get in close contact with various species, mostly endemic but also exotic, in your own town, county, district, province or state at Wildlife Rehabilitation Centres. These centres, usually managed by local or national Non-Profit Organisations or private individuals - rarely local governments, take care and try to rehabilitate wounded or mistreated animals. Animals may have been wounded by hunters or car accidents or have been victims of plain cruelty. Often exotic wildlife that is confiscated by local authorities is handed over to Wildlife Rehabilitation Centres. Rare species illegally imported or detained against the CITES convention (International Convention on Trade of Endangered Species) cannot be released into a foreign habitat and rarely are re-exported to the country of origin.

Wildlife Rehabilitation Centres are always in need of volunteers. They often don't charge any fees and, if they are located near where you live, they may allow you to work just a few hours a week. There are several hundred Wildlife Rehabilitation Centres throughout the world, and they are mostly concentrated in First World countries. We did list a few in this guide as examples because we have had direct communication with them, but it would not be difficult to find a Rehabilitation Centre nearby where you can volunteer for a short period, a weekend or even a few hours a week.

We recommend that you do a web search with the key words "Wildlife Rehabilitation" and the name of the geographical area of your choice, such as Bedfordshire, Oregon, Alberta or New South Wales, depending on where you live or where would you like to volunteer. To help with your search, we have selected a few websites with a comprehensive international list of Wildlife Rehabilitation Centres.

www.catchat.org/adoption/notcats.html

A very thorough list of animal rescue centres in the British Isles, divided by species.

www.ispca.ie/content/links.html

The website of the Irish Society for the Prevention of Cruelty to Animals, a good list of Irish and non-Irish Wildlife Sanctuaries.

http://www.wildliferehabber.org

The Wildlife Rehabilitation Information Directory. A complete list of Centres throughout the US, Canada and the world.

www.greenpeople.org/sanctuary.htm

A list of over 200 sanctuaries in the US, Canada, Australia and throughout the world.

www.wildliferehabilitators.com/links.htm

The link page of the Association of Wildlife Rehabilitators, it has a good list of Wildlife Rehabilitators and Rehabilitation Centres in the US, Australia, Canada and the UK.

Finally Yahoo has a good list of Wildlife Rehabilitation Centres under Wildlife > Rescue and Rehabilitation.

IMPORTANT NOTE AND WARNING

The Editor and Publisher of *Green Volunteers* has decided, both in order to offer prospective volunteers the widest possible choice and to be a valid conservation instrument, to cite, whenever possible, small projects and organisations, particularly in developing countries, for the following reasons:

1) Without *Green Volunteers* many small projects and organisations would not be able to receive volunteers from developed nations. We think that we should help as best as we can this conservation potential, particularly if it comes directly from local organisations, without an input from large organisations from our side of the world.

2) Prospective volunteers, by purchasing this guide, expect to find something different and unique from what is normally offered by large organisations in developed countries.

3) Often small projects require non-paying and long-term volunteers, which is what many of *Green Volunteers* readers expect. These opportunities are also usually offered at extremely affordable costs to the volunteers, which is not the case of projects offered from large organisations, which are often expensive and don't allow long-term volunteering.

Before joining projects and organisations, prospective volunteers should carefully read the following considerations and warnings:

1) Because of obvious cost reasons, which would then reflect on the cover price, the Editor and Publisher cannot personally visit every project listed in this guide but have to trust what projects and organisations (or the websites or previous volunteers) declare.

2) Small projects and organisations, particularly in developing countries, mainly because of shortage of funding or qualified personnel or because of conflicts with local populations and/or local authorities, often change their programmes or even interrupt their activities without informing the Editor and Publisher of *Green Volunteers*.

3) Before joining a project volunteers should verify the validity of what is declared on the project website (if one exists) or in this guide.

4) Prospective volunteers should exchange frequent e-mails, or even fax or phone calls, **with project leaders** and ensure that communication is always prompt and clear. They should also confirm the project details, such as the living, working and safety conditions, prior to departure.

5) Prospective volunteers to any project should ask names and addresses of previous volunteers and correspond with them to further verify the conditions of the projects.

6) Volunteers should never join a project by going directly to the location without previous correspondence and verification of existing conditions.

7) Prospective volunteers should read carefully the WARNING on the third page of this book.

ORGANISATION LIST

A' Pas de Loup 'Volunteers For Nature'

12, rue Malautière
26 220 Dieulefit France
Tel.: ++33 (4) 7546 8018
Fax: ++33 (4) 7546 8018
E-mail: info@apasdeloup.org
www.apasdeloup.org

Desc.: A' Pas de Loup is a conservation volunteering organisation founded in 1994. Its objectives are to support local organisations in both developing and executing their schemes of nature conservation and to improve their local natural environment. 280 volunteers work in the field each year. During an assignment, volunteers are monitored by local staff to ensure quality results.

Spp.: Some projects are wildlife related (seals, elephants, wolves, turtles), others are related to vegetation or reforestation (in France and in Africa).

Hab.: Coastal Mediterranean, African savannah and tropical forests.

Loc.: Europe, Africa and South America.

Dur.: From 1 to 6 weeks.

Per.: In Europe in the summer, year round elsewhere.

Age: Min. 18.

Qualif.: No qualifications required.

Work: Depends on the project, often is mostly manual, such as work planting trees in Togo or cutting young trees for recovering the Grouse habitats in the Alps. Scientific observation is also involved, such as of birds migration or turtles monitoring. Leisure activities and eco-tours are also planned.

Lang.: English, French, Spanish, Italian.

Accom.: Always very simple; in a campsite or in local houses.

Cost: Volunteers must pay for travel and food and must join the organisation (EUR20).

Applic.: Apply on website and send CV with cover letter.

ARCAS – Wildlife Rescue and Conservation Association, Guatemala

Section 717, PO Box 52
Miami, FL 33152-7270 USA
Tel./Fax: ++(502) 7830 1374 / 7830 4273
E-mail: arcasvolunteers@gmail.com
www.arcasguatemala.com

Desc.: ARCAS' flagship project is its Wildlife Rescue and Rehabilitation Centre, established in 1990, in order to rescue, rehabilitate and release wild animals confiscated from traffickers. It releases 300-600 animals of over 40 species per year into the Mayan Biosphere Reserve (MBR). ARCAS' second important project is the Hawaii Sea Turtle Conservation Program on the Pacific coast of Guatemala. ARCAS manages an integrated coastal zone program which includes sea turtle and mangrove conservation, environmental education and community development. Volunteers participate in research and nightly patrols for nesting sea turtles.

Spp.: The centre receives many different species from the MBR, which include 70% parrots, but also spider and howler monkeys, 5 kinds of felines, tiaras, peccaries and kinkajous. The Hawaii Program includes Olive ridley and leatherback sea turtles, migratory birds, mangrove, caimans and iguanas.

Hab.: Dry tropical forest, mangrove coastal wetland.

Loc.: The Wildlife Rescue Centre is next to Petencito Zoo, near the city of Flores, Peten; the Sea turtle Conservation Project is in the Parque Hawaii, Chiquimulilla, Santa Rosa, Guatemala.

Travel: Flight to Guatemala City. For the Wildlife Rescue Centre: bus or plane to Flores, than by boat from El Arco on bridge; for the Sea turtle Project: public bus (via Taxisco) or tourist shuttle to Monterrico, than 8km to the east by bus or taxi.

Dur.: Min. 1 week. For internships or research projects, min. 1 month.

Per.: Year round for the Rescue Centre. July to December for the Sea turtle Project.

L.term: Volunteers can stay for as long as they want. Volunteers can also spend some time in each project.

Age: Rescue Centre: min. 18; Sea turtle Project: min. 16. Under 18 with parents or letter from parents.

Qualif.: No specific skills required for generic volunteers. Candidates for internships or research projects must be students or researchers in a conservation related field. Flexibility, individual initiative, optimism and good team-worker help.

Work: Volunteers help cleaning cages and feeding and caring for the animals. Special projects may include: observing the animals in the rehabilitation area, building cages, animal releases, research. Research and internship opportunities are in the area of wildlife veterinary medicine, wildlife rehabilitation, nutrition, sea turtle conservation and environmental education. At Hawaii volunteers assist in patrolling beaches at night in search of nesting sea turtles, collection and burial of eggs in the hatcheries and collection of data. Volunteers can also take part in caiman and iguana breeding programme and mangrove reforestation. Everyone is expected to help in house cleaning and dish washing.

Lang.: English; basic Spanish is highly desirable.

Accom.: Volunteers live in a comfortable house with toilet and kitchen facilities and electricity. Sheets are provided, own sleeping bag useful in cooler months (December-February), mosquito net is optional.

Cost: US$140/week for room and board at the Rescue Centre. US$75/week for room at the Sea turtle Project. It is possible to eat with local family or cook in the Parque. Additional charge for airport pick-up and transfer to project. Home-stays available.

Applic.: No application needed. For the research and internship opportunities candidates should contact ARCAS directly.

Notes: Apart from the projects mentioned above, ARCAS carries out a range of other conservation and community development projects in which volunteers are always needed. See Voluntary Guidebook on website.

ASVO – Asociacion de Voluntarios para el Servicio en las Areas Protegidas

Programa de Voluntariado
PO Box 11384-1000 San José Costa Rica
Tel.: ++(506) 258 4430 / (506) 223 4260 - Fax: ++(506) 223 4518
E-mail: info@asvocr.com
www.asvocr.com

Desc.:	ASVO is the organisation providing volunteers to Costa Rican National Parks and Reserves, who are needed for research, construction and maintenance work, English teaching, tourist assistance, interpretation and sea turtle conservation programmes on the coasts.
Spp.:	Primates, tropical birds and mammals, sea turtles.
Hab.:	Tropical coast, rainforest, cloud forest, beaches.
Loc.:	Parks and Reserves throughout Costa Rica.
Dur.:	Min. 30 days, 2 months for special projects. Volunteers who stay at least 30 days can work in 2 different projects.
Per.:	Year round.
L.term:	Inquire with organisation.
Age:	Min. 18.
Qualif.:	Flexibility, motivation, a good physical condition and ability to tolerate the tropical climate. 2 reference letters by Costa Rica residents or by organisations in the home country are required along with a copy of passport and 2 photos. Special qualifications are necessary for some research projects.
Work:	Various tasks: construction and maintenance of park structures and trails, providing information to tourists, assisting in research on biodiversity or in wildlife surveys, etc.
Lang.:	Spanish; inquire for English.
Accom.:	In general in rangers' lodges.
Cost:	Approx. US$22/day for room and board. Application fee: US$50.
Applic.:	Online form.
Notes:	Health and repatriation insurance required.

Bergwaldprojekt (Mountain Forest Project)

Stiftung Bergwaldprojekt
Via Principala 49, 7014 Trin
Grisons Switzerland
Tel.: ++41 (81) 650 4040
E-mail: info@bergwaldprojekt.org
www. bergwaldprojekt.org

Desc.:	The foundation has a non-profit purpose: to promote the maintenance, care and protection of the forest and the cultural landscape in mountain regions, especially through care and restoration during work assignments and by encouraging the public's understanding for the forest's concerns.
Spp.:	The ecosystem of the mountain forest.
Hab.:	Mountain forest.
Loc.:	Switzerland, Germany, Austria, Ukraine and Spain.
Travel:	The Volunteers will have to pay for their journey to and from the location of the project.
Dur.:	One week.
Per.:	March to October.
L.term:	Not available.
Age:	Min.18.
Qualif.:	All skills welcome, no specific skills required.
Work:	Through tangible work, the participants experience the fascinating ecosystem of the mountain forest with all their senses. The importance of the protection forest and the measures for its care are experienced directly.
Lang.:	Language of the region of the project.
Accom.:	Simple group accommodations close to the working area are organised and provided by the Bergwaldprojekt.
Cost:	Participation is free of charge for volunteers. The Bergwaldprojekt covers accommodation, meals and project management.
Applic.:	See website.

Biosphere Expeditions

The Henderson Centre
Ivy Road, Norwich NR5 8BF UK
Tel.: +44 (870) 446 0801
Fax: +44 (870) 446 0809
E-mail: info@biosphere-expeditions.org
www.biosphere-expeditions.org

Desc.: The projects are not tours or photographic excursions, but expeditions with real wildlife conservation content. Adventure, remote locations and different cultures are part of them, but also the knowledge to play an active role in conserving part of the planet's biosphere.

Spp.: Large cats, primates, whales, dolphins, rainforest birds, turtles etc.

Hab.: Rainforest, desert, savannah, marine, mountains, etc.

Loc.: Worldwide.

Travel: Volunteers are met in-country and taken to the project area.

Dur.: Min. one week up to 3 months.

Per.: Year round.

L.term: Volunteers can join an expedition for several months.

Age: No age restrictions. Minors with parents' consent.

Qualif.: No specific skills. Disabled/minority expeditioners are encouraged.

Work: Work (e.g., surveying, tracking, identification) is several hours a day, often independently, but never alone. All necessary training is given and a Biosphere Expeditions leader is always present.

Lang.: English.

Accom.: Varies from B&B to research stations to tent camps.

Cost: Variable and depending on project. Expedition contributions start from GB£980/week; for longer periods discounts are available.

Agents: See website for offices in Germany, France, Australia. North American Office: northamerica@biosphere-expeditions.org; tel. toll-free: 800 407 5761; fax toll-free: 800 407 5766.

Applic.: Contact organisation for more details and application forms.

Les Blongios
La Nature en Chantiers
Maison Régionale de l'Environnement et des Solidarités
23 rue Gosselet, 59000 Lille France
Tel.: ++33 (3) 2053 9885 - Fax: ++33 (3) 2086 1556
E-mail: contact@f lesblongios.fr
www.lesblongios.fr

Desc.: Les «Blongios» (*Ixobrychus minutus)* is an NGO which organizes more than 30 workcamps in natural reserves in France and Northern Europe.

Spp.: Trees, vegetation and various species.

Hab.: Various habitats.

Loc.: The Netherlands, Great Britain, Ireland, Belgium.

Travel: Depends on the location, details on the website.

Dur.: From 1 week-end to 1 month.

Per.: Year round.

Age: Min. 18.

Qualif.: No qualifications required.

Work: Maintenance work in natural reserves: habitat restoration (cutting bushes to restore natural sites, digging ponds for amphibians), trail blazing and building board walks, building visitor centres.

Lang.: French, English.

Accom.: In huts, lodges or hostels near natural reserves. Cooking and dish-washing is one of the responsibilities of the group.

Cost: Only travel expenses. Room, accommodation and meals are provided. Membership EUR20 (EUR15 for students or unemployed).

Applic.: Via e-mail or with the online application form available in various languages.

Notes: All the available workcamp locations are on the website.

Blue Ventures

Aberdeen Studios 2D, 22-24 Highbury Grove
London, N5 2EA UK
Tel.: ++44 (207) 7359 1287
Fax: ++44 (800) 066 4032
E-mail: enquiries@blueventures.org
www.blueventures.org

Desc.: An award-winning organisation dedicated to conservation, education and sustainable development in tropical coastal communities. Volunteers work with local biologists, marine institutes, NGOs and communities whose livelihoods depend on coral reefs, to carry out research, environmental awareness and conservation programmes at threatened reef habitats. Blue Ventures offers opportunities and field experiences to people wanting to become actively involved in marine conservation, both beginners and experts.

Spp.: Tropical marine (coral reef) species.

Hab.: Tropical coastal seas.

Loc.: Madagascar, Malaysia, Belize.

Dur.: 6-week expedition (min. 3 weeks).

Per.: Year round.

L.term: Enquire with organisation.

Age: Min. 18.

Qualif.: Blue Ventures offers: Scuba training up to PADI Advanced Open Water (or up to Divemaster on site if required).

Work: Comprehensive marine science training course, learning from international team of marine biologists. Average number of 18 volunteers per expedition. Staff to volunteer ratio of 1:2.

Lang.: English.

Accom.: Comfortable eco-cabins plus excellent food provided.

Cost: From GB£1,300 for 6 weeks, including food, accommodation, equipment and training.

Applic.: See website and fill the online application form.

Brathay Exploration Group

Brathay Hall
Ambleside, Cumbria LA22 OHP UK
Tel./Fax: ++44 (1539) 433 942
E-mail: admin@brathayexploration.org.uk
www.brathayexploration.org.uk

Desc.: Brathay Exploration Group is a non-profit organisation running project-based expeditions, club events and DofE Open Gold. Destinations include The Lake District, Foula (in the Shetland Islands) and Norway. These projects encompass field sciences from glaciology to ornithology.

Hab.: Mountain, countryside, glacial.

Loc.: The Lake District, Scotland, Wales & Norway

Dur.: 3 days to 3 weeks.

Per.: July to August.

L.term: Inquire with organisation.

Age: Min.18.

Qualif.: No qualifications required. Prior experience may vary depending on trip. Sense of adventure and environmental interest is a must!

Lang.: English.

Cost: From GB£20 to £1,300 depending on the expedition.

Applic.: See website.

Notes: BEG is a membership organisation with great benefits including BMC membership – see www.brathayexploration.org.uk/brathay-exploration-club/12-reasons-to-join.html. BEG also offers training such as Mountain Leader and Off-site Safety Management. BEG is always looking for volunteer leaders so please get in touch!

BTCV

Sedum House
Mallard Way
Potteric Carr, Doncaster, DN4 8DB UK
Tel.: ++44 (1302) 388 883 - Fax: ++44 (1302) 311 531
E-mail: information@btcv.org.uk; International@btcv.org.uk;
natural-breaks@btcv.org.uk   www.btcv.org.uk

Desc.:   BTCV is the UK's leading practical conservation charity, connecting people with place, builds healthy, sustainable communities, and increasing people's life skills. It aims to create a better environment where people from all cultures feel valued, included and involved. BTCV supports approximately 300,000 volunteers a year taking hands-on action to improve their urban and rural environments, and a Community Network supports local groups. BTCV offers regular conservation tasks, the BTCV Green Gym, training opportunities and an on-line shop making products and services accessible to all. BTCV organises also holidays travel to some of the most beautiful and amazing locations in the UK, all about improving the environment and making a real difference to the people and visited places.

Spp.:   Large varieties of UK native species, internationally: Reptiles, amphibians, colobus monkeys, sandwich terns, storks, pelicans, avocets and more.

Hab.:   Wetlands, woodlands, grasslands, rainforests, desert, mountains, islands, coastline.

Loc.:   UK, Albania, Bulgaria, Romania, Estonia, Cameroon, Germany, Iceland, Italy, Japan, Kenya, Lesotho, Nepal, New Zealand, Portugal, South Africa, USA.

Dur.:   1 day to 12 weeks. UK holidays: 2-7 days in England, 7-10 days in Scotland.

Per.:   Year round.

L.term: Volunteer Officer positions available. UK holidays: contact organisation for details.

Age: Under 18 with parental consent for UK projects; min. 18 for international projects.

Qualif.:   Some international expeditions and all UK holidays require a reasonable level of fitness.

Work: Diverse, e.g. UK: variety including restoring paths and dry stone walls or hedgelaying. International: revegetation, construction, sustainable development, habitat management or animal research. UK holidays: woodland management, dry stone walling, hedgelaying, fencing, habitat management and beachsweeps.

Lang.:   English. Other languages encountered with various projects.

Cost: From GB£100 for UK (project day tasks free) to GB£210-900 for international projects. UK holidays: GB£100-290.

Applic.:   International projects: GB£100 deposit. UK holidays: full payment required at the time of booking; contact BTCV directly at natural-breaks@btcv.org.uk.

Notes: Conservation Holidays Brochure available on request or visit the online shop.

Selected projects: Shisong, Kumbo, Cameroon.
Skaftafell National Park, Iceland.

Centre for Alternative Technology

Machynlleth, Powys
SY20 9AZ Wales UK
Tel.: ++44 (1654) 705 950
Fax: ++44 (1654) 702 782
E-mail: info@cat.org.uk
www.cat.org.uk

Desc.:	The Centre for Alternative Technology, open to the public since 1975, has working displays of wind, water and solar power, low energy buildings, organic farming and alternative sewage systems. It offers residential courses on topics such as water power, bird watching, organic gardening and rustic furniture making. The Centre also hosts an information service and a bookshop (with mail-order service). The Centre receives 80,000 visitors per year.
Loc.:	Wales, Great Britain.
Dur.:	Short-term volunteer programme of 1-2 weeks.
Per.:	Specified weeks between March and September inclusive.
L.term:	A limited number of long-term volunteers work in specific departments such as engineering, building, gardening and information for 6 months. Prospective long-term volunteers must stay for a 'trial' week before any offer of a placement can be made.
Age.:	Min. 18.
Qualif.:	Particular skills are not needed for short-term volunteers. Certain skills and previous experience may be criteria for the selection of long-term volunteers, as places are limited.
Lang.:	English.
Cost:	Volunteers contribute GB£10 (EUR15) per day for the cost of room and board. Accommodation and food are provided.
Agents:	Contact the Centre directly.
Applic.:	Application forms for the short-term volunteer programme are published in January. Early booking is necessary. Contact the Centre for details on the long-term volunteer programme.

Chantiers de Jeunes Provence Côte D'Azur

La Maison des Chantiers La Ferme Giaume
7 Avenue Pierre de Coubertin
06150 Cannes la Bocca France
Tel.: ++33 (4) 9347 8969 - Fax: ++33 (4) 9348 1201
E-mail: cjpca@club-internet.fr
www.cjpca.org

Desc.:	This organisation offers programmes for teenagers who want to experience community life, work for heritage protection, and spend an unusual summer holiday.
Loc.:	St. Marguerite Island, Cannes, in the Region of Provence, France, and in the region of Piedmont, Italy.
Dur.:	2 weeks.
Per.:	Summer, but also year round during school holidays.
Age:	Min. 13, max. 17.
Qualif.:	No qualifications necessary.
Lang.:	French.
Cost:	Approx. EUR400.
Agents:	Contact the organisation directly.
Work:	Different for each project, from simple construction to trail maintenance.
Applic.:	Call or e-mail the organisation to receive an application form.

Concordia

19 North Street, Portslade
Brighton BN41 1DH UK
Tel.: ++44 (1273) 422 218
Fax: ++44 (1273) 421 182
E-mail: info@concordiavolunteers.org.uk
www.concordiavolunteers.org.uk

Desc.: Most Concordia volunteer projects are environmental or renovation projects as well as play schemes or other social projects. There are also long-term opportunities through the European Voluntary Service and other programmes.

Spp.: Various.

Hab.: Over 60 countries worldwide.

Loc.: Most of the time, camps are in small isolated villages and there is not necessarily a car available on the camp.

Travel: Specific details provided for each volunteer project.

Dur.: 2-4 weeks on average.

Age: Minimum 18. Some projects available for 16 and 17 year olds.

Qualif.: No particular skills required.

Work: Building restoration, conservation and social work. 6hrs/day (Monday-Friday).

Lang.: Mostly English; some projects require German.

Accom.: Self-catered basic accommodation. A common room for sleeping and eating. Sleeping may be on the floor or in tents (varies with each project). Bring a sleeping bag and mat.

Cost: Registration fee: GB£180, including food and accommodation. Travel and personal expenses are not included.

Applic.: Application online or by post.

Notes: Projects in Latin America, Asia and Africa require a preparation weekend in Brighton; contact the office for more info. Bring seasonal clothing, working clothes, shoes, gloves, etc.

Coral Cay Conservation (CCC)

Elizabeth House
39 York Road
London SE1 7NQ UK
Tel: ++44 (020) 7921 0463 - Fax: ++44 (020) 7921 0469
E-mail: info@coralcay.org
www.coralcay.org

Desc.: CCC use the best marine science to support the preservation of coral reefs through learning and education support the dependent communities in the most cost-effective means possible. Volunteers play a crucial role collecting scientific information and working with local communities, governments and NGO's to help formulate sustainable management recommendations. Since 1986, CCC has helped to establish numerous marine reserves and wildlife sanctuaries worldwide and a UNESCO World Heritage Site in Belize.

Spp.: Terrestrial and marine organisms.

Hab.: Coral reefs and tropical rainforests.

Loc.: Cambodia, Philippines and Tobago.

Dur.: Min. 2 weeks.

Per.: Year round.

L.term: Inquire with organisation.

Age: Min. 16.

Qualif.: CCC offers: 1 Scuba Training week, 2 Skills Development and several Conservation weeks. PADI Open Water divers are trained to Advanced Open Water (AOW) and Emergency First Response (EFR) and are accepted directly onto the Skills development Programme.

Work: Training in marine and/or terrestrial ecology, survey techniques.

Lang.: English.

Accom.: Basic on-site accommodation provided.

Cost: Start at GB£850, including room and board, equipment and training. Flights and in country transport not included.

Applic.: See website or call. Monthly presentations are organised in the UK.

Cotravaux

11 Rue de Clichy
75009 Paris France
Tel.: ++33 (1) 4874 7920
Fax: ++33 (1) 4874 1401
E-mail: informations@cotravaux.org
www.cotravaux.org

Desc.:	Cotravaux promotes voluntary work and community projects concerning environmental protection (such as "J'agis pour la nature" program), monument restoration and social projects. It is a platform which gathers several organisations, offering many workcamps in different regions of France. Many of the organisations members of Cotravaux work with foreign partners.
Loc.:	France and worldwide.
Dur.:	2–3 weeks.
Per.:	Year round; most projects run between June and October.
L.term:	Certain projects offer 3-12 months volunteering.
Age.:	Min. 15.
Qualif.:	No specific skills needed.
Lang.:	A few projects require French.
Cost:	Volunteers must pay for their own travel to the camps. Room and board provided (some camps require a daily contribution).
Agents:	Some partner organisations (inquire with Cotravaux).
Applic.:	Contact Cotravaux by fax or mail to obtain the list of partner workcamps in France.
Notes:	The list of Cotravaux member organisations can be obtained on the website www.cotravaux.org.

CTS – Centro Turistico Studentesco e Giovanile

Dipartimento Ambiente, Settore Ecoturismo
Via Celso 4, 00161 Rome Italy
Tel.: ++39 (06) 4411 1351   Fax: ++39 (06) 4411 1901
E-mail: ambiente@cts.it
www.ctsambiente.it

Desc.:	Founded in 1974, CTS is now the largest youth association in Italy. Its Environmental Department organises research activities, ecotourism and environmental education programmes, training courses and workshops. It also publishes books and produces videos on environmental subjects. Projects concern endangered species, animal behaviour, habitat protection, and wildlife management.
Spp.:	Bears, dolphins, sea turtles, wolves.
Hab.:	Alpine, Mediterranean Sea and coast, temperate forest, lagoons.
Loc.:	Italian Alps, Appennines, Mediterranean coasts and islands, often inside protected areas and natural reserves.
Dur.:	Depends on the project; average period is 7-15 days.
Per.:	Summer time.
L.term:	Inquire with organisation.
Age:	Min.18. Younger members with an adult (either parents or a relative).
Qualif.:	Physically fit, flexible, cooperative. Able to swim for marine projects.
Cost:	EUR280-800, excluding food and journey to/from chosen destination.
Lang.:	Italian, English.
Agents:	CTS offices are scattered throughout Italy.
Applic.:	Membership is required to join the expeditions (EUR30).

CVA – Conservation Volunteers Australia / Conservation Volunteers New Zealand

Conservation Volunteers Booking Office
PO Box 423, Ballarat 3353 Victoria Australia
Tel.: ++61 (3) 5330 2600 - Fax: ++61 (3) 5330 2922 (2655)
E-mail: bookings@conservationvolunteers.com.au
www.conservationvolunteers.com.au

Desc.:	Founded in 1982, CVA is a non-profit organisation dedicated to practical conservation. CVA's activities concern environmental topics such as salinity, soil erosion, biodiversity and endangered species. CVA projects offer the opportunity to see parts of Australia, off the regular track, as well as to make international friendships through team activities.
Spp.:	Turtles, penguins, birds, koalas, wallabies, vegetation.
Hab.:	Rivers, coasts, dryland, swamps.
Loc.:	Various locations in Australia and New Zealand.
Travel:	Flight to Australia.
Dur.:	4-6 weeks.
Per.:	Year round.
L.term:	Inquire with organisation.
Age:	Min. 18.
Qualif.:	Experience and qualifications related to the environment are welcome but not essential.
Work:	Contact organisation for details.
Lang.:	English.
Accom.:	Contact organisation for details.
Cost:	AUS$1,500 for 6 weeks, including food, accommodation and project-related transportation within Australia or New Zealand.
Applic.:	Call, write or e-mail Conservation Volunteers Bookings Office for information. Applications are accepted online.

Earthwatch Institute

Mayfield House, 256 Banbury Road
Oxford OX2 7DE UK
Tel.: ++44 (1865) 318 831
Fax: ++44 (1865) 311 383
E-mail: projects@earthwatch.org.uk
www.earthwatch.org/europe

Desc.: Earthwatch Institute is an international charity supporting 61 environmental research projects in 31 countries. It provides funds and pays volunteers who work alongside field scientists and researchers and with people from all over the world, having in common the commitment to doing something to protect the environment. To ensure its research addresses pressing global environmental issues, Earthwatch preferentially funds projects of: sustainable resource management, climate change, oceans, sustainable cultures.

Spp.: Lions, elephants, dolphins, birds, rhinos, Grevy's zebras, brown hyenas, monkeys, sea turtles and many others.

Hab.: Rainforest, desert, savannah, tropical and temperate seas and coasts, arctic, sub-arctic.

Loc.: The Americas, Europe, Africa, Asia.

Dur.: 3-15 days.

Per.: Year round.

Age: Min. 18, unless participating on a special teen or family team.

Qualif.: No specific qualifications. Grants are available for teachers.

Lang.: English.

Cost: Approx. GB£795-1,995, with room and board, training, emergency medical evacuation and the offsetting of greenhouse gas emissions.

Applic.: E-mail to projects@earthwatch.org.uk or call ++44 (1865) 318 831.

Notes: Earthwatch Headquarters are located in USA: 3 Clock Tower Place, Suite 100, Box 75, Maynard, MA 01754. Earthwatch has various national offices: see website for details.

Selected projects: Saving Kenya's Black Rhinos.

The Ecovolunteer Network

Tierra Natuurreizen
Heidebergstraat 311, 3010 Leuven Belgium
Tel.: ++32 (016) 255 616
Fax: ++32 (016) 649 995
E-mail: info@ecovolunteer.org
www.ecovolunteer.be

Desc.: About 30 projects offer hands-on experience in wildlife conservation and research, assisting in fieldwork, monitoring research and in wildlife rescue and rehabilitation centres. Volunteers work with local experts and are expected to adapt to local culture and food.

Spp.: African wild dog, wolf, bear, rhino, elephant, gibbon, orangutan, beaver, otter, dolphin, whale, seal, turtle, horse, sheep, birds, rare breeds of dogs, various species in wildlife rescue centres.

Hab.: Ranging from subarctic to tropical rainforest.

Loc.: Worldwide.

Dur.: Min. 1, 2, 3 or 4 weeks, depending on projects.

Per.: Some projects are seasonal, others are year round.

L.term: Possible with many projects, especially for academic research.

Age: Min. 18-20, depending on projects. Some allow a parent with a minor.

Qualif.: Variable. Physically fit and able to work independently.

Lang.: English; some projects admit people speaking only French, Spanish or Portuguese.

Cost: From EUR115/week. Min. 77-80% of the price goes to projects.

Agents: Agents in various countries are listed in the website.

Applic.: Mail or fax the application form on www.ecovolunteer.org to the nearest agency, or ask for a form in the preferred language.

Notes: For projects and new agencies that would like to be included in the Ecovolunteer Network, contact the central office.

Selected projects: Brown Bear Project, Russia.
Rhino Rescue Project, Swaziland.

EDGE of AFRICA

Suite 88, Private Bag X31
Knysna, 6570, South Africa
Tel.: ++27 (0) 44 382 0122
Fax: ++27 (0) 86 615 1857
E-mail: roger@edgeofafrica.com
www.edgeofafrica.com

Desc.: EDGE of AFRICA is committed to ethical volunteering and responsible travelling. Providing volunteer and internship placements in South Africa for gap years, career breaks, university internships, school groups and corporate team building projects.

Loc.: Garden Route, South Africa.

Travel: Flight in Cape Town/Johannesburg and then domestic flight to George, South Africa.

Dur.: Min. 1 weeks for foreign volunteers; Max 1 year

Per.: Year round. Closure 20 December – 10 January each year.

L.term: With project leaders approval.

Age: Min. 18.

Qualif.: No experience is necessary and volunteers from any background are accepted. Volunteers with a conservation, sports or community development background may consider joining this program for work related experience. Volunteers should be physically fit and mentally positive.

Work: Volunteers are involved in a variety of conservation, community and sports projects run by EDGE of AFRICA.

Lang.: English.

Accom.: Volunteers are based in simple, clean, dorm style accommodation at the cosy volunteers house, located in Knysna, as well as on-site at the various reserves and national parks.

Cost: Project fees start at EUR250 per week including food, accommodation, training, project transport and exclude flights

Applic.: Application form on EDGE of AFRICA website.

Selected projects: Everything Elephants, South Africa

ELIX – Conservation Volunteers Greece

Veranzerou 15,
10677 Athens Greece
Tel.: ++30 (210) 3825 506
Fax: ++30 (210) 3814 682
E-mail: elix@elix.org.gr; volunteers@elix.org.gr
www.elix.org.gr

Desc.: Greek summer work camps, which usually take place in remote areas in co-operation with Forestry Departments, local authorities, cultural associations. Intercultural exchanges and conservation work allow young people to contribute to a hosting community. ELIX is also involved in European Voluntary Service projects.

Spp.: Various: birds of prey, forest flora and fauna.

Hab.: Mediterranean ecosystems, forests and wetlands.

Loc.: Greece, usually remote areas.

Travel: Contact the organisations for specific projects.

Dur.: 2-3 weeks; fixed dates are provided for every project.

Per.: Summer.

Age: Min. 18.

Work: Nature conservation (forest-fire protection, tree-planting, footpath maintenance, construction and placement of signs), cultural heritage (restoration of traditional buildings, ancient cobbled-stone footpaths and help in archaeological digs) or social benefit (people with disabilities, restoration of school buildings, construction of playgrounds). Work is 5-6hrs/day, 6 days/week.

Lang.: English.

Accom.: Hosting is usually in schools and community or youth centres. Sleeping bag and mat are required. Household chores involved.

Cost: Participation fee: EUR100.

Agents: The Alliance of European Voluntary Service Organisations (www.alliance-network.org).

Applic.: Volunteer Exchange Form on website or by Alliance organisations.

EUROPARC Deutschland

Bundesgeschäftsstelle
Friedrichstrasse 60 D-10117 Berlin Germany
Tel.: ++49 (30) 2887 8820 - Fax: ++49 (30) 288 7882-16
E-mail: *info@europarc-deutschland.de;*
freiwillige@europarc-deutschland.de (for VIP)
www.europarc-deutschland.de; www.freiwillige-in-parks.de (for VIP)

Desc.: EUROPARC Deutschland has supported since 1991 the promotion of environmental education and a system's plan of protected areas in Germany to preserve the natural heritage for future generations. Each year, the project «Praktikum fuer Die Umwelt» offers about 40/60 volunteer placements in protected areas to students who would like to contribute their knowledge and skills to the Parks. The Volunteers in Parks Programme (VIP) offers people of every age and qualification a variety of activities in order to maintain the reserves.

Hab.: Temperate forest, coastal habitats, lakes, etc.

Loc.: Germany.

Dur.: 3-6 months for Praktikum; from a few hours to a few months for VIP.

Per.: April to October for Praktikum; year round for VIP.

L.term: Up to 6 months.

Age: Min. 18 for Praktikum; min. 14 for VIP (18 for international VIP).

Qualif.: Education, geography and biology backgrounds are an advantage. Sometimes field experience and a valid driver license are required. Interest in wildlife, nature conservation, environmental education.

Work: Protection and monitoring of species and plants, environmental education, public relations.

Lang.: German.

Accom.: Always provided for Praktikum; provided in some parks for VIP.

Cost: No contributions; most of the positions are paid (for Praktikum).

Applic.: Deadline January for Praktikum; see www.praktikum-fuer-die-umwelt.de. No deadline for VIP; see www.freiwillige-in-parks.de.

Notes: Mandatory work visa requirements for non-EU residents.

Frontier

50-52 Rivington Street
London EC2A 3QP UK
Tel.: ++44 (20) 7613 2422
Fax: ++44 (20) 7613 2992
E–mail: info@frontier.ac.uk
www.frontier.ac.uk

Desc.: Frontier is an international non-profit organisation that carries out sustainable conservation and development projects in partnership with host-country institutions. We have projects located in over 50 countries across the globe. Volunteers can track lions and elephants across the savannah, dive with dolphins and rays, teach English in a rural school, or learn to lead their own expedition. Full training is offered and volunteers can gain unique BTEC qualifications in Tropical Habitat Conservation or Expedition Management (biodiversity research). We also offer free TEFL and FGASA Courses as well as the opportunity to gain UCAS points with our CoPE Certificate.

Hab.: Rainforests, tropical forests, savannah, mangroves, coral reefs, urban and rural environments.

Loc.: Over 50 countries across the globe.

Dur.: 2 weeks and longer.

Per.: Year round.

L.term: Inquire with organisation.

Age: Min. 16.

Qualif.: Applicants must be enthusiastic and have a commitment to conservation and development issues in developing countries.

Work: Biodiversity surveys, habitat mapping, socio-economic work with local communities.

Lang.: English.

Cost: From GB£295, excluding flights, visas and insurance.

Applic.: Contact Frontier for an application form or apply on the website.

Selected projects: Marine Conservation and Diving, Tanzania
Sri Lanka Elephant Conservation Experience

Gapforce

Greenforce, Trekforce, Ozforce, Medforce, Skiforce, Careergap
Gap Year & Career Break Projects
21 Heathmans Road, Parsons Green, London SW6 4TJ UK
Tel.: ++44 (0207) 384 3028
E-mail: info@gapforce.org
www.gapforce.org

Desc.: Gapforce is an expedition company evolved from UK-based charity Greenforce and Trekforce. Keen to continue the legacy of successful conservation expeditions to challenging destinations, Gapforce has taken 20 years of experience and developed it to create a popular gap year and career break organisation. Working with remote communities in far flung corners of the globe, Gapforce combines the rewards of expedition life with sustainable conservation projects, offering also language training, remote trekking, paid placements, diving courses, skiing opportunities, medical internships and customised programmes for mature applicants.

Hab.: Rainforest, coastal, African savannah, Amazon, tropical.

Loc.: Belize, Guatemala, Ecuador, Peru, Tanzania, South Africa, India, Vietnam, Cambodia, Thailand, Nepal, China, Fiji, Bahamas, Borneo, Papua New Guinea, Australia, Canada, Morocco.

Dur.: 2 weeks to 1 year.

Per.: Year round.

L.term: Many participants return for more expeditions at discounted rates. Traineeships are available. The Expedition Leader Training Course offers great pathways into enticing careers.

Age: Min. 17.

Qualif.: No specific skills needed. Training is part of the expeditions.

Lang.: English. Longer programmes involve learning local languages.

Accom.: Varies depending on expedition from hammocks, tents, grass huts (bures), mud huts (bomas) or standard housing.

Cost: Between GB£550 and GB£4,100 depending on expedition length.

Applic.: Apply online at www.gapforce.org or to receive a brochure.

Notes: Open days are organised to discuss projects and meet ex-volunteers.

Geography Outdoors: the Centre Supporting Field Research, Exploration and Outdoor Learning

Royal Geographical Society with IBG
1 Kensington Gore, London SW7 2AR UK
Tel.: ++44 (20) 7591 3030 - Fax: ++44 (20) 7591 3031
E-mail: go@rgs.org   www.rgs.org/go

Desc.:   Geography Outdoors: the Centre supporting field research, exploration and outdoor learning is an office of the Royal Geographical Society with IBG (Institute of British Geographers). It is primarily concerned with advising those who are planning their own expeditions, with an emphasis on field research projects overseas. The Centre provides information on all aspects of expedition planning and organises Explore: the annual RGS-IBG Expedition and Fieldwork Planning Weekend each November. A wide variety of resources are available on the website, including a directory listing over 100 organisations that regularly arrange expeditions from environmental research and conservation work to community projects and adventurous training. Guidelines are given on fund-raising to support participation in these ventures.

Notes: People who are thinking of organising their own field research project should e-mail: go@rgs.org.

Global Service Corps

Earth Island Institute
3543 18th Street, #14
San Francisco, California 94110 USA
Tel.: ++1 (415) 551 0000 ext.128 - Fax: ++1 (415) 861 8969
E-mail: gsc@globalservicecorps.org
www.globalservicecorps.org

Desc.:	Global Service Corps provides opportunities for adult volunteers to live and work on projects in Africa and Southeast Asia. Volunteers work with community members on village-based projects through the Service-Learning Programs or give back to communities through the Volunteer Vacations.
Loc.:	Tanzania, Thailand, Cambodia.
Dur.:	From 2 weeks Volunteer Vacations or Service-Learning programs to long-term projects from 5-8 weeks to 6 months or longer.
Per.:	Monthly start-dates throughout the year.
L.term:	Programs begin with an in-depth, in-country cultural orientation and technical training. Long-term volunteers experience a rare in-depth look at the country, its people and sustainable development.
Age:	Min. 18.
Qualif.:	No specific skills needed beyond good English speaking skills.
Work:	Volunteers choose from a variety of projects: HIV/AIDS education and prevention, sustainable agriculture and food security, international and public health, teaching English, orphanage care, or Buddhist immersion.
Lang.:	English.
Cost:	Volunteer Vacations: from US$1,480; Service-Learning Projects: from US$2,265, including all in-country expenses, cultural orientation and technical training as well as home-stay accommodations. Travel expenses and travel insurance are not included.
Applic.:	Online application process including a CV and personal statement as well as a US$300 refundable deposit.

Global Vision International

Suite 308, 3rd Floor, The Senate, Exeter, Devon EX1 1UG, UK

Tel.: ++44 (0) 1727 250 250 (UK)

 ++1 (888) 653 6028 (toll free from North America)

Fax: ++44 (0) 1727 250 260

E-mail: info@gviworld.com

www.gvi.co.uk; www.gviusa.com

Desc.:	Critical conservation and humanitarian projects in over 40 countries rely on GVI for volunteers, promotion and direct funding. GVI works locally with its partners to promote sustainable development through environment research, conservation and education. Volunteers benefit from exceptional support, training and a Careers Abroad job placement scheme. Projects include: marine research in Mexico and Seychelles; Amazonian and Costa Rican rainforest expeditions; predator research and marine studies in South Africa or Kenya; training as a safari field guide in South Africa; etc.
Hab.:	Rainforests, savannah, tropical coasts, coral reefs.
Loc.:	40 countries worldwide.
Dur.:	2 weeks to 2 years.
Per.:	Year round.
L.term:	Opportunities for those who have completed a 10 week expedition.
Age:	Min. 18.
Qualif.:	No qualifications are necessary, beyond understanding the aims of the project and cultural sensitivities. Full training in the field is provided.
Work:	Data collection, biodiversity surveys, wildlife research, scuba diving surveys, teaching, construction, community volunteering.
Lang.:	English.
Cost:	From GB£595, including room and board; flights and insurance are excluded.
Applic.:	Apply online.
Notes:	US address: 66 Long Wharf, Suite 562 S Boston, MA, 02116, USA.

Hellenic Ornithological Society

Vas. Irakleiou 24
GR-106 82 Athens Greece
Tel.: ++30 (1) 822 8704 /822 7937
Fax: ++30 (1) 822 8704
E-mail: birdlife-gr@ath.forthnet.gr
www.ornithologiki.gr

Desc.:	Protecting bird fauna and important bird areas of Greece.
Spp.:	All endangered species of Greek bird fauna.
Hab.:	All habitats of Greece (forests, lagoons, rivers, sea).
Loc.:	Greece.
Travel:	Bus, train or plane to the project area.
Dur.:	Min. 3 weeks for foreign volunteers; 2 weeks for Greek volunteers.
Per.:	May to October (mostly in the summer); some projects year round.
L.term:	With project leaders approval.
Age:	Min. 18.
Qualif.:	Ability to work also in difficult conditions, to live and work with people from different cultures and to cooperate with the local communities; manual work; reliability. Experience in similar projects or studies in biology, environment, ornithology are more than welcome.
Work:	Work in the field (constructing/monitoring nests, counting birds, feeding, monitoring of the habitats, etc.) and in public awareness.
Lang.:	English.
Accom.:	According to project, either provided by HOS in organized campsites, in rooms rented for the project or different accommodation at special low-cost rates.
Cost:	A EUR60 membership fee is required. Travel, food and personal expenses are not covered. Expenses needed for work during the project are covered by the HOS.
Applic.:	Application form on HOS website, sent by mail, fax or e-mail.
Selected projects:	Conservation of Gialova Lagoon, Greece

Iceland Conservation Volunteers

Umhverfisstofnun, Environment Agency of Iceland
Sudurlandsbraut 24, 108 Reykjavik Iceland
Tel.: ++354 591 2000
Fax: ++354 591 2020
E-mail: volunteer@umhverfisstofnun.is
http://ust.is/

Desc.:	Umhverfisstofnun (UST) is responsible for the management of nature protection areas in Iceland. Volunteers are involved in all aspects of the practical management of these areas including heritage and wilderness management projects, trail construction and maintenance, which helps to protect ecologically fragile areas from tourism pressure and also improves safety for visitors.
Hab.:	Remote upland areas with little vegetation.
Loc.:	Based in Skaftafell, Vatnajökull National Park, includes projects in other protected areas throughout Iceland.
Travel:	Flight to Reykjavik, then bus to Skaftafell, where volunteers are met.
Dur.:	2 weeks – 4 months.
Per.:	May - September.
L.term:	Volunteers may be able to stay for up to 4 months.
Age:	Min 18.
Qualif.:	No previous experience is necessary as full training is offered. Nature conservation skills (e.g. trail construction) are very useful.
Work:	Volunteers work in teams and are guided by experienced leaders. Trail work includes constructing stone drains, steps, timber boardwalks and bridges. Wilderness management also include the removal of an invasive plant species (*Lupinus nootkatensis*).
Lang.:	English is the working language.
Accom.:	Various, including camping and shared rooms in bunkhouses. Personal good quality tents and sleeping bags are a must.
Cost:	Room, board and transfers are covered. Travel expenses are not included.
Applic.:	Apply online: http://english.ust.is/of-interest/ConservationVolunteers/.

International Otter Survival Fund

7 Black Park
Broadford, Isle of Skye
IV49 9DE Scotland UK
Tel./Fax: ++44 (1471) 822 487
E-mail: info@otter.org
www.otter.org

Desc.:	IOSF works to conserve otters by safeguarding areas of good habitat and supporting people working in research and rehabilitation worldwide. The Fund's mission is to protect 13 species of otter worldwide.
Spp.:	Eurasian otter (*Lutra lutra*).
Hab.:	Coastal and rivers.
Loc.:	Hebridean Islands, Scotland.
Travel:	Flight to Scotland.
Dur.:	1 week.
Per.:	May to September.
L.term:	Inquire with organisation.
Age:	Min. 19, no maximum age provided fit.
Qualif:	No specific skills needed but must be physically fit.
Work:	Volunteers learn skills in otter surveying, such as identifying droppings, footprints, etc. They may also take part in surveying particular islands. Since the otters are not nocturnal the chances to observe them are very high.
Lang.:	English.
Accom.:	Volunteers stay in local guesthouses.
Cost:	GB£340-380 depending on the project. Cost includes Bed&Breakfast, but volunteers pay for the other meals. Transport and equipment are provided.
Applic.:	Call or write IOSF for application form.
Notes:	IOSF supports several otter conservation projects overseas.

Involvement Volunteers Association Inc.

PO Box 334, Diamond Creek
Victoria 3089 Australia
Tel./Fax: ++61 (3) 9438 6007
E-mail: ivworldwide@volunteering.org.au
www.volunteering.org.au

Desc.: Involvement Volunteers Association Inc. (IVI) is a non-profit, NGO providing individual programmes for volunteering in one or more countries.

Loc.: Over 50 countries worldwide.

Dur.: 2, 6 or 12 weeks, up to 12 months.

Per.: Some projects are seasonal, others all year round.

Age: Min.18.

Qualif.: Suitable qualifications, determination, enthusiasm or experience.

Work: Various conservation related activities.

Lang.: English or Spanish in some countries.

Accom.: Various, depending on the project and the location.

Cost: Minimum AU$1,200.

Applic.: Contact IVI by e-mail, airmail, fax or telephone.

Notes: IV volunteering is organised to best suit the individual volunteer's needs or the group of individuals taking part.

IUCN – The World Conservation Union

28, rue Mauvernay
1196 Gland Switzerland
Tel.: ++41 (22) 999 0000
Fax: ++41 (22) 999 0002
E-mail: mail@iucn.org
www.iucn.org

Desc.:	Founded in 1948, IUCN – The World Conservation Union brings together more than 1,000 governmental and non-governmental members and 10,000 technical and scientific experts in its six Commissions. IUCN's mission is to influence, encourage and assist societies throughout the world to conserve the integrity and diversity of nature and ensure that any use of natural resources is equitable and ecologically sustainable.
Loc.:	Refer to www.iucn.org – About IUCN – Offices.
Dur.:	Min. 3 months to 1 year.
Per.:	Inquire to the appropriate IUCN Regional/Country Office in the preferred location.
L.term:	Long-term assignments are preferred.
Age:	Min. 21.
Qualif.:	Vary according to specific assignments.
Work:	Assist in collecting information, desk research and report writing. Organise and facilitate meetings and workshops. Develop project proposals and communication materials. Maintain databases and web-pages.
Lang.:	Depends on the location of work (English, French and Spanish are also commonly used)..
Cost:	Conditions vary according to location and assignment.
Agents:	Refer to www.iucn.org - About IUCN – Vacancies – Offices and Members – Directory. Contact the IUCN Regional/Country Office and/or IUCN members in the preferred location.
Applic.:	Send CV and information on availability of time to preferred IUCN Regional/Country Office in the preferred location.

Legambiente

Via Salaria 403
00199 Rome Italy
Tel.: ++39 (06) 862 681 /Volunteer office: ++39 (06) 8626 8323
Fax: ++39 (06) 2332 5776
E-mail: volontariato@legambiente.com
www.legambiente.com/volontariato/campi

Desc.: Founded in 1980, Legambiente is a non-profit organisation involved primarily with public awareness and environmental campaigning activities. Volunteer opportunities include work camps and events such as the 'Clean up the World' day. Current projects include restoration and protection camps in small islands near Sicily, underwater archaeology and ecology camps in Sicily, ecological research in the Italian Alps, archaeological study in southern Italy and many others.

Spp.: Various species of the different habitats.

Hab.: Mediterranean seas, islands and coasts, temperate forest, lagoons, Alps.

Loc.: National Parks and Reserves, Mediterranean islands, Italian Alps, Germany, Brazil, Japan, France, Wales, Czech Republic, Mexico, Belarus, Turkey, Spain, Denmark, Poland, Belgium, Cuba, South Africa, Swaziland.

Dur.: 10-20 days.

Per.: Year round.

L.term: Volunteers can join the medium and long term voluntary programme from 3 weeks to 1 year.

Age: Min.18. Special programmes available for those under 18 and under 14.

Qualif.: No specific qualifications are required.

Lang.: Italian, English.

Cost: Min. EUR120, max. EUR270.

Applic.: Contact Legambiente for information and application forms.

LIPU – Lega Italiana Protezione Uccelli, Birdlife Italy

Italian League for the Protection of Birds
Via Trento 49, 43100 Parma Italy
Tel.: ++39 (0521) 273 043
Fax: ++39 (0521) 273 419
E-mail: info@lipu.it www.lipu.it

Desc.: LIPU, founded in 1965, is the Italian representative of BirdLife International. The aim of the organisation is the protection of nature and in particular of birds. It supports bird rescue centres, research programmes for the conservation of endangered species, awareness campaigns and environmental education programmes.

Spp.: Birds.

Hab.: Mediterranean coasts and islands, temperate forest, Alps.

Loc.: Various locations in Italy.

Dur.: 7-10 days or more.

Per.: April to October.

L.term: Inquire with organisation.

Age: Inquire with organisation. Junior and adult camps.

Qualif.: Previous experience and qualifications are not required. Some camps need expert ornithologists.

Work: Birdwatching, counts, ringing, data collection, fire prevention, trail maintenance and restoration.

Lang.: Italian, English.

Cost: Min. EUR100, max. EUR600.

Applic.: See website for exact programme of camps. Contact LIPU via e-mail for information on international application.

Mingan Island Cetacean Research Expeditions

Mingan Island Cetacean Study, Inc.
378 Rue Bord de la Mer
Longue-Pointe-de-Mingan, Québec, GOG 1V0 Canada
Tel./Fax: ++1 (418) 949 2845
E-mail: mics@globetrotter.net
www.rorqual.com

Desc.:   Volunteers join a team of marine biologists conducting cetacean research in north-eastern Quebec (Canada), Baja California (Mexico), and Azores (Portugal). During research projects, participants spend most of their time on the water, depending on the weather; there is a field station/museum at the site in Québec.

Spp.:   Blue, fin, humpback and minke whales.

Hab.:   Gulf of the St. Lawrence, Sea of Cortez, Azores.

Loc.:   Northeast Québec; during winter in Baja California and spring in Azores islands for blue whale studies.

Travel: Flight to Sept-Iles, Gaspé or Forrestville. For Loreto: stop over at LA. To Azores: flight to Pico or Faial from Lisbon.

Dur.:   7–14-day sessions.

Per.:   June to September in Québec; February to March in Loreto.

L.term: Possible to stay up to 1 month in Mingan.

Age: Min. 12.

Qualif.:   Recommended a fairly good physical condition, in order to spend long periods on the water, up to 10 hours.

Work: Collecting field data: take notes, observe biopsies, photographic work. Organizing daily logistics (gas, food, boat preparation).

Lang.:   English, French, German. Spanish and Portuguese useful.

Accom.:   B&B, inn or hotel.

Cost: Mingan CAD$2,245; Gaspe' estuary blue whale session CAD$2,455; Azores EUR 1700 including transportation, accommodation, and food. US$1,895 in Loreto, transfers are not included.

Applic.:   Request from the organisation registration and medical forms.

The National Trust

Working Holidays Booking Office
Sapphire House, Roundtree Way, Norwich NR7 8SQ UK
Tel.: ++44 (844) 800 3099
Fax: ++44 (844) 800 8497
E-mail: working.holidays@nationaltrust.org.uk
www.nationaltrust.org.uk/volunteering/

Desc.: The National Trust offers around 400 working holidays per year. This includes activities from carrying out a conservation survey and herding goats to painting a lighthouse or planting trees, etc.

Loc.: England, Wales, Northern Ireland.

Dur.: 2-7 days.

Per.: Year round.

L.term: Inquire with the organisation. Many opportunities are listed on the website.

Age: Min. 18. Youth Discovery holidays (UK volunteers only): min. 16.

Qualif.: No specific skills required. Volunteers must be team-worker and adaptable to work also in uncomfortable conditions.

Work: Work involves outdoor countryside conservation. On some holidays there are opportunities to learn specific skills (dry-stone walling, hedge laying etc.). Indoor conservation activities are also available (working with textiles, cataloguing collections, etc.).

Lang.: English.

Accom.: Trust base camp; farmhouse, cottage, or apartment specially converted for group use. Most base camps have a fully equipped kitchen, hot showers, and bunk beds.

Cost: From GB£90 a week, including food and accommodation. Travel and personal expenses are not included. A supplementary charge of GB£5 per person is made on bookings from overseas to cover bank and administrative charges in the UK.

Applic.: On-line application form or call ++44 (844) 800 3099.

Notes: Work permits and visas are the responsibility of the volunteer. Bring a sleeping bag, raingear, work clothes, boots, and gloves.

The Nature Corps

3600 Ridge Road
Templeton, California 93465 USA
Tel.: ++1 (805) 434 0299
Fax: ++1 (805) 434 3444
E-mail: thenaturecorps@gmail.com
www.thenaturecorps.org

Desc.: The Nature Corps recruits volunteers to work on projects in National Parks in California and Hawaii, such as Yosemite, Sequoia, Channel Islands and Hawaii Volcanoes National Park. Projects vary from revegetation and tree planting to species preservation.

Hab.: Rainforest, high sierra.

Loc.: California and Hawaii, USA.

Dur.: 6-8 day excursions.

Per.: May to October.

L.term: Nature Corps will help volunteers make arrangements to stay after the 8-day period.

Age: Min. 18 (12–17 with parents' permission).

Qualif.: No particular skills needed, photography and carpentry skills welcome.

Lang.: English.

Cost: Adults fees start from US$595, including food and camping arrangements. Transportation provided on most excursions. A portion of the adults' contribution goes to supporting the 6-day Youth Expeditions. Youth and students fees are about US$370.

Agents: Contact The Nature Corps directly.

Applic.: Apply on-line at www.thenaturecorps.org or ask for an application form.

Notes: Half of the excursion is devoted to the project and half to guided recreation and education. Further information available from The Nature Corps.

NZTCV – The New Zealand Trust for Conservation Volunteers

Three Streams; 343 S.H.17, R.D.3 Albany
Auckland New Zealand
Tel.: ++64 (9) 889 3711
E-mail: enquiries@conservationvolunteers.org.nz
www.conservationvolunteers.org.nz

Desc.:	The New Zealand Trust for Conservation Volunteers (NZTCV) is New Zealand's premier organisation for conservation volunteerism. Since 1997 NZTCV has served the New Zealand conservation community altruistically by brokering opportunities between conservation project providers and willing volunteers. NZTCV's website promotes conservation projects, registers volunteers and distributes its bi-monthly newsletter.
Spp.:	Various species of New Zealand's flora and fauna.
Hab.:	Coasts, dryland, National Parks and Reserves, forests, wetlands, natural bush
Loc.:	Throughout New Zealand.
Dur.:	1-3 weeks (varies).
Per.:	Year round.
L.term:	Inquire with organisation.
Age:	No age restrictions.
Qualif.:	Experience and qualifications related to the environment are welcome but not essential.
Work:	Projects cover: wildlife and habitat, planting and restoration, sustainability and eco diversity, research and fieldwork, botanical and organic centres.
Lang.:	English.
Cost:	Free accommodation offered with some projects. Food costs for duration of stay, cost of transportation to and from project location and international travel are paid by the volunteer. See website for more information.
Applic.:	Enquiries via e-mail. Visit www.conservationvolunteers.org.nz.

Oceanic Society Expeditions

Fort Mason Quarters 35
San Francisco, CA 94123 USA
Tel.: ++1 (415) 441 1106 /(800) 326 7491 (toll free in North America)
Fax: ++1 (415) 474 3395
E-mail: info@oceanicsociety.org
www.oceanicsociety.org

Desc.:	Founded in 1972, Oceanic Society Expeditions (OSE) is a non-profit organisation that conducts research to protect aquatic environments and promote environmental education. OSE organises over 30 projects classified as 'Natural History Expeditions' (NHE) and 'Research Expeditions' (RE); the latter are designed to accomplish specific scientific objectives. For these projects volunteers work with field biologists, collecting data and logging information.
Spp.:	Dolphins, manatees, corals, seabirds, sea turtles.
Hab.:	Tropical seas, temperate seas, rivers.
Loc.:	Baja California, Caribbean, Belize, Micronesia and various locations in Central, South and North America.
Dur.:	4-10 days for NHE; 1-2 week for RE.
Per.:	Year round.
L.term:	Inquire with organisation.
Age:	Min. 18. Anyone under 18 must be accompanied by a guardian.
Qualif.:	Enthusiasm and willingness to take directions are necessary.
Lang.:	English.
Cost:	Approx. US$1,500-3,000 for NHE, US$1,000-2,000 for RE.
Applic.:	Request application form to be returned with a deposit of US$400/person/trip.
Notes:	OSE also raises contributions through adopt-a-dolphin, adopt-a-whale and adopt-an-atoll programs.

Operation Wallacea

Hope House
Old Bolingbroke, Spilsby
Lincolnshire PE23 4EX UK
Tel.: ++44 (1790) 763 194 - Fax: ++44 (1790) 763 825
E-mail: info@opwall.com
www.opwall.com

Desc.: Operation Wallacea (Opwall) is a series of biological and conservation management research programmes that has operated since 1995 in remote areas across the world. Opwall volunteers join marine, rainforests and desert projects organized by a 150 strong team of scientist from UK, Ireland, US, Canada and other academic institutions.

Spp.: Corals, sponges, fish, birds, bats, butterflies, mammals, macaques, reptiles and amphibians.

Hab.: Coral reefs, rainforest, desert and bush projects.

Loc.: Indonesia, Honduras, Egypt, South Africa, Peru, Mozambique, Cuba.

Travel: Flight to the nearest international airport (see website).

Dur.: 2, 4, 6, 8 or 10 weeks.

Per.: June to September.

L.term: Inquire with organisation.

Age: Min. 16.

Qualif.: Enthusiasm and a positive attitude towards the environment. Full training is given on site.

Work: Volunteers work alongside scientists to complete surveys of the endemic species. Both flora and fauna are surveyed.

Lang.: English.

Accom.: From hammocks under bashas in the rainforest to huts on the beach.

Cost: GB£975-3,350 depending on length of stay. Prices include food, accommodation, dive training to PADI OW and internal transfers. For further information visit website.

Applic.: Contact UK office. University presentations take place in the UK, US and Canada.

Raleigh

Third Floor, 207 Waterloo Road
London, SE1 8XD UK
Tel.: ++44 (20) 7183 1270
Fax: ++44 (20) 7504 8094
E-mail: info@raleigh.org.uk
www.raleighinternational.org

Desc.: Raleigh is a youth and education charity that runs adventure and challenge expeditions for volunteers from a wide range of backgrounds, nationalities and life stages with the aim of increasing the leadership skills of young people and their awareness of their role as active global citizens. Projects vary from country to country and may include rainwater harvesting, building an eco lodge, or building a school in a local community.

Hab.: Various.

Loc.: Borneo, Costa Rica and Nicaragua, India.

Dur.: 4, 5, 7 and 10 weeks (plus 3 weeks training for volunteer managers).

Per.: Year round.

L.term: Raleigh has an alumni of over 30,000 people. Participants are encouraged to continue their involvement with Raleigh as well as other volunteering opportunities on their return home.

Age: 17-24 (Venturers); 25 or over (Volunteer Managers).

Qualif.: Volunteers must be physically fit, able to swim 200 metres and speak basic English. An introduction weekend including physical and mental challenges is required.

Accom.: Tents. Living conditions during the expeditions are very basic.

Cost: GB£1,500-2,995 for Venturers and GB£1,350-1,950 for Volunteers Managers; depending on programme length, excluding travel expenses.

Applic.: Request more information and apply online at www.raleighinternational.org.

RSPB – The Royal Society for the Protection of Birds

The Lodge, Sandy
Bedfordshire SG19 2DL UK
Tel.: ++44 (1767) 680 551
Fax: ++44 (1767) 692 365
www.rspb.org.uk/volunteering/residential

Desc.:	RSPB Residential Volunteering Scheme operates in 43 reserves around the UK, providing an opportunity for those interested in the environment and conservation to gain practical experience of the day-to-day running of a RSPB reserve.
Spp.:	Birds.
Hab.:	Woodland, swamps, ponds, lakes, moorland, coastal lagoons, cliffs.
Loc.:	England, Scotland, Wales, Northern Ireland.
Dur.:	Min. 1 week (Saturday to Saturday); max. 1 month.
Per.:	Year round.
L.term:	Negotiable by arrangement.
Age:	Min.16 (18 for international volunteers and in some reserves).
Qualif.:	Good physical health. Enthusiasm for conservation and the environment.
Work:	Duties vary and may include: habitat and estate management, tourist assistance, reception work, survey/research assistance, working with stock, reed cutting/planting, bird counts, animal population monitoring. Duties allocated according to volunteer knowledge and experience.
Lang.:	English.
Accom.:	Chalets, cottages, houses, cabins, caravans or bungalows. May have to share a room with at least 1 other person of same sex. Bedding is provided (except sleeping bag). Cooking facilities available (volunteers must provide and cook their own food).
Cost:	Free accommodation. Food and travel expenses not included.
Applic.:	See online brochure and application form on the website.
Selected projects:	Rathlin Island Seabird Centre, Northern Ireland.

SANCCOB – The Southern African Foundation for the Conservation of Coastal Birds

PO Box: 1111 6, Bloubergrant
7443 Cape Town South Africa
Tel.: ++27 (21) 557 6155 - Fax: ++27 (21) 557 8804
E-mail: carole@sanccob.co.za; info@sanccob.co.za
www.sanccob.co.za

Desc.: SANCCOB rehabilitates sick, injured, oiled and abandoned sea birds. The species most affected is the African penguin, a bird only found along the southern African coast and classified as 'vulnerable.' The South African route is a popular ship-faring route and is very polluted.

Spp.: African penguin (*Spheniscus demersus*), Cape gannet, Cape, crowned and whitebreasted cormorants, kelp and hartlaub gulls, petrel, tern, albatross.

Hab.: Coastal.

Loc.: 20km north of Cape Town, South Africa.

Travel: Flight to Cape Town.

Dur.: Min. 6 weeks.

Per.: May to October is busy but oil spills can happen any time.

L.term: Possible, with project leaders approval.

Age: Min. 18.

Qualif.: Willingness to work hard with wild, difficult birds.

Work: Keeping the centre clean, scrubbing pools and pens daily (cleaning after 30-200 birds), feeding and stabilizing birds and assisting veterinary staff.

Lang.: English.

Accom.: Bed&Breakfast or contact the organisation for other possibilities.

Cost: Project fee of R1000 for the first 6 weeks and R167 for every week thereafter. Volunteers are responsible for food, transport and accommodation costs, approx. US$30-40/day.

Applic.: Fill out application form from the web page.

SCA – Student Conservation Association, Inc.

PO Box 550
Charlestown, New Hampshire 03603 USA
Tel.: ++1 (603) 543 1700
Fax: ++1 (603) 543 1828
E-mail: admissions@thesca.org
www.thesca.org

Desc.:	SCA is an educational organisation operating volunteer and internship programmes in conservation and natural resource management. The Conservation Internship Programs (CIP) are for anyone to serve alongside seasonal staff for public/private natural resource management agencies. The Conservation Crew Program (CCP) allows high school students to join summer conservation projects.
Loc.:	USA: opportunities exist in all 50 states
Dur.:	Usually 12-52 weeks for CIP; 3-5 weeks for CCP.
Per.:	CIP are available year round, CCP from June to August only.
L.term:	Max. 12 months, depending upon project.
Age:	Min. 18 for CIP, no upper age limit; 15-19 for CCP.
Qualif.:	Good health, enthusiasm, flexibility, fluent English.
Work:	Interns work with wildlife, in back country patrol, trail building, hydrology and resource management, visitor services and interpretation, environmental education with youth, research, public outreach, museum curator positions, etc.
Lang.:	English.
Cost:	No cost. CIP interns receive paid travel (within the US), free housing and related expenses, weekly living allowance of US$75-160 and accident insurance. CCP volunteers receive only free room and board and equipment. Application fee: US$10-40.
Applic.:	An application must be submitted with a medical form and at least 2 references. Request by mail or phone or download from SCA's website. Applicants can apply directly online. No deadline for CIP; deadline for CCP is March 1st, or until all positions are filled.
Notes:	Listings of positions on website. Searchable database updated weekly; applications can also be filled out on website directly.

SCI – The Association of Service Civil International

St-Jacobsmarkt 82
B-2000 Antwerpen Belgium
Tel.: ++32 (3) 226 5727 - Fax: ++32 (3) 232 0344
E-mail: info@sciint.org
www.sciint.org

Desc.: SCI is an international volunteering organisation with more then ninety years of experience in coordinating international voluntary projects. Through these projects SCI wants to break down barriers and prejudices between people of different backgrounds and promote a culture of peace. Ecological projects in SCI vary from planting bamboo trees in Sri Lanka to helping out in an eco-village in Bulgaria.

Loc.: Worldwide.

Dur.: 2-3 weeks.

Per.: Year round, mainly June to September.

L.term: People with experience in short term voluntary projects can join long term projects for 3-12 months.

Age: Min. 18 for Europe; min. 16 for the United States.

Qualif.: Ability to work as part of a team and live simply.

Lang.: English. For other languages, inquire with local SCI office.

Cost: Volunteers must provide transportation; contributions are US$65 in the United States, EUR120 in Europe, EUR250 in Eastern Europe. Accommodation, food and insurance are provided.

Agents: Local SCI offices listed in the above website. SCI has more than branches in the world and cooperates with many organisations: contact the nearest office for information.

Applic.: Standard application; no need to be a member.

Notes: For short term voluntary projects in Africa, Asia or Latin America some previous voluntary experience and attendance of preparation days is required.

Tethys Research Institute

Civic Aquarium
Viale G.B. Gadio 2
20121 Milan Italy
Tel.: ++39 (02) 7200 1947
Fax: ++39 (02) 8699 5011
E-mail: tethys@tethys.org   www.tethys.org

Desc.:	This private non-profit organisation is dedicated to the study and protection of marine habitats, focusing on Mediterranean cetaceans. Founded in 1986, TRI is formed by a team of marine biologists conducting research with the help of volunteers.
Spp.:	Cetaceans.
Hab.:	Mediterranean Sea.
Loc.:	Mediterranean (Italy, Greece).
Dur.:	1-2 weeks.
Per.:	May to October.
L.term:	Biology students or research assistants may assist TRI biologists for 1-2 months upon leader's approval.
Age:	Min.18. Minors may be accepted if accompanied by an adult.
Qualif.:	Volunteers must be enthusiastic and flexible; ability to swim is necessary.
Work:	Assist the researchers with observations, cetacean photo-identification, field data collection and analysis of digital images. Share boat or household duties (shopping, cleaning, cooking).
Lang.:	English, Italian.
Accom.:	Aboard the 21–metre ketch *Pelagos* for research cruises in the Cetacean Sanctuary. In house along the coast for dolphin project in Greece.
Cost:	Approx. EUR695-925 for 6 days. Food included. Travel to and from project not included.
Applic.:	Visit website for detailed information and application forms.
Selected projects:	Cetacean Sanctuary Research, Ligurian Sea. Ionian Dolphin Project, Greece.

United Nations Volunteers (UNV)

PO Box 260-111,
D-53153 Bonn Germany
Tel.: ++49 (228) 815 2000
Fax: ++49 (228) 815 2001
E-mail: information@unvolunteers.org
www.unv.org

Desc.: The United Nations Volunteers programme is open to specialists in various fields. Since 1971 over 30,000 volunteers have joined the programme in over 160 countries (particularly in developing ones), co-operating with local organisations and communities for teaching or offering their professional skills. UNV programmes include: education, environment, peace operations and democracy, humanitarian relief and rehabilitation, technical co-operation and refugee assistance. Today, some 10% of the serving UNVs work with environmental or conservation issues in specific areas such as plant protection, forestry conservation, sanitation/waste disposal, energy engineering, meteorology, coastal erosion, preservation of cultural heritage and tourism. UN Volunteers have been assigned to projects on pandas in a reserve in China or on global warming policy planning in the Maldives.

Loc.: Developing countries throughout the world such as India, Brazil, Mali and Burkina Faso (for the environmental programme).

Dur.: Assignments last from a few months to 1-2 years.

Per.: Year round.

L.term: Some assignments can be extended beyond the 2-year period.

Age: Min. 25, but UNV volunteers are usually older than 35, as a professional working experience is necessary.

Qualif.: Volunteers must be professionals or technicians with at least 2 years of experience. Teachers, medical doctors, nurses, mechanical or electrical engineers, geologists, automotive mechanics, librarians, midwives, etc.

Work: Varies depending on programme and location.

Lang.: English, French, Spanish, Arabic, Portuguese. Language ability of selected volunteers will be tested.

Accom.: Simple accommodation provided for volunteer and dependent relatives (spouse and up to 2 children under 21 years of age). Furniture and utilities are normally provided. If these arrangements cannot be made, the paid rent will be reimbursed.

Cost: UNV volunteers receive a monthly living allowance intended to cover basic living expenses. Upon completion of an assignment, a resettlement allowance will also be paid. Life, health and permanent disability insurance is provided free of charge. Return travel to duty station is also provided (includes direct dependents).

Applic.: Write or call for the PHS (Personal History Statement) form (either in French or English), which must be completed and sent in together with 2 photos and reference forms completed by both professional and personal referees. If the PHS is approved by UNV headquarters, the application is added to the roster of candidates. If a volunteer is selected for a particular post, the PHS is submitted for clearance by a UN agency and for approval by the Government requesting the services of a UNV specialist. Submission and selection of candidates may take several months. Candidates who are accepted must begin the assignment within 8 weeks of being notified of final selection.

U.S. Department of Agriculture – Forest Service

Volunteering in the National Forests
PO Box 96090, Washington, DC 20090-6090 or
1400 Independence Ave., SW Washington, DC USA
Tel.: ++1 (800) 832 1355
www.fs.fed.us (then search for 'employment')

- Region 1–Northern Region, Federal Bldg., PO Box 7669, Missoula, Montan 59807, tel. ++1 (406) 329 3511

- Region 2–Rocky Mountain, PO Box 25127, Golden, Colorado 80401, tel. ++1 (303) 275 5350

- Region 3–Southwestern, 333 Broadway, SE, Albuquerque, New Mexico 87102, tel. ++1 (505) 842 3292

- Region 4–Intermountain, 25th St., Ogden, Utah 84401, tel. ++1 (801) 625 5306

- Region 5–Pacific Southwest, 1323 Club Drive, Vallejo, California 94592, tel. ++1 (707) 562 8737

- Region 6–Pacific Northwest, 333 SW First Avenue, PO Box 3623 Portland, Oregon 97208–3623, tel. ++1 (503) 808 2468

- Region 8–Southern, 1720 Peachtree Rd., NW, Atlanta, Georgia 30309, tel. ++1 (404) 347 4191

- Region 9–Eastern, 626 E. Wisconsin Ave., Milwaukee, Wisconsin 53202, tel. ++1 (414) 297 3600

- Region 10–Alaska, Federal Office Bldg., PO Box 21628 Juneau, Alaska 99802–1628, tel. ++1 (907) 586 8806

- Pacific Northwest Research Station, 333 SW 1st Avenue, PO Box 3890, Portland, Oregon 97208-3623, tel. ++1 (503) 808 2592

- Rocky Mountain Research Station, 240 W. Prospect Road, Fort Collins, Colorado 80526, tel. ++1 (970) 498 1100

- International Institute of Tropical Forestry, PO Box 25000, UPR Experimental Station, 1201 Calle Leiba, Puerto Rico 00928, tel. ++1 (787) 766 5335

Desc.: The Forest Service manages and protects the National Forest System and cooperates with private forest and woodland owners, State and local government agencies and private organisations. It performs research for improving the quality of the forest and forest products. Volunteer service is needed in US National Forests because the Forest Service has a limited budget. The programme goal is to provide fulfilling work experience to volunteers while accomplishing necessary tasks.

Spp.: Various in the United States.

Hab.: Various in the United States.

Loc.: National Forests throughout the United States.

Dur.: Inquire with the National Forest of choice.

Per.: Inquire with the National Forest of choice.

L.term: Inquire with the National Forest of choice.

Age: No age limit. Under 18 with the written consent of a parent or guardian.

Qualif.: No specific skills required. Volunteers must be in good health to allow them to perform their duties without risk to themselves or others. A medical examination may be required for some tasks. Persons with disabilities are encouraged to volunteer.

Work: Maintaining and hosting campgrounds, working at visitor centres and ranger stations, planting trees, presenting environmental education programmes, building and repairing structures, taking photographs. Training provided if necessary.

Lang.: English.

Accom.: Housing may be available. Inquire with National Forest of choice.

Cost: Some expenses such as transportation, lodging, subsistence and uniforms may be reimbursed on a case-by-case basis.

Applic.: Write or call the volunteer coordinator of the region of interest. See list in the previous page or from the directory on the website: www.fs.fed.us/intro/directory/orgdir.shtml (or search for 'directory').

Notes: Non-U.S. citizens are eligible to work for a U.S. Federal Agency only if permanent residents of the U.S. or if non-immigrant aliens with F-1 visa status or if bona fide students residing in the U.S. Enquire with your nearest U.S. Consular Office.

U.S. Fish and Wildlife Service
1849 C Street, NW
Washington DC 20240 USA
Tel.: ++1 (800) 344 WILD (toll free in the USA)
www.fws.gov/volunteers

Desc.:   The USFWS mission is to conserve, protect and enhance fish, wildlife, plants and their habitats. Almost 40,000 volunteers every year perform a variety of task, part or full time or during a particular season or event. Work ranges from ringing birds at a national wildlife refuge to raising fish at a fish hatchery, from conducting wildlife surveys to leading tours or restoring fragile habitat.

Spp.:   Migratory birds, fish and all endangered species.

Hab.:   Various in the United States.

Loc.:   Throughout the United States.

Dur.:   From a few days to several months.

Per.:   Year round.

Age: Min. 18.

Qualif.:   No special skills are required. Experience with the life sciences is preferable. Some positions require teaching, public speaking or other specialized skills. Training provided if necessary.

Lang.:   English.

Cost: Volunteers arrange their travel; assistance available for US applicants. Room and board are usually covered while on duty.

Applic.:   Online form.

Notes: Non-US citizens must plan well ahead and secure a proper visa or entry papers. The USFWS does not work with whales and dolphins. It offers also the Resident Volunteers Program (see www.fws.gov/residentvols/). "RV's" are volunteers who provide their own "homes" (usually a pop-up camper or a van). The agency (or host) provides a variety of support amenities; volunteers in exchange for the right of stay in a beautiful area, perform work as volunteer service.

U.S. National Park Service

National Park Service Headquarters
1849 C Street NW
Washington, DC 20240 USA
Tel.: ++1 (202) 208 6843
www.nps.gov/volunteer/

Desc.: The United States National Park Service is officially entrusted with preserving more than 350 national parks in the US. Through the VIP (Volunteers-In-Parks) Program, anyone can help conserving the parks' natural and historical resources.

Spp.: Various of North America.

Hab.: Various of North America.

Loc.: National parks throughout the United States.

Dur.: Inquire with the park or the field area of choice.

Per.: Inquire with the park or the field area of choice.

L.term: Inquire with the park of choice.

Age: Min. 18. Persons under 18 years of age must have permission of their parents or be accompanied by adults in a family or group.

Qualif.: Various skills and talents desired. Reasonably good health is expected. A medical examination may be required for some jobs. Disabled individuals are encouraged to volunteer.

Work: Providing information at a visitor centre, accessioning artifacts into a park's archaeological or historic collection, conducting surveys of plant and animal species in the park or doing construction and repair work on hiking trails. Accepted volunteers receive appropriate training and orientation at the beginning of the service.

Lang.: English.

Accom.: Some of the larger parks may provide free housing for VIPs. Arrangements made between the volunteer and the park.

Cost: Some parks reimburse volunteers for some expenses, such as local travel costs, meals and uniforms. Volunteers must cover the cost of travel to and from the park.

Agents: Alaska Area Region, 240 West 5th Avenue, Anchorage, Alaska 99501, tel. ++1 (907) 644 3510.

Intermountain Region, 12795 Alameda Parkway, Denver, Colorado 80225, tel. ++1 (303) 969 2500.

Midwest Region, 601 Riverfront Drive, Omaha, Nebraska 68102, tel. ++1 (402) 661 1524.

Northeast Region, U.S. Customs House, 200 Chestnut St. Fifth Floor, Philadelphia, Pennsylvania 19106, tel. ++1 (215) 597 7013.

Pacific West Region, One Jackson Center, 1111 Jackson Street, Suite 700, Oakland, California 94607, tel. ++1 (510) 817 1304.

Southeast Region, 100 Alabama St., SW, 1924 Building, Atlanta, Georgia 30303, tel. ++1 (404) 562 3100.

Applic.: The website lists hundred of opportunities (click on opportunities) and gives detailed application contacts for each position. Addresses of parks can be obtained from the Regional offices listed above. Ask for a VIP application form. Prospective volunteers can apply to more than 1 park. Selection for summer positions are usually made between February and April.

Notes: Non-U.S. citizens are eligible to work for a U.S. Federal Agency only if permanent residents of the U.S. or if non-immigrant aliens with F-1 visa status or if bona fide students residing in the U.S. Enquire with your nearest U.S. Consular Office.

Volunteer Latin America

PO Box 585, Rochester
Kent ME1 9EJ UK
Tel.: ++44 (20) 7193 9163
E-mail: info@volunteerlatinamerica.com
www.volunteerlatinamerica.com

Desc.: Volunteer Latin America provide a personalised information service on free and low cost volunteer opportunities in Central and South America, as well as referrals to good Spanish and Portuguese language schools.

Spp.: Various species of Latin America: birds, reptiles, mammals, etc.

Hab.: Various of Latin America: tropical coasts, rainforest, pampas, altiplanos, etc.

Loc.: All the countries of Central and South America.

Travel: Independent travel to project site.

Dur.: Varies depending on project: from 1-2 weeks to several months.

Per.: Projects take place year round.

L.term: Many projects accept long-term volunteers.

Age: Min. 18 - max. 65.

Qualif.: No particular qualifications required. Inquire with organisation. Full training provided in projects that require specific skills.

Work: Various research and conservation work. Many projects give an excellent opportunity to gain fieldwork experience and to learn about conservation efforts.

Lang.: English or Spanish.

Accom.: In several projects volunteers receive free board and lodging.

Cost: Volunteers are exclusively responsible for their own travel. Some projects require an affordable contribution from the volunteers.

Applic.: Visit VLA website for further details.

Selected projects: Jaguar Conservation, Brazil.
Penguin Research, Argentina and Chile.

Volunteers for Outdoor Colorado (VOC)

600 South Marion Parkway
Denver, Colorado 80209-2597 USA
Tel.: ++1 (303) 715 1010
Fax: ++1 (303) 715 1212
E-mail: voc@voc.org
www.voc.org

Desc.: This non-profit organisation, founded in 1984, promotes and fosters citizen and visitor responsibility for Colorado's public lands. VOC organises 1-day to week-long conservation projects and provides volunteer resources to land management agencies, non-profits and user groups. VOC also manages Volunteers Outdoors (www.volunteeroutdoors.net), a state-wide clearinghouse for public lands volunteer opportunities. Land managers and non-profits post hundreds of opportunities to volunteer in Colorado's public lands.

Hab.: Urban gardens and parks, streams, lakes, mountains.

Loc.: Urban and natural areas, National Parks, National Forests, State Parks, public lands, Colorado, USA.

Dur.: 1 day to 4 months.

Per.: Year round.

L.term.: No.

Age: Min. 8 for VOC projects; under16 must be accompanied by an adult.

Qualif.: Desired experience varies from none to skilled.

Lang.: English.

Cost: No cost.

Applic.: Sign up online.

Notes: The VOC website has an excellent list of links to other volunteering organisations in the US and in Colorado.

The Wilderness Foundation UK

47-49 Main Road, Broomfield,
Chelmsford, Essex, CM1 7BU UK
Tel.: ++44 (1245) 443 073
Fax: ++44 (1245) 445 035
E-mail: info@wildernessfoundation.org.uk
www.wildernessfoundation.org.uk

Desc.:	The Wilderness Foundation UK charity promotes self-financed adventurous journeys on foot, horseback and by canoe into the last remaining wilderness areas across the world. Additional volunteer and guide training programmes focus on rural communities, conservation, teach wilderness skills for groups of young people and adults. Groups size is from 6 to 8 people.
Loc.:	Trails are held in Wales, Scotland, Tanzania, South Africa and USA.
Dur.:	Min. 7 days, max. 30 days for adults and students.
Age:	Min. 15.
Qualif.:	No specific qualifications required. Must be reasonably fit.
Lang.:	English.
Cost:	Costs on average are GB£75 per person per day. This excludes travel to and from destination but includes food, guides and equipment. Apart from travel to and from the destination this is all inclusive.
Accom.:	Normally in the open or in remote bush camps for journeys in Africa and USA. Basic bunkhouse accommodation is provided in Wales and Scotland.
Notes:	Trails focus on the ethics and values of wilderness experience. Tailor made programmes can be put together for groups of 4 or more.

WWF International
WWF Secretariat
Av. du Mont-Blanc 27
1196 Gland Switzerland
Tel.: ++41 (22) 364 9111
Fax: ++41 (22) 364 8836
www.panda.org

Desc.: WWF is one of the largest environmental associations in the world, managing more than 1300 conservation projects everywhere. The vast majority of these focus on local issues, ranging from school nature gardens in Zambia, to the restoration of orangutan habitats to the establishment of giant panda reserves. Besides, its work involves partnerships with local non-profit agencies and other NGOs. Volunteers are recruited for field study projects, restoration activities and conservation workcamps.

Spp.: Birds, wolves, sea turtles, whales, dolphins, bears.

Hab.: Sea, mountains, wetlands, lakes.

Loc.: All over the world.

Dur.: Min. 5 days; max. 2 weeks.

Per.: Year round.

L.term.: Inquire with organisation.

Age: Min. 18.

Qualif.: Previous experience and specific qualifications maybe required according to chosen field.

Lang.: According to country of destination.

Cost: Inquire with organisation.

Agents: WWF has offices in many countries. Contact national WWF office for information on workcamps in your country or on international volunteering opportunities. For a complete list of national offices see: www.panda.org/how_you_can_help/volunteer/index.cfm.

Applic.: Request an application form. Volunteers must be WWF members to participate.

YCI – Youth Challenge International

20 Maud Street, Suite 305
Toronto, Ontario M5V 2M5 Canada
Tel.: ++1 (416) 504 3370
Fax: ++1 (416) 504 3376
E-mail: generalinfo@yci.org
www.yci.org

Desc.:	Youth Challenge International combines community development, health promotion and environmental work in adventurous projects carried out by teams of volunteers aged 18-30. Volunteers are accepted from across Canada and represent different backgrounds. Experienced staff teams ensure projects are dynamic and results oriented. Self-discovery, personal growth and community development are key elements.
Spp.:	Rainforest and riverine/coastal fauna.
Hab.:	Rainforest, coast, mountains.
Loc.:	Costa Rica, Ghana, Guatemala, Guyana, Uganda, Nicaragua, Kenya, Tanzania.
Dur.:	5, 6, 8, and 10 week projects.
L.term.:	Placements for field staff are for 4-6 months at a time. Upon review, volunteers can work for another placement period.
Age:	Min. 18 - max. 30.
Qualif.:	No specific qualifications are needed.
Lang.:	English.
Cost:	USD$2,500-3,900, travel expenses excluded. Volunteers must pay for inoculations and personal equipment.
Applic.:	Participants and field staff can apply at any time; applications can be submitted on-line.
Notes:	Due to insurance limitations YCI can only accept applications from Canadian citizens, residents or landed immigrants.

PROJECT LIST

ACE – American Conservation Experience, Arizona USA

418 S Leroux Street
Flagstaff, Arizona 86001 USA
Tel.: ++1 (928) 226 6960
E-mail: kazuko@usaconservation.org
www.usaconservation.org

Desc.:	ACE organises volunteer work adventures in America's most stunning National Parks and allows to experience a different range of conservation opportunities throughout the Southwest U.S. Typical projects include trail reconstruction, habitat surveys and planting, revegetation in remote sections of the Grand Canyon, Zion and other National Parks. Work is physically demanding and production oriented in a supportive multi-cultural atmosphere.
Spp.:	Work with flora and fauna ecosystems ranging from low desert to 3,500ft (1,200 m) mountains.
Hab.:	Grand Canyon desert, high elevation mountain forests, and everything in between.
Loc.:	Grand Canyon, Zion and other National Parks and Forests. Home base in Flagstaff, Arizona, and Santa Cruz, California.
Dur.:	8-12 weeks (longer terms possible).
Per.:	Year round.
L.term:	Inquire with organisation
Age:	Min. 18 - max. 35.
Qualif.:	Physically capable of hiking and camping in remote areas. Sense of adventure. Enthusiastic work ethic.
Work:	Trail construction and restoration, planting/revegetation, forest restoration, habitat survey.
Lang.:	English.
Cost:	Travel expenses. Booking fees through international partners apply, typically US$300-500 for 12-week program. Visit the registration page of the website for details.
Applic.:	Register online at www.usaconservation.org. Accepting applications year round.

Adriatic Dolphin Project, Croatia

Blue World
Kastel 24 51551
Veli Losinj Croatia
Tel./Fax: ++385 (51) 604 666
E-mail: info@blue-world.org
www.blue-world.org

Desc.: Since 2000 the research has been carried out by a local NGO, Blue World, in cooperation with international researchers. In 2003 Blue World constructed an educational centre in Veli Losinj which provides a professional environment to study cetaceans. The ADP studies the bottlenose dolphin population of the Northern Adriatic. This project looks at the fields of population dynamics, behaviour and acoustics. Data is taken in the field and analysed in the offices above the Losinj Marine Education Centre located in the picturesque harbour of Veli Losinj. The standard research procedure includes photo-ID, acoustic and behavioural sampling. Dolphin habitat use, association patterns and reproductive rate are also recorded.

Spp.: Bottlenose dolphin (*Tursiops truncatus*). Other marine species occasionally observed: marine turtles, blue sharks, tuna, cormorants.

Hab.: Coastal waters.

Loc.: Cres–Losinj archipelago, northern Adriatic Sea (Croatia).

Travel: The island of Losinj can be easily reached by bus, via Rijeka, from Trieste (Italy), Zagreb (Croatia) and Ljubljana (Slovenia), or (during the summer) by ferry from Venice or hydrofoil from Trieste (Italy); the nearest airports are in Rijeka and Pula.

Dur.: 12 days. Up to 5 volunteers can participate in each stage.

Per.: May to September.

L.term: Extra days beyond the initial 12 can be arranged.

Age: Min.18. Younger volunteers may apply, but must be accompanied by one parent.

Qualif.: Interest in the research and positive motivation is required. Volunteers must be physically fit and able to endure long hours, possibly in hot sun or in harsh sea conditions on a small boat.

Work: Behavioural observations, acoustics and photo-ID of the dolphins from the inflatable boat. With good weather researchers and volunteers conduct boat surveys. With bad weather volunteers may work in the centre, entering and analysing data and matching the catalogued dolphins.

Lang.: English, Croatian, Italian and German are spoken by researchers.

Accom.: Shared rooms in a house in Veli Losinj. Volunteers take part in cooking and housekeeping.

Cost: Min. EUR700, max. EUR950, depending on the season. Volunteers must confirm that they have personal insurance. Fees do not include travel expenses. All tourists coming to Losinj are required to pay the local tourist fee (about EUR1/day for the duration of the programme).

Applic.: A downloadable application form is available on the website. Early booking is suggested.

Notes: Volunteers must be aware that they are participating in scientific research rather than a vacation programme.

African Impact Lion Rehabilitation Programmes, Zambia

African Impact
6 Carlton Close, Noordhoek, 7985 Cape Town   South Africa
Tel: ++27 (217) 854 319 / 0800 520 0926 (UK toll free)
E-mail: info@africanimpact.org
www.africanimpact.com

Desc.: By volunteering with this project, you can contribute to the welfare and rehabilitation of the cubs as they undertake pre-release training in the Mosi-oa-Tunya National Park; take part in a research program to better understand the ecology of elephants in the Park and join our conservation education and community programs to involve communities in conservation as part of our holistic approach.

Spp.: Lions, elephants and free roaming wildlife.

Hab.: The banks of the Zambezi river, in the Mosi-oa-Tunya National Park.

Loc.: Livingstone, southern Zambia.

Travel: Plane to Livingstone; the Park is in the outskirts of the city.

Dur.: 2-6 weeks.

Per.: Year round.

Age: Min 17, max dependent on participants health.

Qualif.: No previous experience necessary, training will be given.

Work.: Data gathering and observation of lions behaviour, meat preparation, bottle feeding of cubs, boundary patrols and snare sweeps in the reserve. Supervision of cubs and adolescent lions out in the bush.

Lang.: English.

Accom.: Comfortable twin thatched rooms with adjacent clean ablutions.

Cost: US$3,395/GB£1,885 for 1 month, including room and board, airport transfers and a project donation.

Applic.: Via e-mail or with Green Volunteers Standard Application Form.

Altai Snow Leopards Survey Expedition, Russia

Ivy Road, Norwich NR5 8BF UK
Tel.: +44 (870) 446 0801
Fax: +44 (870) 446 0809
E-mail: info@biosphere-expeditions.org
www.biosphere-expeditions.org

Desc.:	This expedition takes place in the high mountains of Central Asia to survey snow leopards and their prey animals like the argali mountain sheep and the Altai ibex, as well as other animals like marmots and birds.
Spp.:	Snow leopards, argali mountain sheep, Altai ibex and others.
Hab.:	High mountains.
Loc.:	Altai Republic, Russia, Central Asia.
Travel:	Flight to Novosibirsk, where participants are welcomed.
Dur.:	Minimum 2 weeks.
Per.:	July to August.
L.term:	Stays up to 6 weeks possible.
Age:	Min. 18.
Qualif.:	No particular skills or knowledge are needed.
Work:	Volunteers will be covering ground in Land Rovers and on foot, looking for tracks, kills, scats and the animals themselves. True expedition-style base camp conditions, testing but satisfying mountain surveying and offroad driving.
Lang.:	English.
Accom.:	Tent camp of one and two person dome, mess and kitchen, as well as shower and toilet tents.
Cost:	GB£1,690 for two weeks.
Applic.:	Applications via www.biosphere-expeditions.org/availability

The American Bear Association, USA

The Vince Shute Wildlife Sanctuary
PO Box 77, Orr
Minnesota 55771 USA
Tel.: ++1 (218) 757 0172
E-mail: bears@americanbear.org
www.americanbear.org

Desc.:   An NGO dedicated to promoting the well-being of the black bear, other wildlife and natural resources through education and research. The Vince Shute Wildlife Sanctuary is the best place in North America to observe and photograph wild black bears, featuring environmental education, conservation efforts, and wildlife co-existence.

Spp.:   American black bear (*Ursus americanus*).

Hab.:   Forest.

Loc.:   Northwoods of Minnesota, USA.

Travel: Flight to Duluth, Minnesota.

Dur.:   Min. 1 week - max. 5 months, for volunteers and interns.

Per.:   Summer (early May through early October).

L.term: Volunteers can stay up to 5 months with director's approval.

Qualif.:   Volunteers must read the Volunteer Handbook and complete a liability waiver. When possible, jobs will be matched to the specific interests and skills of the volunteer. Students are encouraged to apply.

Work: Visiting with visitors on and off the viewing platform and interpreting bear behaviour, assisting in construction projects, conducting daily clean-up chores, cooking, completing routine maintenance projects, grounds-keeping, maintaining records on bear activity, etc.

Lang.:   English.

Accom.:   All services available in the towns of Orr and Nett Lake. Campgrounds and numerous resorts are at nearby Pelican Lake. On-site lodging may be possible.

Cost: Volunteers are responsible for off-site lodging and extras.

Applic.:   Contact the Association for more information.

Andean Bear Research Project, Ecuador

Andean Bear Foundation
Reina Victoria N 26-125 y La Nina
Quito Ecuador
Tel.: ++593 (2) 2683 647
E-mail: volunteer@andeanbear.org
www.andeanbear.org

Desc.: The only project in the world that radiotracks Andean bears in the wild. It is part of ongoing efforts to expand protected areas and prevent the extinction of the species. The primary purpose is to determine the use of the habitat, activity patterns and size of home range and core area of the Andean bear.

Spp.: Andean Spectacled Bear (*Tremarctos ornatus*).

Hab.: Andean cloud forest.

Loc.: Intag region, north-western Ecuador.

Travel: Flight to Quito. Transportation to project area is provided.

Dur.: Min. 2 max. 5 weeks.

Per.: Year round.

L.term: Available only for Ph.D researchers and Volunteer Coordinators.

Age: Min. 19.

Qualif.: No special qualifications requested; volunteers should be fit.

Work: Following roads or trails and listening for signals from the bears by means of radio-telemetry equipment, clearing trails to be used for tracking, collecting samples, recording marking behaviour.

Lang.: English or Spanish.

Accom.: Traditional Andean house with electricity, running water. Volunteers sleep in a large dormitory room.

Cost: US$390 for 2 weeks, US$660 for a month, including 3 meals/day, accommodation, transportation to project site. Local transportation costs not included (approx. US$15-20 per month).

Applic.: A simple application via e-mail. Include possible dates.

Andean Condor and Puma Surveys, Peru

Mundo Azul
Calle Enrique del Horme 214
Lima - Miraflores Peru
Tel.: ++51 (1) 9947 3336
E-mail: mundoazul@terra.com.pe
www.mundoazul.org

Desc.:	Volunteers will accompany researchers on trekking surveys in the central Peruvian Andes between 3,500 and 5,000 meters of altitude in order to survey condor and puma populations, as well as other species.
Spp.:	Andean condor, puma, vicuna, birds of prey, humming birds, etc.
Hab.:	Andean mountains.
Loc.:	Chancay valley, central Andes, Peru.
Travel:	Flight to Lima, airport pick-up, overland travel in 4 wheel drive cars, trekking.
Dur.:	Each survey lasts 2 weeks.
Per.:	Year round.
L.term:	Inquire with the organisation.
Age:	Min. 16 - max. 50. Older if fit; people with heart problems should not apply.
Qualif.:	No special skills required, other than English knowledge and physical fitness. Training will be given on-site.
Work:	Surveying species.
Lang.:	English; some Spanish knowledge is an advantage.
Accom.:	Hostels, tents.
Cost:	EUR1,600 for 2 weeks, all inclusive.
Applic.:	Fill out the application form on: www.mundoazul.org, section "conservation volunteers".

Animal Aid Unlimited, India

Chota Hawala, Udaipur Rajasthan 313001 India
Tel.: ++91 (0294) 251 3359
6900, 37th Ave SW, Seattle WA 98126 USA
Tel.: ++1 (206) 935 2670 /(995) 053 1639
E-mail: info@animalaidunlimited.com
www.animalaidunlimited.com

Desc.:	Animal Aid's aim is to save the lives of injured and ill dogs, cats, birds, donkeys, cows, and monkeys in Udaipur, India, learning that suffering is preventable. Long-term and short-term volunteers brighten the lives of animals by giving walks, baths, coaxing scared animals to eat, play-time for puppies, and love.
Spp.:	Dogs, cats, birds, monkeys, donkeys, cows, buffaloes.
Hab.:	Semi-desert and city.
Loc.:	Udaipur, Rajasthan, India.
Travel:	Animal Aid is reachable by train, plane, and bus.
Dur.:	Even an hour can brighten the life of a recovering animal.
Per.:	Year round.
L.term:	Long-term volunteers are welcome
Age:	Min. 13.
Qualif.:	Experience with animals helps, but all skill levels, together with compassion and love, can do great work and save lives at AAU.
Work:	Giving walks to recovering dogs, baths, groom donkeys and dogs, coaxing sick and scared animals to eat, playing with puppies, feeding orphaned babies.
Lang.:	English and Hindi are spoken.
Accom.:	Accommodation is not provided, but all price-ranges of hotels are nearby.
Cost:	There is no charge for volunteers, but donations are encouraged as running the hospital depends on each generous contribution.
Applic.:	Send e-mail at info@animalaidunlimited.com for information.

Antigua Nesting Turtles Arché Project, West Indies

A.R.C.H.E'. Research and Educational Activities for Chelonian Conservation
Via Mulinetto, 40/A-I, 44100 Ferrara Italy
Tel.: ++39 (0532) 767 852 - Mob.: ++39 (348) 393 7924
Fax: ++39 (1782) 253 279
E-mail: archeturtle@tiscali.it   www.archeturtle.org

Desc.:	The project focuses on the nesting turtles, nest protection, educational activities for the local people.
Spp.:	Hawksbill, Loggerhead, Green sea turtle.
Hab.:	Atlantic and Caribbean Sea.
Loc.:	Antigua and Barbuda, West Indies.
Travel:	Flight to Saint Johns.
Dur.:	Min. 12 days.
Per.:	July, August.
L.term:	There is no limit for long-term stays.
Age:	Min. 24.
Qualif.:	No special qualifications, other than ability to work in team, enthusiasm, adaptability, love for animals and willingness to work long hours. Respect to other people.
Work:	Early morning walk on the beaches where the turtles lay the eggs, to protect females and, if necessary, to relocate the nests because of predators. In the afternoon, insert the collected data and educational activities for the local people and tourists in the hotels.
Lang.:	English.
Accom.:	At bungalows with cooking and washing facilities in shared rooms.
Cost:	EUR650/12 days. Food and accommodation included. Travel and personal expenses are not included.
Applic.:	Via e-mail or by filling the online application form.

APES-Umpalazi Community and Wildlife Project, South Africa

PO Box 443 Greytown
3250 KwaZulu/Natal South Africa.
Tel.: ++27 (0) 72 306 5664
E-mail: apes1@gom.co.za
www.apes.org.za

Desc.: A wildlife sanctuary specialised in primates, providing refuge also for other displaced animals. This project incorporates local community upliftment, including skills training and aid work, with the rehabilitation of injured and/or orphaned wildlife for future release and monitoring.

Spp.: Primates (i.e. vervet monkey), domestic and farm animals (dogs, cats, donkeys, cows, chickens, goats, geese).

Hab.: Subtropical.

Loc.: Greytown (Umvoti) area, KwaZulu-Natal, South Africa.

Travel: Flight to Johannesburg, stay at Shoestrings Airport Lodge, then by bus to the pick-up location at Mooi River.

Dur.: Minimum 4 weeks.

Per.: Year round.

L.term: Volunteers are invited to stay long-term.

Age: Min. 18. Younger with parents' permission (min. 16).

Qualif.: No particular skills are needed; experience in carpentry, zoology, veterinary, etc. is appreciated but not essential.

Work: Animal food preparation, enclosure cleaning, wildlife rescue/rehabilitation, construction work, trap clearing, environmental management, assistance at local rural Zulu school, skills training for local people.

Lang.: English.

Accom.: In a basic but comfortable house with bunk beds (bed linen provided). Sleeping bags are required for outdoor camping if desired.

Cost: GB£610/month, including accommodation, laundry and meals. Volunteers are collected and returned at the pick-up location.

Applic.: Via e-mail or standard application form on website.

The Ara Project, Costa Rica

Apdo 1904-4050 , Alajuela Costa Rica
Tel./Fax: ++ (506) 833 4329
E-mail: richmar@racsa.co.cr; hatchedtoflyfree@gmail.com
thearaproject @gmail.com
www.thearaproject.org

Desc.: This is an NGO dedicated to the conservation of the 2 endangered species of macaws found in Costa Rica. Activity is focused on breeding and re-introduction into their native habitat. A world first was achieved with pairs (one bird handreared and one bird parent reared) producing youngsters in the wild. It also runs a refuge with various endemic birds and an education program for local schools.

Spp.: Scarlet (*Ara macao*) and Great Green macaw (*Ara ambiguus*), 4 species of Amazon parrot, 2 of Toucan, 2 of Aracari and various small parakeets.

Loc.: Central Valley, near Alajuela town and San José airport, Costa Rica.

Dur.: Min. 1 month at the Breeding Centre; 2 or more in the field.

Per.: Year round.

L.term: No long term limits.

Age: Min.18.

Qualif.: No qualifications necessary, but experience with birds would be useful. Students in the field of biology are preferred for field work.

Work.: Breeding Centre: feeding, aviary maintenance, perching and cleaning, making toys, playing with babies. In the field: working with biologist in the field research program.

Lang.: English; Spanish helpful in the field.

Accom.: Homestay with shared facilities or private room with shower.

Cost: Breeding Centre: US$4 a day to the project. US$18/day for lodging, 3 meals and laundry. In the field: free accommodation, but food has to be bought in the village (a charge of US$8).

Applic.: Via e-mail or by telephone.

Notes: Field research opportunities are available, as well as gardening fund raising and educational activities.

Azafady, Madagascar

Studio 7, 1a Beethoven Street
London W10 4LG UK
Tel.: ++44 (20) 8960 6629
Fax: ++44 (20) 8962 0126
E-mail: info@azafady.org
www.madagascar.co.uk

Desc:	Azafady is a grassroots organisation tackling conservation issues and extreme poverty in Madagascar. Volunteers can embark on a Lemur Venture, join Azafady's award winning Pioneer Program, or join one of the short term volunteering schemes just for a few weeks.
Spp.:	Lemurs (ring tailed, Verreaux's sifaka, brown collared), amphibians and various botanical species.
Hab.:	Littoral forest (tropical coastal forest), spiny desert.
Loc.:	South-east Madagascar.
Travel:	Flight to Antananarivo, then to Fort Dauphin.
Dur.:	2-10 weeks.
Per.:	Year round.
L.term:	Long-term stay as a coordinator or specialist may be possible.
Age:	Min. 18. Over 55 with doctor's agreement.
Qualif.:	No special skills needed; enthusiasm and sensitivity are a must; practical and research experience welcome.
Work:	The Pioneer Program combines sustainable development work, health infrastructure and education, and environmental conservation. Lemur Venture provides opportunities to study wild lemurs and their habitat. Short-term placements also available.
Lang.:	English; intensive course in Malagasy is given.
Accom.:	Basic camping facilities are provided throughout the scheme.
Cost:	Volunteers must cover personal costs (flight, insurance, medical expenses, visa and equipment) and raise a minimum donation ranging from GB£600-2,000 depending on project or duration. All donations go to support Azafady's work in Madagascar.
Applic.:	Download an application form from the website

BDRI – Bottlenose Dolphin Research Institute: Dolphins, Education and Research, Italy

Via Diaz 4
07020 Golfo Aranci (Olbia-Tempio) Italy
Tel.: ++39 (346) 0815414
E-mail: info@thebdri.com
www.thebdri.com

Desc.:	BDRI carries on scientific research and education programmes to contribute to the conservation of bottlenose dolphins and of the marine environment. Motivated volunteers can participate with BDRI in comprehensive and intensive periods of training in the study of wild bottlenose dolphins.
Spp.:	Bottlenose dolphin (*Tursiops truncates*).
Hab.:	Mediterranean coast.
Loc.:	Golfo Aranci, Emerald coast, Sardinia, Italy.
Travel:	Olbia airport is connected both with Italian and European airports. Bus, taxi or train to Golfo Aranci (project area).
Dur.:	6 or 13 days or more.
Per.:	Year round.
L.term:	Volunteers can join a project for a longer period.
Age:	Min. 18.
Qualif.:	A strong interest and motivation to participate to dolphin research and conservation campaigns. No background knowledge of cetaceans is required.
Work:	Boat-based research surveys investigating ecology and behaviour of bottlenose dolphins. Data collection and analyses as part of an ongoing research (communication, social life, photo-identification).
Lang.:	English, Spanish, Italian or Portuguese.
Accom.:	Comfortable house close to a beautiful beach, in rooms with bunks and/or single beds. Private rooms available. Linens are required.
Cost:	EUR70-100 per day, including food, accommodation, research field costs and training. Transportation is not included.
Applic.:	Download application form from website or request it via e-mail.

Bimini Lemon Shark Project, Bahamas

Bimini Biological Field Station
c/o RSMAS University of Miami
9300 SW 99 Street, Miami, Florida 33176-2050 USA
Tel./Fax: ++1 (305) 274 0628
E-mail: sgruber@rsmas.miami.edu
www.miami.edu/sharklab/

Desc.:	Study of the feeding, predator-prey relations, growth, survival, movements and community relations of the lemon shark using field techniques and computer modelling/simulations. Disciplines of systems ecology, bioenergetics, life history studies, population genetics, ethology and sensory biology involved.
Spp.:	Lemon shark (*Negaprion brevirostris*) and its prey organisms, primarily mojarra fish (*Gerres spp.*) as well as other local elasmobranch species.
Hab.:	Coastal reefs, mangrove forest, seagrass meadows.
Loc.:	Bimini Bahamas, 85km east of Miami, Florida, USA.
Travel:	Flight to Fort Lauderdale, then flight to Bimini Island.
Dur.:	Min. 1 month.
Per.:	Year round.
L.term:	With project leader's approval.
Age:	Min. 20 - max. 35.
Qualif.:	Students or graduates with a biology background are encouraged, preferably with an interest in graduate school or to pursue a career in marine biology. Boating skills, swimming and computer literacy.
Work:	Field research on boats in shallow water all hours of the day; cooking, household and mechanical maintenance, etc.
Lang.:	English.
Accom.:	Wood frame, air-conditioned house with bunk beds for 21 persons.
Cost:	Room and board approx. US$695/month. Transportation not included. Round trip flight from Fort Lauderdale to Bimini: approx. US$290.
Applic.:	Contact Dr. Samuel H. Gruber (sgruber@rsmas.miami.edu).

BioMindo, Ecuador

PO Box #8990, Quito
Puerto Quito, Pichincha Ecuador
Tel.: ++593 (9) 030 7932
E-mail: biomindo@hotmail.com
www.virb.com/biomindo

Desc.:	Biological research and sustainable living: a combination based on permaculture and environmental conservation focused on researching the cloudforest and its biodiversity in western Ecuador.
Spp.:	*Anolis proboscis*, *Rupicola peruviana*, *Cinclus leucecophalus*, *Anturium mindoense*, *Tremarctos ornatos*.
Hab.:	Cloud forest, tropical area.
Loc.:	Perto Quito, Pichincha-Ecuador.
Travel:	Flight to Quito, then 3.5 hours by bus.
Dur.:	Minimum 2 weeks.
Per.:	Year round.
L.term:	Preferable long-term volunteers.
Age:	Min. 18; families with children are also accepted.
Qualif.:	Biologists, ecologists, photographers, graphic designers and nature enthusiasts.
Work:	Making an inventory of biodiversity, opening (interpretative) trails in the forest, constructing with renewable materials (bamboo, palm leafs etc.), organic gardening and permaculture.
Lang.:	Spanish, English, German.
Accom.:	Bamboo cabins, shared or private rooms, provided with kitchen, solar shower, composting toilet, social area with hammocks, pizza oven etc; sleeping bag required.
Cost:	US$70/week or US$250/month including accommodation and food; transportation not included.
Applic.:	Standard form to fill out.

Black Howler Monkey Project, Argentina
Center Rescue, Rehabilitation and Conservation of Primates
(Orphanage of Primates)
Paraje Tiu Mayu, La Cumbre, CP 5478 Cordoba Argentina
E-mail: carayaproject@yahoo.com.ar; proyectocaraya@yahoo.com.ar
www.volunteer-with-howler-monkeys.org
www.proyectocaraya.com.ar

Desc.: The centre takes care of black howler monkeys, that have been former pets. The monkeys are rehabilitated physically, psychologically and socially. After rehabilitation they are able to live freely in the forests in social groups of more than 100 primates.

Spp.: Black howler monkey (*Alouatta caraya*) and Capuchinos. Other animals: pumas, llamas, donkeys, horses, vizcachas farm animals.

Hab.: Andean foothills with some little tree groups and pine forests.

Loc.: La Cumbre, province of Cordoba, Argentina.

Travel: Flight to Cordoba; then bus to La Cumbre and taxi to the refuge.

Dur.: Min. 3 weeks - max. 3 months.

Per.: Year round.

L.term: After 3 months special arrangements can be fixed for volunteers who want to stay longer.

Age: Min. 18 years.

Qualif.: Patience, dedication, love for animals and no fear of dogs, since there are many. It's not necessary to be a university or high school student.

Work: Feeding and observing monkeys, study and data input of free social groups, care for orphan monkeys and other animals, cleaning and maintenance of the areas in the centre, construction and repair of refuges and airways, assisting in the capture and handling of monkeys, tree plantation (only in wintertime).

Lang.: Mainly Spanish, English is optional.

Accom.: In a hut with several rooms for 2-3 volunteers each and very basic sanitary facilities.

Cost: EUR500/3 weeks; EUR600-800-900 for 1, 2 or 3 months.

Applic.: Via e-mail. Project director: Alejandra Juarez.

Black Sheep Inn, Ecuador

PO Box 05–01–240 Chugchilan
Cotopaxi Ecuador
Tel.: ++593 (3) 2814 587
Fax: ++593 (3) 2814 588 (call ahead)
E-mail: info@blacksheepinn.com
www.blacksheepinn.com

Desc.: A small award winning Eco-Lodge high in the Ecuadorian Andes. Eco-permaculture features: solar panels, adobe construction, composting toilets, recycling, roof-water collectors, gray-water systems, community education work, reforestation and erosion control. Volunteers help run Inn and learn about sustainability.

Spp.: No species are studied but there are over 172 spp. of birds in the outlying area.

Hab.: High Andean Sierra and Humid Andean Cloud Forest.

Loc.: Western Cordillera Andes, Cotopaxi, Ecuador.

Travel: Flight to Quito, then 5+ hours by bus to Chugchilan and to the Inn.

Dur.: Min. 8 weeks; preferably 3 months or more.

Per.: June to August; November to March.

L.term: Welcome after initial period. The Inn is looking for full-time managers.

Age: Min. 22. Mature and physically capable volunteers.

Qualif.: Useful skills: small business administration, farm work, trip leading, hotel service, computer skills. No allergies to animals.

Work: Volunteers primary help in guest lodge and take care of guests. Also general maintenance, gardening, cooking and cleaning, animal care, some hiking. Possible teaching in community, helping with library and recycling project.

Lang.: English and Spanish are essential.

Accom.: Comfortable shared room at the Inn with full bedding, hot water, towels and access to all guest services.

Cost: US$15/day for a trial period of 2 weeks. Thereafter, room and board are usually free.

Applic.: Via e-mail or on website. The Inn generally takes 1 volunteer at a time.

Blue Mountains Conservation, Iceland

SEEDS Iceland
Klappastigur, 16
101 Reykjavik Iceland
Tel.: ++354 (8) 456 178
E-mail: seeds@seedsiceland.org
www.seeds.is

Desc.:	The aim of the project is to halt the erosion of vegetation and soils and to strengthen the ecosystem of the area by enhancing its natural vegetation. Through the process of using organic waste materials as fertilizing means, a double dividend is achieved. Close to 70% of the total population of Iceland lives in this area of the country and the area has suffered of overgrazing and volcanic activity; some areas are stripped entirely of top soil.
Hab.:	Volcanic mountain range, glacial lake.
Loc.:	Bláfjöll mountains, Iceland.
Travel:	Flight to Reykjavik, then Bus to Central station.
Dur.:	2 weeks.
Per.:	June to July.
L.term:	Inquire with organization.
Age:	Min. 16.
Qualif.:	No particular skills or knowledge are needed.
Work:	Fertilising the slopes in Bláfjöll by yard-waste cover, monitoring the survival and growth rate of tree plantations, cleaning up in the vicinity of caves in the Bláfjöll area.
Lang.:	English is the language of the camp; high proficiency is not required.
Accom.:	Volunteers are lodged most of the time directly in the area of Bláfjöll in a fully equipped skiing hut and part of the time in a local house in the city of Reykjavík. Food is provided.
Cost:	Participation fee EUR 180.
Applic.:	Application should come through sending organizations and partners in volunteers' home countries.

Bohorok Environmental Centre, Indonesia

Jl. Wahid Hasyim No 51, Medan 20154
Sumatera Utara Indonesia
Tel./Fax: ++62 (61) 451 4363 /451 4360
E-mail: lawang@indosat.net.id; mail@paneco.ch
www.sumatranorangutan.org; www.paneco.ch

Desc.:	The Centre was born in 1995 to help control the environmental impact of tourism on the Orangutan Rehabilitation Station of Bohorok. It has input in the town planning process and in environmental management programmes, including also environmental education in schools and development of eco-tourism.
Spp.:	Orangutan.
Hab.:	Tropical rainforest.
Loc.:	Bukit Lawang, Bohorok, Langkat, North Sumatra, Indonesia.
Travel:	Flight to Medan, then bus to Bukit Lawang.
Dur.:	Min. 2 weeks - max. 4 months.
Per.:	Year round.
L.term:	Inquire with the organisation.
Age:	Min. 21.
Qualif.:	Specific skills are required depending on the topic. Teamwork capacities and interest in Indonesian culture are important.
Work:	Environmental education and management (waste, water bio-filtration), ecotourism. No work at the Orangutan Quarantine Station.
Lang.:	English. Bahasa Indonesian would be helpful.
Accom.:	Simple local accommodation. Free housing food not included.
Cost:	US$600 for students, US$1,200 for persons with regular income, travel and insurance are covered by the volunteer.
Agents:	PanEco Foundation, Ms. Cornelia Jenny, Chileweg 5, CH-8415 Berg am Irchel, Switzerland, tel.: ++41 (52) 318 2323, fax: ++41 (52) 318 1906, e-mail: mail@paneco.ch.
Applic.:	Download and mail the application form, from www.paneco.ch.

Brown Bear Project, Russia

The Ecovolunteer Network
Meyersweg 29, 7553 AX Hengelo The Netherlands
Tel.: ++31 (74) 250 8250
Fax: ++31 (74) 250 6572
E-mail: info@ecovolunteer.org
www.ecovolunteer.org

Desc.:	Orphan bear cubs are rescued from hunters in order to raise them and release them into the wild. The cubs need to be fed for about 3 months. In the spring, 1-year old bear cubs are released and some are equipped with radio-collars, to record their daily movements.
Spp.:	Brown bear (*Ursus arctos*).
Hab.:	Typical southern taiga.
Loc.:	Isolated biological station approx. 400km west of Moscow.
Travel:	Flight to Moscow then train to Staraya Toropa, meeting is at the train station. Private transportation by car from Moscow can be arranged for an extra cost of EUR110.
Dur.:	Minimum 1 month.
Per.:	February to October.
L.term:	Inquire with the organisation.
Age:	Min. 18
Qualif.:	February-April: some practice and experience of animal handling is preferred. May-October: be very fit, long and strenuous walking may be required.
Work:	February-April: preparing food for and feeding of brown bear orphan cubs. May-October: radio-tracking daily movements of released 1-year old bear cubs.
Lang.:	English or Russian.
Accom.:	Simple rooms at a biological station.
Cost:	Approx. US$1,590 for 1 month; US$211 for the following weeks.
Agents:	The Ecovolunteer Network at www.ecovolunteer.org.
Applic.:	The Ecovolunteer Network (see Organisation list).

California Wildlife Center, California USA

PO Box 2022, Malibu
California 91302 USA
Tel.: ++1 (818) 222 2658 (administration) - Fax: ++1 (818) 222 2685
E-mail: volunteer@californiawildlifecenter.org;
jo@californiawildlifecenter.org
www.californiawildlifecenter.org

Desc.: California Wildlife Center is an NGO dedicated to the rescue, rehabilitation and release of sick, injured and orphaned native wildlife. It provides expert medical care and community outreach and education, and responds to wildlife emergencies in Los Angeles County for a wide variety of species: from raptors and songbirds to pelicans, sea lions, coyotes and deer. The Center works with a small staff, as trained interns, volunteers and consulting veterinarians.

Spp.: Birds (65%), native mammals (squirrels, opossum, coyotes and deer). Marine mammals are rescued from the Malibu's coastline.

Hab.: Southern California.

Loc.: Southern California, Los Angeles County.

Travel: Flight to either Burbank, CA or Los Angeles, then by car.

Dur.: Minimum of 3 months.

Per.: Volunteers are accepted year round, but are needed most during the busy season: March to September.

Age: Min. 18.

Qualif.: Ability to work in a team, experience with animal care is a plus.

Work: Volunteers will go through mandatory training classes, including but not limited to basic training, dispatch (how to handle calls from the public), baby bird, squirrel and Marine Mammal Rescue training. Volunteers prepare food, feed animals, clean enclosures, wash dishes, do laundry, answer phones, and do administrative support as necessary. Shifts of 8-10hrs/day depending on season.

Lang.: English.

Accom.: No accommodations available.

Cost: Volunteers must provide accommodation, food and transportation. There is no public transportation to the site.

Cambodian Marine Biodiversity Monitoring and Conservation

Marine Conservation Cambodia (Group 8, Centre 2, Quarter 3)
Mittapheap District, Sihanoukville Cambodia
Tel.: ++855 (11) 462 336
E-mail: info@marineconservationcambodia.org
www.marineconservationcambodia.org

Desc.: Cambodia has an extremely rich and diverse marine environment with many endangered species such as seahorses, dugongs and horseshoe crabs. Volunteers work to help protect and maintain this threatened Coral Reef ecosystem with the use of visual census methodologies and research dives.

Spp.: Seahorses (*H. hippocampus, H. histrix, H. kuda*), Dugong (*Dugong dugong*) and horseshoe crabs.

Hab.: Tropical oceans.

Loc.: Sihanoukville, Cambodia.

Travel: Flight to Phnom Penh; then a 3 hour transfer is organized to bring volunteer to Sihanoukville.

Dur.: Project can be extended for internship purpose up to 6 months.

Per.: Year round.

Age: Mi. 18; younger with parents' permission.

Qualif.: No particular skills needed, Scuba diving certification are available on-site.

Work: After training marine conservation volunteers will join research expedition and collect data on coral reef health status. Also local communities work will be a compulsory part of the program.

Lang.: English.

Accom.: Accommodation is rustic and consists of several dormitory-style bungalows. Single/twin/double accommodation is also available.

Cost: GB£300-335 per week, including food, accommodation, dives, equipment and transportation.

Applic.: The Green Volunteers Standard Application Form is welcome.

Cano Palma Biological Station, Costa Rica

COTERC, Canadian Organization for Tropical Education and
Rainforest Conservation
PO Box 335, Pickering, Ontario L1V 2R6 Canada
Tel.:++1 (905) 831 8809 - Fax: ++1 (905) 831 4203
E-mail: info@coterc.org
www.coterc.org

Desc.:	The station serves as a facility for visiting biologists and student groups interested in studying various aspects of neo-tropical lowland forest biology. It also supports a volunteer programme.
Spp.:	Over 300 bird species, 120 mammal species, 100 reptile and amphibians.
Hab.:	Lowland Atlantic tropical wet forest.
Loc.:	9km north Tortuguero National Park, north-eastern Costa Rica.
Travel:	Tortuguero is accessible only by bus then boat, or by small airplane from San José; there are no roads nearby.
Dur.:	Min. 2 weeks.
Per.:	Year round.
L.term:	Applicants with useful skills will be taken into consideration.
Age:	Min. 18. Under 18 must be accompanied by an adult taking responsibility.
Qualif.:	Volunteers should be enthusiastic, self-starting, in good physical condition and able to fit in with remote field station conditions.
Work:	Participation in the station's activities, including grounds and equipment maintenance, helping out in the kitchen, etc. Assisting visiting researchers.
Lang.:	English, Spanish.
Cost:	A dormitory with bunks capable of sleeping 30 persons. Bedding is provided, but volunteers should bring mosquito nets. Conditions are basic but clean and comfortable.
Accom.:	US$180 or equivalent per week, in cash. No travellers cheques or personal cheques. Tortuguero has no banks.
Applic.:	Contact COTERC in Canada: info@coterc.org.

Cape Tribulation Tropical Research Station, Australia

PMB 5, Cape Tribulation
Qld. 4873 Australia
Tel./Fax: ++61 (7) 4098 0063
E-mail: austrop@austrop.org.au
www.austrop.org.au

Desc.:	An independent field research station open to all researchers, funded through the Australian Tropical Research Foundation. It conducts many projects: radio-tracking bats, rainforest rehabilitation, weed control, alternative technology, design of GPS animal tracking systems. Researchers must provide a proposed research summary.
Spp.:	About 12 micro bats and 4 mega bats; figs: min. 12 spp.; angiosperm plant spp., many rare and locally endemic. Captive colony of flying foxes (*Pteropus spp.*) at the Station.
Hab.:	Lowland rainforest and tropical coastal communities.
Loc.:	Australia (coastal far north Queensland).
Travel:	Contact the station for travel details (hugh@austrop.org.au).
Dur.:	After initial 2 weeks volunteers can negotiate a longer stay.
Per.:	Year round.
L.term:	Encouraged and negotiable after the first stay.
Age:	Over 23 preferred.
Qualif.:	Any skills: carpenters, botanists, computer programmers, etc.
Work:	Routine maintenance, forest regeneration, helping with research projects.
Lang.:	English.
Accom.:	The station has bunkhouse accommodation and 2 air-con labs.
Cost:	US$30/day for room and board. Interns, students and researchers pay more. Negotiable rates. See www.austrop.org.au/aboutus.pdf.
Applic.:	Applications should be sent via e-mail to the Station director with CV with photo and a statement of experience.
Notes:	The climate conditions (Nov.-April) can be wet in this remote area.

Cardigan Bay Marine Wildlife Centre, Wales UK

Patent Slip Building, Glanmor Terrace, New Quay
Ceredigion, West Wales SA45 9PS UK
Tel.: ++44 (1545) 560 032
E-mail: volunteer@cbmwc.org
www.cbmwc.org

Desc.:	A research and education project focusing on cetaceans and other marine life. Assist with CBMWC's ongoing research and education programmes concerning the marine wildlife of Cardigan Bay, including photo-identification of bottlenose dolphins.
Spp.:	Bottlenose dolphins, harbour porpoise, Atlantic grey seals, sunfish, jellyfish and other marine fauna.
Hab.:	Temperate seas, coasts.
Loc.:	Wales, United Kingdom.
Travel:	Train to Aberystwyth or Carmarthen, then bus to New Quay.
Dur.:	Volunteering opportunities from 4 weeks to 6 months or more.
Per.:	Year round (focus April to November).
L.term:	Long term positions up to 6 months available.
Age:	Min. 16. There is no maximum age. Something for everyone.
Qualif.:	Willingness to work in a conscientious, responsible and reliable manner; enthusiasm, hard work and interest in marine wildlife and conservation.
Work:	Land and boat based data collection and input, staffing the visitor centre and dealing with enquiries, environmental education activities.
Lang.:	English.
Accom.:	Local accommodation can be arranged, please contact CBMWC for further information.
Cost:	GB£55/week for accommodation. Volunteers are responsible for their own food, travel and accommodation costs.
Applic.:	Please contact CBMWC for information on how to apply.

Caretta Research Project, Georgia USA

Savannah Science Museum
PO Box 9841
Savannah, Georgia 31412 USA
Tel.: ++1 (912) 447 8655 - Fax: ++1 (912) 447 8656
E-mail: wassawcrp@aol.com
www.carettaresearchproject.org

Desc.:	Since 1973, the Savannah Science Museum has been conducting a research and conservation programme on the endangered loggerhead sea turtle. The program's purpose is to learn more about population levels, trends, and nesting habits of loggerheads. It also hopes to enhance the survival of eggs and hatchlings and to involve the public in this effort.
Spp.:	Loggerhead sea turtle (*Caretta caretta*).
Hab.:	Coastal barrier island.
Loc.:	Wassaw Island, about 5 miles south of Savannah.
Travel:	Bus or airplane to Savannah, then boat to Wassaw. The island is accessible only by boat.
Dur.:	1 week, Saturday to Saturday.
Per.:	May to September.
L.term:	Inquire with organisation.
Age:	Min. 15.
Qualif.:	No previous experience required.
Work:	Volunteers patrol the beaches in search of female turtles, tag and measure the animals, record data, monitor the nests and escort hatchlings to the sea.
Lang.:	English.
Accom.:	Rustic cabins (dormitory style).
Cost:	Check website for fees. Most of the fee is tax-deductible (for US citizens); it includes lodging, meals, leadership/instruction and transportation to and from the island.
Applic.:	Full payment must accompany the application.

Cats of Rome, Italy

Torre Argentina Cat Sanctuary
Largo Argentina
00100 Rome Italy
Tel./Fax: ++39 (06) 4542 5240
E-mail: torreargentina@tiscali.it
www.romancats.com

Desc.:	An international group of volunteers, working together to raise the quality of life of Rome's abandoned cats. Approximately 600 cats get abandoned annually at the Sanctuary, which shelters anywhere from 250 to 300 cats. The Sanctuary promotes spay/neuter, proper animal care, adoptions and education projects through public relations events. All funding comes from the 8,000 tourists who visit every year.
Spp.:	Domestic cat.
Loc.:	In the archaeological ruins of Largo Argentina.
Dur.:	Minimum 1 week with a full or part time schedule.
Per.:	All year round.
L.term:	Inquire with the sanctuary.
Age:	No age limits.
Qualif.:	No particular qualifications other than strong motivation, flexibility and love of animals, especially cats.
Work:	Cleaning cages, distributing food and treating sick cats, clerical work such as stuffing envelopes, making photocopies and various other administrative tasks. People who are able to speak to the many tourists who visit, give a tour of the sanctuary (mostly in English) and eventually ask for contributions.
Lang.:	English, other languages useful but not necessary.
Accom.:	Housing is available, consisting usually of a nice room in someone's apartment with private bath.
Cost:	Volunteers are responsible for travel, housing, food and personal expenses. Ask the organisation for the cost of a private room.
Applic.:	Prospective volunteers must send a resumé with a short letter about themselves.

Cats Unlimited Wildlife Foundation, Namibia

Mossinkserf 20
7451 XE Holten, The Netherlands
Tel.: ++31 (0) 53 302 0009
E-mail: contact@catsunlimited.nl
www.catsunlimited.net

Desc.:	A non-profit wildlife conservation foundation, which aims to protect and research large carnivore populations in central Namibia. Volunteer expeditions are organised to research and monitor these predators and other game species in the ecosystem.
Spp.:	Leopard, Brown Hyena, Hartmann's Mountain Zebra, White Rhino, Cheetah and several prey species.
Hab.:	Inland plateau, scrublands.
Loc.:	Khomas Hochland region, central Namibia.
Travel:	Flight/bus to Windhoek; pick-up from Windhoek to project.
Dur.:	2 week expeditions; extension is possible.
Per.:	Year round.
L.term:	Volunteers may stay for a longer period if they wish.
Age:	Min.17. No max age but fitness and good health are required.
Qualif.:	No particular skills needed; enthusiasm and interest in wildlife.
Work:	Each expedition has a different research programme which can include predator tracking and monitoring, game surveys, wildlife population research, feeding injured animals and general farm work (clearing bush and fencing). Groups are 8 volunteers max.
Lang.:	English.
Accom.:	Camping (single/shared tent). Self (group) catering. Camps are at different locations, both near a farm and in the bush.
Cost:	EUR949 for 2-week expedition, including accommodation, 3 meals per day, training, leisure activities and transport to and from Windhoek.
Applic.:	Via Cats Unlimited website application form or via e-mail.

Centre for Dolphin Studies (CDS), South Africa

Orca Foundation
PO Box 1812
6600 Plettenberg Bay South Africa
Tel.: ++27 (44) 533 5083
E-mail: bookings@orcafoundation.com
www.orcafoundation.com

Desc.: A non-profit marine research trust, which aims to promote responsible research and effective conservation of whales, dolphins, seals and other marine animals. Volunteers are encouraged to help: observe and conserve.

Spp.: Bottlenose and humpback dolphins Southern right, humpback and Bryde's whales, Cape fur seals.

Hab.: Coastal beaches, temperate ocean.

Loc.: Plettenberg Bay, South Africa.

Travel: Flight to Cape Town; plane/bus to George/Plettenberg Bay; bus/taxi to Plettenberg Bay.

Dur.: Min. 1 week; 2-3 months is ideal.

Per.: Year round.

L.term: Volunteers may stay for a longer period if they wish.

Age: Min.18. No max age but fitness and good health are required.

Qualif.: No particular skills needed; enthusiasm and interest in marine life.

Work: Marine mammal surveys (land and boat); dietary analysis; course work on biology of marine mammals and research techniques; photo identification and cataloguing of whales and dolphins; environmental education with local school children.

Lang.: English.

Accom.: Bunk house (5 rooms with bunk beds) with lounge/dining/kitchen area, showers, toilets, TV and DVD. Outside deck overlooks Elephant Park. Linens and laundry provided.

Cost: GB£280 or 350/week, including accommodation, evening meal, linens, laundry and transport to and from the office (weekdays).

Applic.: The Green Volunteers Standard Application form is welcome.

Centre for Wolf Studies, Russia

Lupus Laetus
P/o Pozhnia, Toropetsky raion, Tverskaya oblast
172862 Russian Federation
Tel.: +7 482 682 7938
E-mail: lupuslaetus@free.fr
www.lupuslaetus.org

Desc.:	A non-profit organization that includes a centre for rehabilitation of bear cubs and wolf pups. Research on ecology of wild wolves has been conducted for 15 years. Volunteers are encouraged to help.
Spp.:	European Grey Wolf, *Canis lupus lupus*.
Hab.:	Southern boreal forest.
Loc.:	Bubonitzy village, Toropets district, Tver region, Russia.
Travel:	Flight to Moscow; train/bus to Staraya Toropa; taxi to Bubonitzy.
Dur.:	Min. 2 weeks; max. 3 months.
Per.:	Winter (December-March) and summer (July-August).
L.term:	Volunteers may stay for a longer period if they wish, but need to renew visa.
Age:	Min.16. No max age but fitness and good health are required.
Qualif.:	No particular skills needed; enthusiasm and interest in wolf and forest.
Work:	Wolf tracking in winter: daily 10km ring and registration of prints (wolf, lynx, fox, moose, wild boar, marten, hare, and squirrel), with special attention to wolf tracks (scats and prey remains). Wolf howling in summer: Night is devoted to listening and localizing wolves' howling.
Lang.:	English.
Accom.:	Local house in winter: rooms for 1 or 2 persons, common toilet and bathroom common. Tent in summer: tent and air mat are provided, toilet and washing in the bush.
Cost:	GB£160/week, including accommodation and food.
Applic.:	The Green Volunteers Standard Application form is welcome.

Cercopan, Nigeria

4 Ishie Lane, HE PO Box 826, Calabar, Cross River State Nigeria
Mob.: ++234 (0802) 827 5428
Aintree Cottage, Low Street, Sloley, Norwich Norfolk NR12 8HD UK
Tel./Fax: ++44 (1692) 538 342 - Mob.: ++44 (7789) 557 258
E-mail: info@cercopan.org claire.coulson@cercopan.org
www.cercopan.org www.facebook.com/cercopan

Desc.: An NGO dedicated to tropical rainforest conservation through primate rehabilitation, education and research.

Spp.: Red-capped mangabey (*Cercopithecus torquatus*) and forest guenons (*Cercopithecus spp.*).

Hab.: Tropical rainforest.

Loc.: South-east Nigeria (close to Cameroon border).

Travel: Flight to Lagos; internal flight Lagos-Calabar.

Dur.: Short-term volunteers: min. 2 weeks - max. 3 months.

Per.: Any time of the year. Rainy season is June to September.

L.term: Min. 1 year with coordinator's permission.

Age: Short-term volunteers: min. 21; long-term volunteers: min. 23.

Qualif.: Short-term volunteers: field experience, building skills, biological surveying. Long-term volunteers: veterinary, building skills, biological research.

Work: Varies with skills and needs of the project.

Lang.: English.

Accom.: At forest site: bush sheds with tent/mosquito net, fridge, outdoor showers and toilets. In Calabar: shared house/room, electricity and running water.

Cost: Short-term volunteers: room and board (GB£200/week). Long-term volunteers: room and board provided.

Applic.: Send letter of interest with CV by snail mail or e-mail without attachments to CERCOPAN.

Cetacean Research & Rescue Unit (CRRU), Scotland UK

PO Box 11307, Banff
Scotland AB45 3WB UK
Tel: ++44 (1261) 851 696
E-mail: info@crru.org.uk
www.crru.org.uk

Desc.:	The CRRU is a small, non profit research organisation dedicated to the understanding, welfare, conservation and protection of whales, dolphins and porpoises in Scottish waters through scientific investigation, environmental education and the provision of professional veterinary assistance to sick, stranded and injured individuals.
Spp.:	Primarily the bottlenose dolphin (*Tursiops truncatus*) and minke whale (*Balaenoptera acutorostrata*).
Hab.:	Marine, coastal.
Loc.:	Moray Firth, north-eastern Scotland.
Travel:	By plane, bus or train to Aberdeen, then bus to Banff.
Dur.:	11 days.
Per.:	May to October.
L.term:	Possible for outstanding volunteers.
Age:	Min. 17 – max. 65.
Qualif.:	Commitment to wildlife conservation and positive attitude towards living and working in a small group of enthusiastic people from different backgrounds and cultures is essential.
Work:	Counting animals, recording behaviour, determining geographical positions and taking photographs under scientific supervision. On shore: identifying animals, cataloguing slides, inputting data.
Lang.:	English.
Accom.:	Researchers and volunteers together in 1 or 2 furnished houses.
Cost:	GB£795 for 11 days including food, accommodation, field equipment (clothing) and supplies.
Applic.:	By e-mail or post.

Cetacean Research Project, Scotland UK

The Hebridean Whale and Dolphin Trust, HWDT
28 Main Street, Tobermory, Isle of Mull
Argyll PA75 6NU Scotland UK
Tel.: ++44 (1688) 302 620
E-mail: volunteercoordinator@hwdt.org
www.hwdt.org

Desc.: The Trust aims to conserve the whales, dolphins and porpoises found off the West Coast of Scotland through various research and education programmes.

Spp.: Whales, dolphins, porpoises, seals, otters, basking sharks and sea birds.

Hab.: Temperate sea and coast.

Loc.: The Hebrides, western coast of Scotland.

Travel: From Glasgow train or bus to Oban; ferry from Oban to Isle of Mull; bus from ferry terminal to Tobermory.

Dur.: Either 9 or 10 days.

Per.: May to September.

L.term: No.

Age: Min. 18 - max. 75; older if fit.

Qualif.: No qualifications are required. Volunteers must be enthusiastic, friendly, and team-worker. Good eyesight and hearing.

Work: Volunteers work alongside HWDT scientists using a combination of visual and acoustic methods to monitor for cetaceans, marine debris and boat traffic.

Lang.: English.

Accom.: All nights are accommodated on HWDT yacht. Sleeping bags are not required as all bedding is provided.

Cost: GB£900-1,200, depending on time and length of survey. Please contact the volunteer coordinator for more information.

Applic.: Apply through the HWDT website or contact the HWDT volunteer coordinator for an application form.

Cetacean Sanctuary Research, Italy and France

Tethys Research Institute
c/o Civic Aquarium, Viale G.B. Gadio 2
20121 Milan Italy
Tel.: ++39 (02) 7200 1947 - Fax: ++39 (02) 8699 5011
E-mail: tethys@tethys.org   www.tethys.org

Desc.:   «Cetacean Sanctuary Research» is a long term project on the ecology and conservation of cetaceans in the western Ligurian Sea. Research is carried out in two main habitats: the continental slope zone and the pelagic environment. In the continental slope the focus is on odontocetes such as sperm whales, Risso's dolphins, striped dolphins and other dolphin species. In the pelagic environment the research focuses on fin whales and long-finned pilot whales. The study area includes the waters of the Pelagos Sanctuary for the Conservation of Mediterranean Cetaceans. Through a multidisciplinary approach, the researchers investigate different aspects of cetacean biology and ecology (distribution, abundance and population dynamics, behaviour, social organisation) and the impact of human activities like unregulated whale watching, in order to suggest effective conservation measures.

Spp.:   Fin whale (*Balaenoptera physalus*), striped dolphin (*Stenella coeruleoalba*), Risso's dolphin (*Grampus griseus*), sperm whale (*Physeter macrocephalus*), long-finned pilot whale (*Globicephala melas*), Cuvier's beaked whale (*Ziphius cavirostris*), short-beaked common dolphin (*Delphinus delphis*), common bottlenose dolphin (*Tursiops truncatus*).

Hab.:   Pelagic and coastal waters.

Loc.:   Ligurian Sea, Mediterranean Sea.

Travel: Departure and arrival is in San Remo (Portosole), Italy. Airplane to Nice, Genoa or Milan, then train to San Remo.

Dur.:   6 nights on board.

Per.:   May to October.

L.term: Consecutive cruises can be booked. Discount granted to university students less than 26 years old.

Age: Min. 18 years.

Qualif.: No qualifications required. Volunteers should be able to swim. Flexibility, enthusiasm and willingness to help with all research and household activities are necessary.

Work: Volunteers will be trained at the beginning of the cruise and then will assist with research activities (data collection, observations, photo-ID, etc.). Lectures on cetacean biology and research methods are carried out by the researchers. In bad weather conditions the boat stays in a safe harbour; volunteers may decide to stay on board, helping researchers entering and analysing data and matching digital photos, or visit the area.

Lang.: Italian, English.

Accom.: On board the 21-metre ketch *Pelagos*, up to 12 participants will be hosted in a 6 bed room and 2 quadruple cabins, with bunk beds. Sleeping bags, bed sheets and pillow case required. There are 4 showers and 4 toilets.

Cost: Costs range between EUR850-925 for a 6-day cruise, depending on the season. Food (except for restaurants and alcoholic beverages) and fuel are included. Travel to San Remo is not included.

Agents: Tethys Research Institute (see Organisation list).

Applic.: Request a standard application form to be completed and returned to the Tethys Research Institute. Early booking is suggested.

Charles Darwin Foundation, Galapagos

Volunteer and Scholarship Program Charles Darwin Research Station
Casilla postal 17-01-3891 Quito Ecuador
Tel.: ++ 593 (5) 252 6146/147
Fax: ++ 593 (5) 252 6146/147 (ext.102)
E-mail: vol@fcdarwin.org.ec
www.darwinfoundation.org

Desc.:	In 1971 the Charles Darwin Foundation (CDF) began the National and International Volunteer Programme. Its purpose is to collaborate with the training of university and undergraduate students, who focus their careers in biology and conservation science and those who want to improve their skills through field experience in the Galapagos Islands.
Spp.:	Terrestrial and marine flora and fauna of the Galapagos.
Hab.:	Various marine and terrestrial habitats of the Galapagos.
Loc.:	Galapagos Islands, Ecuador. Stations on 4 different Islands.
Travel:	Flight to Quito or Guayaquil, then Puerto Ayora, Galapagos.
Dur.:	Min. 6 months, sometimes shorter projects are available.
Per.:	Year round.
L.term:	Duration is set by the project.
Age:	Min. 20.
Qualif.:	Qualifications vary according to position available. Volunteers must be at least a second year undergraduate.
Work:	4 areas of investigation: vertebrate ecology monitoring, invertebrate research, botany, marine investigation and conservation. Non-scientific areas: communication, participation, education, institutional development. Volunteers can choose any of them.
Lang.:	English and Spanish. Fluency not essential.
Accom.:	Dormitory in the Station or apartment or hotel in town.
Cost:	Volunteers are responsible for their own travel expenses, their room and board and their own accident and life insurance coverage for the travel and for the duration of the volunteer period.
Applic.:	Detailed info, application form and available openings on website.

Cheetah Conservation Fund, Namibia

711, Quail Ridge Road
Aledo, Tx., 76008 2870 USA
Tel.: ++1 (817) 441 7205
Fax: ++1 (817) 441 9079
E-mail: ccfinfo@iway.na
www.cheetah.org

Desc.: CCF sponsors scientific research and education programmes in areas such as cheetah population biology, ecology, health and reproduction and human impacts; it works with all stakeholders to achieve best practice in the conservation and management of the world's cheetahs.

Spp.: Cheetah *(Acynonix jubatus)*.

Hab.: Semi-arid, bush-encroached savannah.

Loc.: Central Namibia, Southwest Africa.

Travel: Flight to Windhoek International Airport; shuttle bus or taxis to city centre.

Dur.: 2-4 weeks.

Per.: Year round.

L.term: Depending on the needs of CCF.

Age: Min. 18; under 18, please contact the organisation previously.

Qualif.: No particular skills required.

Work: Cheetah collecting, feeding and care; habitat monitoring of game and vegetation; assisting with data input, mapping, radio tracking; assisting with goat, sheep and livestock guarding dog healthcare and education programmes.

Lang.: English.

Accom.: Two-person thatched huts with beds: detached latrine block. All bedding is provided.

Cost: US$3,150 for 2 weeks, US$5,250 for 4 weeks (student interns and zookeepers: US$ 2,020 per month). Includes food and accommodations, plus additional fee for Namibian Work Visa (US$130) required for all volunteers

Applic.: Contact the organisation at the above address or the agents Earthwatch or African Conservation Experience.

Cheetah Conservation Botswana

Mokolodi Nature Reserve
Private Bag 0457
Gaborone Botswana
Tel./Fax: ++ (267) 350 0613
E-mail: info@cheetahbotswana.com
www.cheetahbotswana.com

Desc.: CCB addresses threats to the long term survival of the national cheetah population and that of other large predators. Using scientific research to inform its community outreach and education programmes CCB works with communities affected by conflict with predators, to promote the adoption of livestock management practices and non-lethal methods of predator control. CCB has opportunities for researchers interested in carrying out postgraduate research on predator related studies, in collaboration with a university, i.e. MSc's and PhD's. CCB also has a short term volunteer programme.

Spp.: Cheetah (*Acinonyx jubatus*).

Hab.: Semi-arid savannah and acacia bush lands.

Loc.: Mokolodi Nature Reserve, Jwaneng Game Reserve or Ghanzi Farmlands, Botswana.

Travel: Flights to Johannesburg, then Gaborone or Maun, then by vehicle to CCB camps.

Dur.: Researchers: dependant on required time for research study. Short term volunteer programme: min. 1 month - max. 3 months.

Per.: March to May and August to October.

L.term: Occasional opportunities for longer term volunteers, by application for specific roles as required. Opportunities will be posted on website and to CCB's e-mail list.

Age: Min. 21.

Qualif.: For researchers: BSc or MSc in wildlife related field. For short term volunteers: Wildlife background useful but not essential. Strong passion for conservation and a desire to learn new skills. Ability to work long days, often in heat during summer, or cold during winter. Ability to live in the bush with a small group of people.

Work: Schedules vary however activities may include assisting with spoor surveys, camera trapping, possible capture and release, school presentations, community visits, data input, camp maintenance, administration.

Lang.: English, Setswana.

Accom.: Very basic small chalets for 2 people sharing. Electricity and shared kitchen and bathroom facilities.

Cost: Approx. US$2,500/month for room and board (reviewed annually, check CCB website).

Applic.: For researchers and volunteers: by e-mail or by mail via application form on the web site. Include current CV. E-mail to research@cheetahbotswana.com. For more information check CCB's website www.cheetahbotswana.com under Volunteers.

Chiloé Silvestre Wildlife Rehabilitation Centre, Chile

Las Américas 1060, Ancud.
Provincia de Chiloé, Regiòn de los Lagos Chile
E-mail: voluntariado@chiloesilvestre.cl
www.chiloesilvestre.cl

Desc.: A conservation, wildlife rehabilitation, education and investigation project of Chiloé Island species in south of Chile, specialising in 3 areas: education; rescue, clinic and rehabilitation; investigation.

Spp.: Several species of Chiloé Island: penguins, pudùs, foxes, birds and other marine and terrestrial mammals.

Hab.: Island, Valdivian rainforest, coast.

Loc.: Chiloé Island, Los Lagos District, southern Chile.

Travel: Flight to Santiago of Chile, then by plane or bus to Puerto Montt, then by bus to Ancud.

Dur.: Min. 3 weeks, with previous project leader approval. For shorter periods, inquire with the organisation.

Per.: Year round.

L.term: Unlimited, after the regular volunteer period.

Age: Min. 15; if younger inquire with the organisation.

Qualif.: No particular skills needed. Experience with animals and team working are welcome

Work: Building and repairing enclosures, animal rescue, cleaning, feeding, monitoring and medicine; taking part in pre-released or released animal watching, animal tracking and sampling, taking part in education programs.

Lang.: English; Spanish is useful but not essential.

Accom.: In a house or a tent. Sleeping bags required.

Cost: Lodging is free; food is the volunteer's responsibility.

Applic.: Write to the organisation asking for the form.

Notes: For further information, visit www.chiloesilvestre.cl.

Cochrane Ecological Institute (CEI), Canada

Cochrane Wildlife Reserve Society
PO Box 484, Cochrane, Alberta, T4C 1A7 Canada
Tel.: ++1 (403) 932 5632
Fax: ++1 (403) 932 6303
E-mail: cei@nucleus.com
www.ceinst.org

Desc.:	The CEI rescues, rehabilitates and releases injured or orphaned wildlife, breeds and implements the reintroduction of the swift fox, provides environmental education services, and develops methods of non-intrusive wildlife survey as well as Field Station facilities for environmental research.
Spp.:	Swift fox (*Vulpes velox*) and all wildlife of western Canada.
Hab.:	Foothills of the Rockies, short, mixed grass, and fescue prairie.
Loc.:	Rocky Mountains, 45min. by car from Calgary Airport, western Canada.
Travel:	At easy travelling distance from Calgary, but no public transport.
Dur.:	Min. 1 month.
Per.:	May to October.
L.term:	Suitable volunteers may be able to stay for 10 months.
Age:	Min. 18. Volunteers must be fit.
Qualif.:	Volunteers must be team-worker and have self-initiative. Training is provided. Driving license essential. Veterinary experience useful.
Work:	Repairing and building enclosures and animal housing, collecting injured or orphaned wildlife, collecting food, preparing food, cleaning enclosures, cleaning all areas where food is prepared (for both people and animals) record keeping, general maintenance and working in the boarding kennel.
Lang.:	English.
Accom.:	Small shared apartment
Cost:	US$12/day for accommodation. The price is cheaper in case of shared accommodation.
Applic.:	E-mail to Clio (cei@nucleus.com) or Pat (patricia@happytailsretreat.com).

Comunidad Inti Wara Yassi, Bolivia

Parque Machia
Villa Tunari
Chapare, Cochabamba Bolivia
Tel.: ++ 591 (44) 136 572
E-mail: info@intiwarayassi.org
www.intiwarayassi.org

Desc.:	A sanctuary that rescues and rehabilitates native wild animals taken from unsuitable captive environments. Aims of the project include: confiscation of animals from illegal markets; rehabilitation where possible; education and awareness to prevent illegal trading of wildlife.
Spp.:	Wild cats, including pumas and ocelots. Monkeys, including Capuchins and black spiders, tropical birds and reptiles.
Hab.:	Tropical rainforest.
Loc.:	Between Cochabamba and Santa Cruz, Bolivia.
Travel:	Flight to La Paz or Santa Cruz, then bus to project.
Dur.:	Minimum 2 weeks. Staying at least 1 month is encouraged.
Per.:	Year round.
L.term:	Long-term volunteers are encouraged.
Age:	Min.18, due to strenuous work and basic living conditions.
Qualif.:	No qualifications required. Experience with animals is useful, but also carpentry and building skills. Volunteers must be hard working and committed.
Work:	Work is physical and includes: maintenance, building cages and fences, clearing forest areas, care and supervision of animals and basic husbandry tasks such as preparing food and cleaning. Working days can be long and in a humid climate.
Lang.:	English; Spanish is an advantage.
Accom.:	Basic shared rooms, with communal bathroom and kitchen areas.
Cost:	Accommodation is US$158-190 for the first 15 days, then US$6.5-8 daily thereafter. Food is approx. US$5/day.
Applic.:	Verify the website for full details. Work is allocated on arrival.

Conservation of Gialova Lagoon, Greece
Hellenic Ornithological Society (HOS)
Vas. Irakleiou 24, 10682 Athens Greece
Tel./Fax: ++30 (210) 822 8704
E-mail: info@ornithologiki.gr
www.ornithologiki.gr

Desc.:	The project aims at implementing conservation actions in Gialova lagoon, in Greece. It includes monitoring of highly endangered species of reptiles, bird counts, public awareness and visitor access management.
Spp.:	Reptiles, water birds.
Hab.:	Mediterranean wetland, sand dunes.
Loc.:	Peloponnese, Greece.
Travel:	Flight to Athens, bus to Pylos.
Dur.:	Min. 3 weeks.
Per.:	July to end October.
L.term:	Up to 6 months after approval.
Age:	Min. 20 - max. 40; older if fit.
Qualif.:	Background in biology, zoology, environmental studies or previous experience is preferred. Students for research are welcome.
Work:	Monitoring and protection of nests, public awareness, wardening, maintenance and infrastructure work, guided tours, bird monitoring, data entering.
Lang.:	English.
Accom.:	Tents in organised camping.
Cost:	Participation fee: EUR60; transport, food and accommodation are not included.
Applic.:	Apply on website.
Notes:	The project runs since 1998 and 450 volunteers have participated. Conservation must be volunteers priority.

Conservation Volunteering in St. Lucia, Caribbean

Durrell Wildlife Conservation Trust
Les Augres Manor
Trinity Jersey Channel Islands JE3 5BP UK
Tel.: ++44 (153) 486 0031
E-mail: charlotte.linney@durrell.org   www.durrell.org

Desc.: An ideal project for conservationists and field biologists. Volunteers can join for a 3 month or 6 month period. Work can be hard but rewarding and it is a great way to make a vital difference to species conservation.

Spp.: Various Caribbean Islands species.

Hab.: Coastal and dry forest tropical.

Loc.: St Lucia, Caribbean.

Travel: Flight to Saint Lucia; further details provided on application.

Dur.: 3 month or 6 month period.

Per.: Year round.

L.term: Inquire with organisation.

Age: Min. 21.

Qualif.: Preference to candidates with previous experience in projects in the tropics, and/or with a background in the biological sciences.

Work: Most activities are field-based and involves population monitoring and management for a variety of threatened species. Ability to handle wild animals, and to work with local people are required.

Lang.: English.

Accom.: Shared apartment, but volunteers are asked to bring their own camping equipment.

Cost: GB£600-1,200 for 3 or 6 months to cover costs, plus flights, vaccinations, full insurance.

Applic.: Recruiting up to 4 times per year; for further information and details, contact: recruitment@durrell.org.

CREES Volunteer Programme, Peru

CREES - The Rainforest Education and Resource Centre
Calle San Miguel 250, Cusco Peru
Tel.: ++51 (84) 262 433
E-mail: info@crees-expeditions.com
www.crees-expeditions.com

Desc.: An opportunity to live, work and train in one of the most bio-diverse regions tropical rainforests on earth. Volunteers contribute to a variety of ongoing conservation, sustainability and educational projects at the MLC Research Facility in the Manu Biosphere Reserve.

Spp.: Tropical rainforest species of birds, mammals, insects, amphibians, reptiles and plants.

Hab.: Tropical rainforest.

Loc.: Manu Biosphere Reserve (MBR), south-eastern Peru.

Travel: Flight to Cusco, then by bus and river boat to the MBR.

Dur.: Min. 4 weeks.

Per.: Year round.

L.term: Long term volunteers are welcome.

Age: Min. 18.

Qualif.: Volunteers should speak either fluent English or Spanish, be in good health and fit enough to participate in physical activity.

Work: Wildlife monitoring projects; sustainable development projects; local education projects.

Lang.: English and/or Spanish.

Accom.: Comfortable shared accommodation and facilities (catering provided).

Cost: US$2,100 for 4 weeks. Price includes: training, accommodation, transport (to and from Cusco), meals, 4 day Amazonian expedition.

Applic.: Online at: www.crees-expeditions.com.

Crocodile Conservation Volunteer, India

WAVA - Work and Volunteer Abroad
67-71 Levisham High Street
London SE13 5JX UK
Tel.: ++44 (020) 8297 3278
E-mail: info@workandvolunteer.com
www.workandvolunteer.com

Desc.: 30 years ago 8 acres of land on India's east coast south of Chennai (formerly Madras) became a trust for the conservation and study of India's three types of crocodile, the Mugger, the Gharial and the Saltwater. Starting with 30 adults, the trust has now bred over 5,000 and currently cares for over 2,400 crocodiles. This animal conservation volunteer programme gives the chance to experience a unique journey by getting close to some endangered species.

Spp.: Crocodiles, turtles, tortoises, king cobras, monitor lizards, pythons and iguanas.

Hab.: Coastal beaches, Indian wetlands.

Loc.: Chennai, Tamil Nadu, India.

Travel: Flight to Chennai, where pickup is arranged.

Dur.: Min. 1 month.

Per.: Year round.

L.term: Max. 4 months.

Age: Min.18. No max age.

Qualif.: No particular skills needed other than genuine interest in reptiles.

Work: Feeding the animals, cleaning out and maintaining the enclosures; helping with research projects and collecting data; supporting the environmental awareness camps by giving presentations.

Lang.: English.

Accom.: Basic accommodation within the center, 2 meals/day provided.

Cost: GB£1,190 one month, GB$2,090 for 3 months.

Applic.: Via website.

Dolphin Research Center, Florida USA

Volunteer and Internship Program
58901 Overseas Highway
Grassy Key, Florida 33050-6019 USA
Tel.: ++1 (305) 289 1121 ext. 230 - Fax: ++1 (305) 743 7627
E-mail: drc-vr@dolphins.org
www.dolphins.org

Desc.:	Dolphin Research Center (DRC) is a NGO dedicated to marine mammal research and education. It offers volunteers unique opportunities for learning about dolphins and various aspects of the daily operations of a marine mammal care facility. It also offers internships involving concentration in a specific department.
Spp.:	Bottlenose dolphin, California sea lion.
Loc.:	Grassy Key, Florida, USA.
Travel:	Flight to Miami, then by bus to Marathon.
Dur.:	1-4 months for volunteers; 3-4 months for internships.
Per.:	Year round.
L.term:	Available for local residents.
Age:	Min. 18.
Qualif.:	Good physical shape (able to lift 30 lbs/15 kg).
Work:	Assist in animal food preparation, monitor visitors and answer questions, assist staff in conducting public interactive programmes, perform various facility maintenance tasks and provide administrative support. Interns duties vary depending upon the specific internship (animal care and training, dolphin-child therapy, research, education and visual communications).
Lang.:	English fluency is a requirement.
Accom.:	Not provided, DRC assists with house sharing information.
Cost:	Living expenses can be as much as US$1,500/month.
Applic.:	Application available on website or mailed upon request.
Notes:	Individuals desiring a shorter, more interactive learning experience may be interested in the week-long DolphinLab class. See website or contact for info: drc-ed@dolphins.org

Dolphins & Sea Life Around The Maltese Islands, Malta

The Biological Conservation Research Foundation (BICREF)
PO Box 30, Hamrun HMR Malta
Tel.: ++(356) 2122 4502 /9942 9592
E-mail: bicref@gmail.com
www.bicref.org

Desc.:	The project consists in boat or SCUBA research surveys during the year to observe and study different marine organisms, analysing the associations between environmental variables.
Spp.:	Dolphins, sea turtles, birds, whales, manta rays and sharks; coastal/marine biodiversity is also studied.
Hab.:	Mediterranean coastal and offshore/pelagic waters.
Loc.:	The Maltese Islands, Mediterranean.
Travel:	Flight to Luqa International Airport, Malta, or ferry from Sicily.
Dur.:	Any duration can be arranged according to project and activity.
Per.:	Year round; summer is most intense.
L.term:	Possible.
Age:	Min. 18 - max. 45, depending on the work chosen by volunteers.
Qualif.:	A background in biology is preferable but not required. Sea-faring stamina and interest or experience in marine research and conservation are required.
Work:	Field observations and data recording during research surveys; assist in data upload on computer and analyses after the surveys.
Lang.:	English or Italian.
Accom.:	Various accommodations are available in Malta, but they have to be arranged by the volunteer.
Cost:	EUR40 once to join research boat surveys; it does not cover any travel, accommodation or maintenance.
Applic.:	Send a brief CV, letter of interest and application form 6-4 months prior to the volunteering period.
Notes:	Any special needs should be stated in the application letter.

Donkey Sanctuary Bonaire, Netherlands Antilles

PO Box 331
Bonaire Netherlands Antilles
Tel.: ++ (599) 9560 7607
E-mail: info@donkeysanctuary.com
www.donkeysanctuary.com

Desc.: Donkey Sanctuary Bonaire is a non-profit foundation taking care of about 450 wild donkeys of the Island of Bonaire, particularly the abused, injured and orphaned donkeys who lost their mothers in car accidents.

Spp.: Donkeys.

Hab.: Caribbean Island farmland.

Loc.: The Sanctuary is 100ha estate, located in the middle of the island.

Travel: Flight to Bonaire, airport pick-up is available.

Dur.: Min. 6 weeks.

Per.: Year round.

L.term: There is no limit of time for long-term stays.

Age: Min. 20. Good physical condition is important.

Qualif.: No particular qualifications required, just a strong motivation and love for animals.

Work: Feeding the animals, facility maintenance, assistance with the educational programmes for school kids, record keeping and observation of the donkeys, cleaning stables, care of injured animals, selling souvenirs and give tourist information.

Lang.: English and Dutch required.

Accom.: Private small house on the compound, with kitchen, shower and toilet.

Cost: Accommodation is provided at no cost.

Applic.: Via e-mail with the subject heading: 'Volunteer program'. In the text, include CV, letter of intentions and possible dates.

Notes: Personal medical insurance required. Only non-smokers accepted.

Earthwise Valley Sustainable Living Programme, New Zealand

Earthwise Valley Conservation Volunteer Projects
PO Box 5, Thames, 3540 Waikato, New Zealand
Tel.: ++64 (0) 9355 0333
E-mail: volunteer@earthwisevalley.org
www.earthwisevalley.org

Desc.:	Earthwise Valley is a New Zealand based, charitable, volunteer run, sustainable living and conservation project. This volunteer programme suits people interested in learning about sustainable living, enjoying the outdoors, and living a saner, richer and simpler life.
Spp.:	Marine mammals, sea birds, kiwi, insects, native flora, reptiles.
Hab.:	Coasts, temperate rainforest.
Loc.:	Coromandel Peninsula, New Zealand.
Travel:	Fly to Auckland, pickup from there or bus to Coromandel.
Dur.:	Three months is considered ideal but longer or shorter is ok.
Per.:	Year round.
L.term:	Up to 1 year placements.
Age:	Min.18.
Qualif.:	No skills required but willing to learn about sustainability and forest conservation desired.
Work:	Revitalising degraded farmland, growing and planting trees, controlling animal pests and weeds, using organic and permacultural techniques, and native bush research.
Lang.:	English.
Accom.:	Shared room or tent with 1-2 other people. Sleeping bags required.
Cost:	Visitors to the Sanctuary are asked to make a contribution of NZ$645 per week. This includes food, accommodation and recreation trips.
Applic.:	Application forms availible on our website. Scholarship positions are possible.

East African Whale Shark Trust, Kenya

PO Box 933
80400 Ukunda Kenya
Tel.: ++ 254 (72) 0293 156
E-mail: nimu@giantsharks.org
www.giantsharks.org

Desc.: An education and research project dedicated to whale shark conservation along the Kenya coast giving the opportunity to monitor and study the local whale shark population and raise awareness in local schools. It works alongside stakeholders with the emphasis being on the value of the whale shark alive.

Spp.: Whale shark (*Rhincodon typus*).

Hab.: Tropical oceans.

Loc.: Diani beach, south coast of Kenya, east Africa.

Travel: Flight to Nairobi and/or direct to Mombasa, then a 2 hour drive south to Diani beach. Volunteers will be met.

Dur.: Shorter terms possible. Longer terms welcome upon application.

Per.: Year round, whale shark season is October to March.

L.term: Longer periods welcome upon application.

Age: Min. 18. No maximum age if fit, healthy and motivated.

Qualif.: Volunteers should be fit, physically active. Useful skills are experience in marine biology and SCUBA diving.

Work: Collect whale shark data, give presentations, work with local fishermen.

Lang.: English; Swahili helpful.

Accom.: Comfortable double rooms in the EAWST accommodation centre on the beach, a short drive from the research base.

Cost: US$750/month with room and board. Travel expenses excluded.

Applic.: Send e-mail or use the Green Volunteers Standard Application Form.

Notes: Vaccinations, anti-malaria tablets and insurance required. Most visitors to Kenya also require a visa. The organisation has a blog on whale sharks at: www.whalesharks.wildlifedirect.org.

Eco-City in Bahia de Caraquez, Ecuador

Planet Drum Foundation
PO Box 31251
San Francisco, 94131 California USA
Tel.: ++1 (415) 285 6556
E-mail: planetdrumecuador@yahoo.com
www.planetdrum.org/volunteerbahia.htm

Desc.: A 8km revegetation/restoration project to stabilize severely eroded hillsides and prevent devastating mudslides. The Foundation also runs a Bioregional Education Program for school children.

Spp.: All species native to this dry tropical rainforest ecosystem.

Hab.: Dry tropical rainforest.

Loc.: Bahia de Caraquez, Ecuador.

Travel: Flight to Quito or Guayaquil, then by bus to Bahia de Caraquez.

Dur.: One month.

Per.: Year round.

L.term: Unlimited.

Age: Min. 18.

Qualif.: Interest in ecological sustainability, willingness to work with community and nature in a third world environment.

Work: Revegetation and restoration work.

Lang.: English, Spanish.

Accom.: PDF's office/apartment can accommodate 6 volunteers. Additional inexpensive housing is also available.

Cost: $15/month.

Applic.: Via e-mail at: planetdrumecuador@yahoo.com. Include the Green Volunteers Standard Form.

El Eden Flora Y Fauna: Animal Rescue and Rehabilitation, Argentina

Villa Rumipal
Cordoba Argentina
Tel.: ++54 (351) 457 6364
E-mail: eleden@grandeslagos.com.ar
www.eledenflorayfauna.org

Desc.:	A Centre in the mountains, 25ha, with almost 500 animals of 60 species. Volunteers are able to do: feeding, vet help, interaction, help and care of new members or baby animals, observation, general duties (cleaning cages, construction of new places for animals) riding horses. Volunteers can also have cultural interactions.
Spp.:	Over 60 spp.: pumas, howler monkeys, ponies, donkeys, capybaras, parrots, farm animals, flamingos, buffalo, llamas, horses.
Hab.:	Mountain.
Loc.:	Villa Rumipal, Cordoba, Argentina.
Travel:	Flight to Buenos Aires, then plane or bus to Cordoba, where volunteers are met.
Per.:	Volunteers can stay up to 1 year.
Age:	Min.18 or 17 with parents' permission. No maximum age.
Qualif.:	No particular skills needed, just a strong motivation and love for animals.
Work:	Feeding, vet help, interaction, help and care of newcomers or babies, cleaning, general maintenance, rescue.
Lang.:	Spanish or English.
Accom.:	Typical rancho lodging, with beds, bathroom with hot/cold water, heat in winter, kitchen.
Cost:	US$400-600 per month, including all food, accommodation, internet, rides to town.
Applic.:	No application form, just inquire via e-mail.

Elephant Nature Park, Thailand

209/2 Sridornchai Road
Chiang Mai 50100 Thailand
Tel.: ++66 (53) 818 932 /818 754 /272 855
Fax: ++66 (53) 818 755 /904 033
E-mail: info@elephantnaturepark.org
www.elephantnaturepark.org

Desc.:	Thai elephant population is struggling for its very survival with existing numbers down to some 3,000. As the population grows, this majestic gentle giant is finding it harder to find places to live without exploitation by humans. The Park, founded in 1966, is located in a valley surrounded by jungle mountains and bordered by a river and provides a home for over 30 elephants.
Spp.:	Asian elephant (*Elephus maximus*), dogs and cats.
Hab.:	Tropical rainforest.
Loc.:	Northern Thailand, 60km from the city of Chiang Mai.
Travel:	About 1 hour from Chiang Mai. Transport is provided. No public transportation available.
Dur.:	Min. 1 week, max. 1 month (12 volunteers at a time).
Per.:	Year round.
L.term:	Only after initial period and approval by project manager.
Age:	Min. 18 in good physical health. Children may participate if accompanied by their legal guardian.
Qualif.:	No particular skills needed. Constant instruction and supervision by park staff is provided.
Work:	Volunteers help with a variety of tasks including basic elephant health care and park duties.
Lang.:	English.
Accom.:	Simple bamboo tree huts, with toilet and shower, in the centre.
Cost:	About US$400/week (includes lodging, food, local transport).
Applic.:	See 'volunteer' section of website.
Notes:	Health insurance is required.

Endangered Species Conservation, South Africa

Wildlife ACT
27 Breda Park, Breda Street Cape Town
8001 Western Cape South Africa
Tel.: +27 (82) 879 7298
E-mail: jo@wildlifeact.com www.wildlifeact.com

Desc.: Real Africa - Real Conservation. Get hands-on experience helping to save endangered and priority African wildlife species like the wild dog, cheetah, rhino, elephant, leopard and lion. Situated in Zululand, South Africa, Wildlife ACT team members work across a number of reserves in the area, each with its own unique focus.

Spp.: Wild dogs, cheetahs, rhinos, elephant, leopard, hyena, and more.

Hab.: African Savannah.

Loc.: Zululand, South Africa.

Travel: From Johannesburg fly to Richards Bay, where volunteers are picked up and driven to camp.

Dur.: Minimum 2 weeks.

Per.: Year round.

L.term: Max. 6 months.

Age: Min. 18. Volunteers need to be young at heart and in reasonably good condition.

Qualif.: A positive attitude, being able to communicate in English, and a desire to make a real conservation difference.

Work: Tracking, via radio telemetry equipment; GPS mapping of sightings; creation/updating of identity kits; animal behavioural research; game counts; radio collaring animals; relocation, re-introduction of game; bird ringing.

Lang.: English.

Accom.: Volunteer house with kitchen, hot water and electricity.

Cost: 2 weeks: US$1,550; 4 weeks: US$ 2,725; every extra 2 weeks: US$115. Food, accommodation and training included.

Applic.: An application form will be sent to you on request.

Everything Elephants, South Africa

EDGE of AFRICA
Suite 88, P.O. Box X31
Knysna, Western Cape 6570 South Africa
Tel.: +27 (44) 382 0122
E-mail: info@edgeofafrica.com
www.edgeofafrica.com

Desc.: This journey takes volunteers through all the aspects of elephant conservation in Africa.

Spp.: Elephant and general game reserve species (possibility of view the big 5 at ADDO Elephant Park).

Hab.: Coast, forest, fynbos and semi-desert.

Loc.: Garden Route, South Africa.

Travel: Fly to George from Johannesburg, Cape Town or Port Elizabeth.

Dur.: Minimum 2 weeks, max 3 months.

Per.: Year Round.

L.term: Inquire with organization.

Age: Min. 18. No age limit as long as fit.

Qualif.: No particular skills or knowledge are needed.

Work: Behavioural studies, community education and empowerment, participating in dynamic current projects as well as possibility for own project development depending on skills; park and reserve management.

Lang.: English.

Accom.: Volunteers are based in simple, clean, dorm style accommodation at the volunteers house, located in Knysna, as well as on-site at the various reserves and national parks. Private, twin or family rooms are available on request.

Cost: US$1,135 for two weeks.

Applic.: Via e-mail, Green Volunteers standard form is welcome.

Faia Brava Reserve, Portugal

ATN - Associação Transumância e Natureza
Travessa Serpa Pinto, 3
6440-118 Figueira de Castelo Rodrigo, Guarda Portugal
Tel.: ++351 (271) 311 202
E-mail: geral@atnatureza.org
www.ATNatureza.org

Desc.:	Faia Brava Reserve, at the Côa Valley SPA, is a multi-task conservation project (ecology, forest engineering, organic agriculture). This area has high biodiversity levels, due to its river canyon species and magnificent cork oak woodlands.
Spp.:	Bonelli's Eagle, Golden Eagle, Griffon Vulture, Egyptian Vulture, Black Stork, European Rabbit, Red Partridge.
Hab.:	River canyons, cork oak woodland, agricultural mosaic.
Loc.:	Figueira de Castelo Rodrigo, Guarda, Portugal.
Travel:	Flight to Oporto or Lisbon; train or bus to Figueira de Castelo Rodrigo or Guarda; transport to the project is provided.
Dur.:	From 1 week to 1 year.
Per.:	Year round.
L.term:	Inquire with the organisation.
Age:	Min. 18 – max. 65. Volunteers need to be fit and able to work in rough terrain.
Qualif.:	Interest and basic knowledge on conservation biology; no other skills are required.
Work:	Activities may change year round. For example: reforestation, traditional pigeon house maintenance, fire surveillance and fauna monitoring (including raptor species nest monitoring), nature trail maintenance, etc.
Lang.:	English.
Accom.:	Camping in tents or housing can be arranged.
Cost:	Exclusive for ATN members: EUR15; work material, t-shirt and hat, daily transportation included, and participation certificate included.
Applic.:	Send CV; the Green Volunteers Standard Application Form is welcome.

Fauna Forever Tambopata, Peru

c/o TReeS PO Box 33153, London NW3 4DR UK
TReeS-Peru PO Box 28
Puerto Maldonado, Madre de Dios Peru
Tel.: ++44 (208) 883 8137
E-mail: info@faunaforever.org
www.faunaforever.org/fft

Desc.:	Asociaciòn Fauna Forever Tambopata is a long-term wildlife and ecotourism monitoring project based on the Amazon rainforest of Peru. This region lies on the eastern edge of the Tropical Andes biodiversity hotspot, the richest and most diverse area on earth.
Spp.:	Reptiles, amphibians, mammals, birds (macaws, parrots, harpy eagle).
Hab.:	Lowland tropical rainforest.
Loc.:	Tambopata, Madre de Dios, Peru.
Travel:	Flight to Lima; then domestic flight to Puerto Maldonado (PEM). Volunteers will be met at PEM airport.
Dur.:	3-6 weeks. Shorter research trips possible by prior arrangement.
Per.:	Year round.
L.term:	Maximum 1 year. Extension as intern possible.
Age:	Min. 18. Volunteers must be in good health.
Qualif.:	A keen interest, educational qualifications and previous experience in a related biological field would be an advantage.
Work:	Wildlife surveys (mist-netting, point census, transect surveying, track traps, night surveying) and vegetation surveys.
Lang.:	English; Spanish useful.
Accom.:	Research stations or tourist lodges, with bunk beds and/or tents. Sleeping bags required.
Cost:	USD 1,300-$2,150 for 3-6 weeks, with room, board and local transfers.
Applic.:	By e-mail. Deadline 60 days before project starts.
Notes:	Volunteers may collect data for their own project or thesis.

Flat Holm Island, Bristol Channel UK

Flat Holm Project
C/O Cardiff Harbour Authority, Queen Alexandra House
Cargo Road, Cardiff Bay CF10 4LY UK
Tel.: ++44 (029) 2087 7912
E-mail: flatholmproject@cardiff.gov.uk
www.flatholmisland.com

Desc.:	Flat Holm Island is a site of special scientific interest, geological conservation review site and local nature reserve. Education, conservation and buildings management go hand in hand. Home to one of the largest Lesser Black Backed Gull colonies in Wales and home to the rare Wild Leek.
Spp.:	Shelduck, lesser lack-backed gulls, butterflies, moths.
Hab.:	Limestone Grassland, rocky shore, scrub habitats.
Loc.:	Bristol Channel, Wales, UK.
Travel:	Flight to Cardiff, train to Barry Island Station, 10 minute walk.
Dur.:	Minimum 2 weeks; preferably commitment of 6 months to 1 year.
Per.:	Year round.
L.term:	Up to 1 year.
Age:	Min. 18.
Qualif.:	No specific qualifications required. Keen interest in conservation, education and a general level of practical ability.
Work:	Species monitoring, habitat management, buildings maintenance, livestock husbandry, environmental education, guided tours.
Lang.:	English.
Accom.:	House with bunkbeds. May need to share room. Sleeping bags required.
Cost:	GB£10.50/day with food and accommodation for short stay (2 weeks). Free for long term volunteers of 6 months.
Applic.:	Cover letter stating interest and abilities to flatholmproject@cardiff.gov.uk.

Fundaciòn Proyecto Ecologico Chiriboga, Ecuador

Puruha 267 y Epiclachima
Ciudadela San Jose, La Magdalena, Quito Ecuador
Tel.: ++593 (2) 265 2128
E-mail: ecoproye@andinanet.net
http://chiribogaecuador.wordpress.com

Desc.:	The Foundation Proyecto Ecologico protects a reserve in the region of Chiriboga focused on reforestation work and protection of nature. Nowadays the Foundation works also in other places of Ecuador promoting environmental education in schools and working with children with disabilities.
Spp.:	Various species of birds and mammals, such as small jaguars, collared peccaries, etc.
Hab.:	Cloudy Forest.
Loc.:	Chiriboga, south-west of Quito, Ecuador.
Travel:	Travel instructions to get to the projects can be found on the website.
Dur.:	Minimum 4 weeks, but a shorter stay can be arranged.
Per.:	4 workcamps per year in spring and summer.
L.term:	Only for qualified or outstanding volunteers.
Age:	Min. 18.
Qualif.:	Special skills are required only for medium or long-term volunteers.
Work:	Reforestation and protection of the baby trees area, feeding animals, making any ecological work. After 2 weeks volunteers travel to the coast to teach English in some schools of other communities. Training and supervision by the workers of the Proyecto are provided.
Lang.:	Basic Spanish knowledge. Volunteers with no Spanish knowledge will be assisted by other volunteers.
Accom.:	At the Proyecto Chiriboga: in the house of the Foundation or in lodges. In communities: home stay with the families of the schools.
Cost:	US$480 for 4 weeks, including accommodation, 3 meals/day and a donation to the foundation. Transports are not included.
Applic.:	Send CV with a motivation letter. Send confirmation via e-mail.

Giant Panda Reserve, China

I to I Volunteer Adventure
Woodsid House, 261 Low Lane
Leeds LS18 5NY UK
Tel.: ++44 (011) 3205 4620
E-mail: info@i-to-i.com
www.i-to-i.com

Desc.: In Shaanxi province there are about 270 giant pandas living in Panda Reservations. At the centre in Louguantai where volunteers will be working they are currently looking after and monitoring fifteen giant pandas. Help is needed to preserve some of the world's most endangered species.

Spp.: Giant panda, black deer, lesser pandas (red pandas), monkeys, peacocks as well as other animals.

Hab.: National forest park.

Loc.: Lougantai, Shaanxi province, China.

Travel: Flight to Xian, where pickup is arranged.

Dur.: Min. 2 weeks, max 1 month.

Per.: Year round.

L.term: Max. 1 month.

Age: Min.17.

Qualif.: No particular skills needed.

Work: Cleaning animal enclosures and waterholes; feeding the animals and observing their behaviour during feeding and cleaning times; maintenance activities including plant control and fencing.

Lang.: English.

Accom.: On-site accommodation at the park, 3 meals a day included.

Cost: GB£750 for 2 weeks, GB£950 for 3 weeks, GB$1,150 for 1 month.

Applic.: Via website.

Gibbon Rehabilitation Project, Thailand

The Wild Animal Rescue Foundation of Thailand (WARF)
65/1 Sukhumvit 55, Wattana
Bangkok 10110 Thailand
Tel.: ++66 (2) 712 9515 - Fax: ++66 (2) 712 9778
E-mail: volunteer@warthai.org
www.warthai.org

Desc.:   «The first gibbon project in the world.» The sanctuary is located on the remote area of Phuket which houses over 70 gibbons. Its aim is the rehabilitation of gibbons back to their natural habitat additionally providing ongoing care to those unsuitable for repatriation.

Spp.:   White-handed gibbon (*Hylobates lar*).

Hab.:   Tropical rainforest.

Loc.:   Bang Pae Waterfall, Khao Phra Thaew non-hunting area, Phuket, Thailand.

Travel: Flight to Bangkok, then bus or plane to Phuket.

Dur.:   Min. 3 weeks.

Per.:   Year round.

L.term: Students and graduates in biology, anthropology and veterinary medicine are especially welcome to stay for long periods.

Age: Min. 18.

Qualif.:   Good physical condition, enthusiasm and ability to work without assistance. Experience with animals or skills in construction, tourist assistance, public relations, etc.,

Work: Quarantine and rehabilitation, reintroduction, conservation, education and fund-raising. Volunteers work 6 days/week.

Lang.:   English.

Accom.:   Bungalows for 2 or more persons located close to the sanctuary, with toilet, shower and cooking facilities.

Cost: 3 weeks: THB38,550 (approx. US$1,100), THB4,410 (approx. US$125) for additional weeks. 8 weeks: THB35,740 (approx. US$1,030), THB4,410 for additional weeks.

Applic.:   On www.warthai.org (Wild Animal Rescue Foundation of Thailand) or www.ecovolunteer.org (Ecovolunteer Network).

GOECO, Israel

Rozanis 13,
Tel Aviv Israel
Tel.: ++972 (036) 499 146-1 /(050) 576 2797 /(054) 734 5643
E-mail: goeco@goeco.org; goeco@goeco.co.il
www.goeco.org; www.goeco.co.il

Desc.: GoEco and the Israel Nature & Parks Authority are leading a conservation and animal care work at the Yotvata Wildlife Preserve, whose mission is to establish reproduction groups for populations of wild animals that are mentioned in the Bible, but have disappeared from the landscape, as well as for other endangered desert animals.

Spp.: African donkeys, onagers, addax, ostrich, Arabian and scimitar oryx, wolves, sand and Afghan foxes, fennecs, leopards, caracals, wild and sand cats, striped hyenas, birds of prey, desert reptiles.

Hab.: The reserve is dotted with Acacia trees and includes a variety of desert habitats: an Acacia forest, a salt marsh, and sand dunes.

Loc.: Yotvata, around 40km north of Eilat.

Travel: Flight to Tel Aviv. Further details upon application.

Dur.: 2 week period volunteer projects will be posted on the website.

Per.: Year round.

L.term: Available; min. 4 weeks for long term position.

Age: Min. 18

Qualif.: Strong motivation, good health/fitness, interest in animal conservation.

Work: Feeding animals, cleaning habitats, maintenance, observations, data collection, accompanying/assisting park rangers, field work, constructing enrichment facilities. Long-term volunteer may be asked to lead short-term workcamps of 6 volunteers at the preserve.

Lang.: A good level of English is required.

Accom.: In a kibbutz, in apartments with shared rooms, bathroom and kitchen. Food isn't included and costs around US$5-10/day.

Cost: 300 USD one time registration fee.

Applic.: Through website www.goeco.org/Israel.

La Gran Vista Agroecological Farm, Costa Rica

El Peje de Repunta de Pérez Zeledòn
San Isidro de El General 1000
San José Costa Rica
Tel.: ++506 506 8924 8983 /2200 3443
E-mail: lagranvista@hotmail.com
www.lagranvista.com

Desc.: La Gran Vista is a non-profit project aimed at spreading awareness of environmentally sustainable agricultural methods to other farmers in the region. The project manager, Donald Villalobos, is an agricultural engineer who has worked with the Ministry of Agriculture for 31 years and has seen first hand how traditional farming practices have contributed to habitat degradation in Costa Rica.

Spp.: Various species of mammals, such as opossum (*Philander opossum, Caluromys derbianus*) and many others.

Hab.: Rainforest.

Loc.: County of Peréz Zeledòn, 3 hours south of San José, Costa Rica.

Travel: Flight to San José, then 3 hours by bus to San Isidro, stopping next to the Super Weber supermarket in a village called Repunta.

Dur.: Min. a week.

Per.: Year round.

L.term: Volunteers can join the project for a longer period.

Age: Min. 18 - max. 30 is preferred.

Qualif.: A positive, hard-working attitude.

Work: Construction, feeding animals, planting seeds, soil conservation, maintenance of medical plants, using and producing organic fertilizer, maintaining spring-water wells, harvesting crops.

Lang.: English or Spanish.

Accom.: Home-stay in a rustic cabin with bunk beds or open place to set tents.

Cost: US$23/day for room and board. Volunteers must have their own medical and travel insurance, including a cancellation policy.

Applic.: Send Green Volunteers Standard Application Form via e-mail.

Great Whales in their Natural Environment, Canada

ORES - Foundation for Marine Environment Research
Postfach 1252, 4502 Solothurn Switzerland
Tel./Fax.: ++41 (32) 623 6354
E-mail: utscherter@ores.org
www.ores.org

Desc.: The coastal ecosystem in the St. Lawrence estuary in Eastern Canada is known for the near-shore abundance and diversity of its marine life, especially whales. ORES marine biologists, with the help of volunteers, study the feeding behaviour, distribution and habitat utilisation of the abundant minke whales applying non-intrusive research methods. During the course, volunteers will have daily encounters with different species and are actively involved in data collection., They will also learn to identify individuals and what whales are doing and why. Research results, conservation issues and general knowledge on whales are shared on the water and during several comprehensive presentations.

Spp.: Harbour porpoise, beluga, sperm whale, minke, humpback, finback and blue whale, several seal species.

Hab.: Protected estuarine waters in a dynamic marine ecosystem.

Loc.: St. Lawrence-Saguenay Marine Park, province of Québec, Canada.

Travel: Flight to Montreal or Québec City, then by bus (or car) to Les Bergeronnes.

Dur.: General Interest Course (GIC) of 2 weeks with daily field trips.

Per.: July to September.

L.term: Please contact the office.

Age: Min. 18. 16 with parents' permission.

Qualif.: No particular skills or knowledge are needed apart from basic knowledge of English.

Work: Observation and data gathering daily (weather permitting) by small research teams from an open inflatable boat. Protected waters offer encounters with whales without any seasickness. Studies carried out among others: feeding strategies and techniques, ventilation recording, spatial and temporal distribution, photo-identification.

Lang.:   English. ORES personnel also speak French and German.

Accom.:   Near Les Bergeronnes. In spacious and heated cabins (2-3 beds) at the research station overlooking the estuary, well-equipped with kitchen, lecture hall and an extensive multi media library.

Cost: Fee for GIC: CHF1,600 (approx. US$1,700, EUR1,200, GB£1100). Fees for ISC on request.

Applic.:   Apply directly via e-mail to receive detailed information and an application form. Due to the high demand, it is recommended to contact ORES early in the year. After enrolment, participants will receive a comprehensive booklet on the project.

Notes: Canada Field Office open from June to October: Ocean Research and Education Society (ORES), PO Box 117, Les Bergeronnes, Quebec, G0T 1G0.

Grey Wolf Recovery & Sanctuary, Oregon and Idaho USA

Wolf Education and Research Center (WERC)
Business Office: 3909 NE MLK Blvd, Suite 202, Portland, OR 97212 USA
Programs&Outreach: 517 Joseph Ave, PO Box 217, Winchester, ID 83555
Tel.: ++1 (888) 422 1110 - Fax: ++1 (208) 924 6959
E-mail: info@wolfcenter.org   www.wolfcenter.org

Desc.:	Public information, education and research concerning endangered species, with an emphasis on the grey wolf, its habitat and ecosystem in the northern Rocky Mountain region. WERC cares for 2 captive packs of wolves: «The Sawtooth Pack: Wolves of the Nez Perce and the Owyhee Pack newly rescued from Idaho». WERC is in partnership with the Nez Perce Tribe, which handles the wolf management and reintroduction for Idaho.
Spp.:	Grey timber wolf (*Canis lupus*).
Hab.:	Camas prairie, timber.
Loc.:	North-central region of Idaho; near the borders of Idaho, Washington and Oregon, USA.
Travel:	From Lewiston, ID take Highway 95 south to Winchester, ID. Follow signs for the Winchester Lake State Park. The centre is approximately 1mi past the State Park.
Dur.:	Varies with prior agreement between individual and WERC.
Per.:	Year round; the need is greater from June to September.
L.term:	Possible: inquire with the project.
Age:	Min.18.
Work:	Volunteers are involved in maintenance and/or construction, building, staffing the visitor centre; providing educational programmes, assisting with membership documentation and generally helping where needed.
Lang.:	English.
Accom.:	Local off-site lodging facilities can be recommended.
Cost:	Max. US$20/day; excluding meals and transportation.
Applic.:	Request information and application form via e-mail or mail.

Griffon Vulture Conservation Project, Croatia

Eco-center Caput Insulae – Beli
Beli 4, 51559 Beli Croatia
Tel./Fax: ++385 (51) 840 525
E-mail: caput.insulae@ri.t-com.hr
www.supovi.hr

Desc.: The griffon vulture has disappeared from many European countries and is declining in its south-eastern European range. The Croatian population includes approx. 100 breeding pairs. The aim is to study their biology and ecology to determine the critical factors for surviving on the islands and to develop new conservation strategies.

Spp.: Griffon vultures (*Gyps fulvus*), golden (*Aquila chrysaetos*) and short-toed eagle (*Circaetus gallicus*), peregrine falcon (*Falco peregrinus*), eagle owl (*Bubo bubo*), shag (*Phalacrocorax aristotelis*).

Hab.: Mediterrannean sea-cliffs, oak forests and grasslands.

Loc.: Island of Cres, Kvarner Archipelago, Northeast Adriatic, Croatia.

Travel: Flight to Zagreb or Trieste (Italy); then bus or train to Rijeka; then bus or catamaran to Cres.

Dur.: Min. 10 days.

Per.: March 1st to October 31st.

L.term: Possible, for extremely motivated volunteers.

Age: Min. 18.

Qual.: Strong motivation and love for nature.

Work: Recording colonies, noting all sightings at feeding station, taking care of ill or exhausted birds in the Rehabilitation Center, repairing stone-walls, cleaning fresh-water ponds, informing visitors.

Lang.: English.

Accom.: Eco-center: 26 beds, 4 toilets, hot showers, fully-equipped kitchen.

Cost: EUR250 for 10 days. Food is not included (approx. EUR8.50/day).

Agents: The Ecovolunteer Network at www.ecovolunteer.org.

Applic.: Application form on website.

Grupo Lobo, Portugal

Fac. Ciências de Lisboa
Dept. de Biologia Animal, Bloco C2, 1749-016 Lisboa Portugal
IWRC, Quinta da Murta. Apartado 61, 2665-150 Gradil Portugal
Tel: ++351 (261) 785 037 (IWRC) - Fax:++351 (261) 788 047 (IWRC)
E-mail: globo@fc.ul.pt
http://lobo.fc.ul.pt/

Desc.: Grupo Lobo is an NGO which has worked since 1985 on wolf conservation and its habitat in Portugal, where the wolf is in danger of extinction. The Iberian Wolf Recovery Center (IWRC) was created by GL in order to provide a suitable environment in captivity for wolves that can no longer live in the wild.

Spp.: Iberian wolf (*Canis lupus signatus*).

Hab.: Atlantic ecosystem.

Loc.: Malveira, 25km north of Lisbon, Portugal

Travel: Flight to Lisbon; then by bus or car to Vale de Guardia-Malveira.

Dur.: Minimum 15 days.

Per.: Volunteers are accepted year round.

L.term: Volunteers can stay up to 1 month.

Age: Min. 18.

Qual.: Ability to work as part of a team. Anyone is welcome to join and apply their skills and interests.

Work: Several tasks can be performed by volunteers: monitor and feeding the wolves; maintenance of the infrastructures; clearing the grounds outside enclosures; reforestation; prevention of fires.

Lang.: English or Portuguese.

Accom.: In a new chalet-type house with a double room and a 4-bed room, fully equipped with all modern conveniences.

Cost: EUR17.50-24/night for accommodation. Volunteers must provide for their own meals and transportation.

Applic.: Online application form.

Notes: Accident and health insurance is mandatory.

Hawaiian Forest Preservation Project, Hawaii USA

Kokee Resource Conservation Program c/o Garden Island Resource Conservation and Development Inc.
PO Box 1108, Waimea, Hawaii, 96796 USA
Tel.: ++1 (808) 335 0045 - Fax: ++1 (808) 335 0304
E-mail: rcp@aloha.net   www.krcp.org

Desc.:	In the Hawaiian Islands over 1,000 flowering plant species evolved, and the forests of Kokee State Park contain many species found nowhere else in the world as well as over 50% of the US Federally listed endangered plant species. This project removes invasive weeds from selected areas of the mountain state park in order to restore those forested areas to their native state.
Spp.:	Weed species: strawberry guava, blackberry, kahili ginger.
Hab.:	Mesic montane Koa-dominated forests, wet montane Ohia-dominated forests, mixed-bog communities.
Loc.:	Kokee State Park, Kauai, Hawaii.
Travel:	Flight to Kauai.
Dur.:	1 week to 1 month.
Per.:	Year round.
L.term:	Possible, inquire with organisation.
Age:	Min. 21, or enrolled in an environmentally oriented degree.
Qual.:	Volunteers must be physically fit. Training is provided. Priority is given to volunteers with a degree and/or experience in ecology, conservation or botany.
Work:	Under supervision, volunteers use herbicides and hand weed to maintain the nearly native state. Work is 8 hours/day, often involving strenuous hiking in mountainous areas.
Lang.:	English.
Accom.:	Rustic housing in historic camp (bunk beds). Groups are welcome but space is limited to parties of 14.
Cost:	Volunteers pay for their own food and must rent a car.
Applic.:	Request application form via e-mail.

Hellenic Wildlife Hospital, Greece

Hellenic Wildlife Hospital
PO Box 57, 18010 Aegina Greece
Tel.: ++30 (229) 703 1338 /(697) 331 8845
Fax: ++30 (229) 702 8214
E-mail: ekpaz@ekpazp.gr
www.ekpazp.gr

Desc.:	Founded in 1990, this is the oldest and largest wildlife rehabilitation centre in Greece dedicated to rehabilitation of wildlife, education and information of the public on wildlife protection issues, protection of endangered species, research on threats to wildlife (illegal shooting, trapping, poisoning, pollution, habitat degradation) and preventative action, cooperation with public authorities, national and international NGO's with similar goals.
Spp.:	Indigenous and exotic species (may be rare or threatened).
Hab.:	All the animals are found in Greece, but can be migrating birds or illegally transported animals from all over the world.
Loc.:	Island of Aegina, 10km from Aegina near Pachia Rachi.
Travel:	Flight to Athens, then by ferry to Aegina from Piraeus.
Dur.:	Min. 10 days, max. 1 year.
Per.:	Year round.
L.term:	Long-term is preferable, with a maximum duration of 1 year.
Age:	Minimum 18.
Qualif.:	No special skills required. Team work. All skills are welcome, especially veterinarian, wildlife expertise.
Work:	Cleaning of outdoor/indoor, food preparation, feeding/watering, maintenance/construction work, help in treatments, information work and other duties depending on experience. Training opportunities for veterinarian, biology or administration students or graduates.
Lang.:	English.
Accom.:	There is a house for volunteers in the centre.
Cost:	No fees, volunteers pay own living costs and travel expenses.
Applic.:	Application and agreement forms can be found on the website.

Hoedspruit Endangered Species Centre, South Africa

PO Box 1278, Hoedspruit, 1380
Limpopo Province South Africa
Tel.: ++27 (15) 793 1633
E-mail: students@cheetahcentre.co.za
www.wildlifecentre.co.za

Desc.:	A research and breeding project on feline species especially cheetah. Based in South-Africa Limpopo province, 40km from Kruger Park. Educational programme with hands on veterinary experiences. Cultural and tourism activities included with accommodation and all meals provided. Lectures on S.A. wildlife followed by practical sessions.
Spp.:	Cheetah, wild dog, African wild cat, lion, rhino, buffalo, black footed cat, caracal, serval, ground hornbill.
Hab.:	African savannah.
Loc.:	South-Africa, Limpopo Province, Hoedspruit.
Travel:	Airplane to Johannesburg and from there to Eastgate / Hoedspruit airport for pick-up.
Dur.:	21 days/3 weeks. It is a set programme.
Per.:	Year round; 3 weeks per month.
L.term:	Possibilities for longer stay depending on coordinator.
Age:	Min. 16 - max. 55. Most volunteers are between 18 and 25.
Qualif.:	No particular skills needed.
Work:	Food preparation and feeding of animals. Helping out at centre.
Lang.:	English.
Accom.:	Huts with 2 beds per hut in a camp within a big 5 area with electricity and warm showers, bedding provided.
Cost:	US$2.700 for 3 weeks, all inclusive.
Agents:	African Conservation Experience
Applic.:	Ask via e-mail for application form.

Iguana Research and Breeding Station (IRBS), Honduras

Bay Islands Foundation (FIB)
Iguana Station Utila, Iguana Road, Island Utila
Islas de la Bahia Honduras
Tel.: ++ (54) 425 3946
E-mail: volo@utila-iguana.de   www.utila-iguana.de

Desc: The IRBS is a conservation center that works for the protection of the wildlife of Utila -a Caribbean island of Honduras- through the breeding and reproduction project of a banner species: Ctenosaura bakeri, an endemic iguana. This is done through scientific research and community awareness improvement.

Spp.:   Mostly reptiles and insects, but also occasionally mammals, birds, plants.

Hab.:   Mangrove forest, Caribbean dry forest, beach, savannah.

Loc.:   Utila Island, in the Caribbean coast of Honduras.

Travel: Fly to San Pedro Sula. Reach La Ceiba by bus and via ferry to the island.

Dur.:   Min. 3 weeks.

Per.:   Year round.

L.term: There is no limit of time for long-term stays.

Age: Min. 18.

Qualif.:   Motivation and willingness to dedicate time and work.

Work: Feeding the animals, facility maintenance, assistance with the ecological educational programmes, wildlife record keeping and observation, assistance on wildlife rehabilitation.

Lang.:   English, Spanish.

Accom.:   Double bedrooms at the first floor of the wooden station building.

Cost: EUR55/week, including accommodation, showers, use of kitchen. Food and beverages are not included.

Applic.:   Via e-mail, please refer to website.

Notes: Health insurance and vaccinations (hepatitis, tetanus) mandatory.

International Conservation Volunteer Exchange, Nevada USA

Great Basin Institute
M/S 0099, University of Nevada Reno, Reno, Nevada 89557 USA
Tel.: ++1 (775) 784 1192 - Fax: ++1 (775) 327 2307
E-mail: icve@thegreatbasininstitute.org
www.thegreatbasininstitute.org (see «International Volunteering»)

Desc.: Over the past few field seasons, GBI has collaborated with numerous international environmental exchange programs, attracting over 350 students and young professionals from over 40 countries worldwide to serve on conservation projects throughout Nevada. Volunteers spent their time in the US working side-by-side with Nevada Conservation Corps members and GBI students at Lake Tahoe, Lake Mead, the Santa Rosa Mountains, and the Black Rock Desert, assisting with field research and restoration projects. In exchange for their service, ICVE volunteers are lead on educational trips, introducing them to premier spots in the west: central Sierra hot springs, Yosemite National Park, Big Sur coastal beaches, and high desert ranges.

Loc.: Projects in locations throughout the state of Nevada.

Travel: Flight to Reno or San Francisco (bus or train from S.F.).

Dur.: 1-6 months.

Per.: Year round (see website for specific dates).

L.term: Inquire with the organisation.

Age: Min. 18 - max. 35. Volunteers must be in good physical shape.

Qual.: No qualifications required.

Work: Work is 10hrs/day. 4 days in the field, with 3 days off or 8 days in the field with 6 days off.

Accom.: Camping during field work dormitory style cabin when off-time.

Cost: Volunteers pay for travel, travellers' insurance and required gear. Food while in and out of the field is provided.

Applic.: Contact Jeff Bryant, ICVE Program Director.

Notes: Projects change frequently and descriptions are provided for a general idea of what projects may entail.

Ionian Dolphin Project, Greece

Tethys Research Institute
Istituto Tethys, Viale G.B. Gadio 2
20121 Milan Italy
Tel.: ++39 (02) 7200 1947
Fax: ++39 (02) 8699 5011
E-mail: tethys@tethys.org www.tethys.org

Desc.:	This is the first long-term project on cetaceans in Ionian Greece, initiated in 1991 by the Tethys Research Institute (see Organisation list), with the goal to study the socio-ecology of common and bottlenose dolphins that live in the coastal waters of Ionian Greece. Common dolphins are now declining in the Mediterranean, owing to overfishing, by-catch and habitat degradation. By monitoring this community, researchers are promoting proper conservation measures.
Spp.:	Short-beaked common dolphin (*Delphinus delphis*), bottlenose dolphin (*Tursiops truncatus*), striped dolphin (*Stenella coeruleoalba*) and other marine megafauna can be observed.
Hab.:	Ionian Sea, Mediterranean Sea, Greece.
Loc.:	Gulf of Corinth.
Travel:	Flight to Athens or ferry to Patra, then bus or taxi. Very easy to reach.
Dur.:	6 days.
Per.:	June to August.
L.term:	Consecutive shifts can be booked.
Age:	Min. 18.
Qualif.:	No particular skills are required. Volunteers should be interested and very motivated in dolphin research and conservation; flexibility, positive attitude and commitment to team work are required.
Work:	Surveys at sea with 5.8m inflatable craft; observation of dolphin groups and collection of behavioural data; individual photo-identification of the animals.
Lang.:	English.

Accom.: Comfortable apartment with patio located in the beautiful village of Galaxidi, near the archaeological site of Delphi.

Cost: EUR695–745 for 6 days, depending on the season, including food, membership, insurance, field work and lectures by the researchers. Special price for students. Fees do not include travel.

Applic.: Application form to be completed and returned to the Tethys Research Institute. Early booking suggested.

Notes: Only 5 volunteers can participate in each course. The small size of the boat and the low-noise engine allow an easy approach of the dolphins and their following at close range without modifications of their behaviour.

Iracambi Atlantic Rainforest Research and Conservation Center, Brazil

Fazenda Iracambi, Rosàrio da Limeira
36878-000 Minas Gerais Brazil
Tel.: ++55 (32) 3723 1297 - Fax: ++55 (32) 3711 1086
E-mail: iracambi@iracambi.com Skype ID: iracambi
www.iracambi.com

Desc.:	Iracambi is committed to making the preservation of the rainforest more attractive than its destruction. It is seeking ways that will not only arrest the rate of destruction, but reverse it, whilst providing at the same time a higher standard of living for the local farmers.
Spp.:	Inventories of flora and fauna are being carried out.
Hab.:	Semi-deciduous rainforest.
Loc.:	South-eastern Brazil in the State of Minas Gerais.
Travel:	Flight to Rio de Janeiro, bus to Muriaé and Rosàrio da Limeira.
Dur.:	Minimum 1 month.
Per.:	Year round.
L.term:	Visa allows max. 180 days. Longer stays require special visa.
Age:	Min.18.
Qualif.:	Volunteers with skills and expertise, as well as plenty of dedication and enthusiasm, are always welcome. IT, GIS and mapping specialists, tropical botanists and zoologists are especially needed.
Work:	4 research priority areas: land use management, forest restoration, income generating alternatives, community understanding and engagement, as well as improvement of the capacity of the Centre.
Lang.:	Portuguese and English.
Accom.:	Shared room in traditional farm house; shared room in cabins are available at higher price.
Cost:	First month: BRR1,200 (approx. US$705); second month: BRR 1,150 (approx. US$675); third and subsequent months: BRR 1,100 (approx. US$650), including full board self catering accommodation.
Applic.:	Send CV via e-mail. No deadlines or forms to fill in.

Irish Seal Sanctuary, Ireland

Tobergregan, Garristown,
Co Dublin Ireland
Tel.: ++353 (1) 835 4370
E-mail: info@irishsealsanctuary.ie
www.irishsealsanctuary.ie

Desc.: The Irish Seal Sanctuary is Ireland's only full-time, 24 hour, wildlife rescue and rehabilitation facility. It is sustained entirely by voluntary effort and in field conditions. The Sanctuary currently deals with more than 1,000 telephone calls per year reporting injured or distressed seals, or marine related incidents.

Spp.: Marine mammals, primarily pinnipeds (mainly: Grey Seal, Harbour Seal). Occasionally: cetaceans, birds and small mammals.

Hab.: Species rescued from anywhere on the 6,000 mile Irish coastline.

Loc.: North County Dublin, Ireland.

Travel: Short travelling distance from Dublin but there is no public transport to the Sanctuary. Pick-up can be arranged in Dublin.

Dur.: Min. 3 months.

Per.: May to March.

L.term: Suitable volunteers may be able to stay for up to 10 months.

Age: Min. 20.

Qual.: The work is based outdoors and is physical so volunteers must be fit and team-worker. A driving license is essential. Training will be given. Animal handling experience useful but not essential.

Work: Full-time volunteers are required to make up a team of handlers to rehabilitate the seals that come into the sanctuary: cleaning seal pens, preparing food for the seals, force feeding sick pups, record keeping, general maintenance, seal rescues and releases.

Lang.: English.

Accom.: A small shared apartment.

Cost: Room and board provided. Volunteers must arrange their own travel.

Applic.: Volunteer application forms available from the website.

Ischia Dolphin Project, Italy

Oceanomare Delphis Onlus
Via G. Marinuzzi 74
00124 Roma Italy
Tel./Fax: ++39 (06) 509 10 791
E-mail: barbara@oceanomaredelphis.org
www.oceanomaredelphis.org

Desc.:	The waters of Ischia Marine Protected Area are known for their pelagic biodiversity and as a feeding and breeding ground for sperm and fin whales, striped and Risso's dolphins. Furthermore, the area has been listed in the last IUCN Cetacean Action Plan as critical habitat for the endangered short beaked common dolphin.
Spp.:	Various spp. of dolphins: common (*Delphinus delphis*), striped (*Stenella coeruleoalba*), bottlenose (*Tursiops truncatus*), Risso's (*Grampus griseus*); pilot whale (*Globicephala melas*), sperm whale (*Physeter macrocephalus*), fin whale (*Balaenoptera physalus*).
Hab.:	Coastal and pelagic Mediterranean waters.
Loc.:	Mediterranean sea, Ischia Island, Italy.
Travel:	Plane/train to Naples, bus to Beverello, ferry/hydrofoil to Ischia island.
Dur.:	1 week.
Per.:	June to October.
L.term:	Maximum stay is 3 weeks with project's leader's approval.
Age:	Min. 15.
Qualif.:	No particular skills are required, just good physical health.
Work:	Helping in data collection: watching, underwater camera monitoring, behavioural data collection, photo-identification.
Lang.:	English, Italian, French or Spanish.
Accom.:	On board of 'Jean Gab', a 17.70 m wooden cutter, equipped with towed hydrophones and underwater videocamera.
Cost:	US$1020-1055, GB£580-660, EUR750-850, with room and board, drinks, petrol, port fee, crew. Travel to/from Ischia is excluded.
Applic.:	Via e-mail. A 50% deposit for reservation is needed with the application.

Jaguar Conservation, Brazil

Volunteer Latin America
PO Box 585, Rochester
Kent ME1 9EJ UK
Tel.: ++44 (20) 7193 9163
E-mail: info@volunteerlatinamerica.com
www.volunteerlatinamerica.com

Desc.: This project assesses the ecological, behavioural, and habitat use of jaguars. One of its objectives is to train volunteers in field methodology and techniques to study the jaguar. Internships are offered to students and professionals of biology, veterinary science, ecology and affiliated areas.

Spp.: Jaguar.

Hab.: Savannah, wetlands.

Loc.: Brazil.

Travel: Travel to campsite is responsibility of the volunteer.

Dur.: Min. 1 month.

Per.: Inquire with organization.

L.term: Up to 6 months

Age: Min.18. No max age but fitness and good health are required.

Qualif.: No specific qualifications required. Interns are expected to treat all data-collecting activities with responsibility and seriousness.

Work: Field research activities: monitoring through radio telemetry; setting and checking camera traps; checking cattle killed by jaguars.

Lang.: English and Portuguese.

Accom.: Lodging is provided at the study area (shared rooms) but interns buy and prepare their own meals.

Cost: GB£80/140 per month depending on the month of participation. Expect to spend around GB£30 per month on food.

Applic.: Contact Volunteer Latin America.

Jatun Sacha, Ecuador

Fundaciòn Jatun Sacha
Eugenio de Santillàn N34-248 y Mauriàn, Sector Rumipamba
Quito 1712867 Pichincha Ecuador
Tel.: ++593 (2) 243 2240 - Fax: ++593 (2) 331 8156
E-mail: volunteer@jatunsacha.org
www.jatunsacha.org

Desc.:	Jatun Sacha Foundation is an Ecuadorian NGO whose main objective is conservation of the environment. Jatun Sacha has 8 biological stations located in different areas of Ecuador: Amazon, coast and highlands, Galapagos Islands.
Spp.:	Various species of Ecuadorian fauna and vegetation.
Hab.:	Andean cloud forest.
Loc.:	Ecuadorian coast, highlands and Amazon, Galapagos Islands.
Travel:	Flight to Quito, then bus or truck from Quito to the stations.
Dur.:	Min. 15 days.
Per.:	Year round.
L.term:	Possible, inquire with the organisation.
Age:	Min. 18. Younger with parents' permission.
Qualif.:	Volunteers must be dynamic and interested in conservation.
Work:	Reforestation, agro-forestry, organic agriculture and farming, community extension projects, general maintenance, meteorological and other environmental data collection, trekking, visits to communities, aquaculture work.
Lang.:	English; basic Spanish is recommended, but not required.
Accom.:	Shared cabins, in some cases without electricity, with toilets outside.
Cost:	Continental stations: application fee US$47, room and board: US$475/month. Galapagos Islands: application fee US$67, room and board: US$840/month.
Applic.:	Send by regular mail: CV, a cover letter, 2 passport size photos, medical certificate, and a US$47 or 67 application fee.

Karumbé Sea Turtles Project, Uruguay

Karumbé: Sea turtles of Uruguay
Av. Giannattasio Km 30,500, Canelones
Rocha state Uruguay
Tel.: ++ (598) 999 178
E-mail: volkarumbe@gmail.com
www.karumbe.org

Desc.: Karumbé is an NGO devoted to the conservation of the sea turtles of Uruguay. The organization combines conservation and research activities in different areas such as environmental education, monitoring sea turtles feeding areas and bycatch in artisanal and industrial fishing fleets.

Spp.: Green turtle (*Chelonia mydas*).

Hab.: Coastline and shallow rocky oceanic areas.

Loc.: Cerro Verde marine protected area , Uruguay.

Travel: Flight to Montevideo or ferry from Buenos Aires (Argentina) to Montevideo, where volunteers are met.

Dur.: Min. 15 days, max. 3 months.

Per.: January to April.

Age: Min. 18 - max. 60.

Qualif.: No specific qualifications are required. Veterinary or biology studies, and good physical condition helpful but not essential.

Work: Sighting and capturing, with nets, juveniles of green turtle; 25km walks, searching for stranded turtles; help researchers with necropsies of dead turtles; collecting data of the artisanal fishery; talks and workshops for the community and tourists; rehabilitation of sick and weak turtles; help in the field station duties.

Lang.: Spanish and English.

Accom.: Shared or individual tent accommodation with indoor bathroom and shower, as well as electricity.

Cost: US$15/day including: room, accommodation and simple meals.

Applic.: Via e-mail with subject "Volunteer Cerro Verde", in the text, include CV, photograph, letter of intents.

KIDO – WIDECAST Sea Turtle Nesting Monitoring, Grenada

YWF-Kido Foundation
Carriacou, Grenada West Indies
Tel.: ++1 (473) 443 7936
E-mail: marina.fastigi@gmail.com
www.kido-projects.com

Desc.: A Leatherback and Hawksbill turtles conservation and monitoring project in Carriacou Island, Caribbean Sea. Volunteers will help to protect these critically endangered species and their eggs, still hunted and poached, and to collect data for their long-term survival.

Spp.: Leatherback turtle (*Dermochelys coriacea*), Hawksbill turtle (*Eretmochelys imbricata*).

Hab.: Tropical coasts.

Loc.: Carriacou Island, Grenadines of Grenada, West Indies.

Travel: Flight to Grenada; plane/ferry to Carriacou Island; then 15min. by bus.

Dur.: Min. 1 month, max. 6 months.

Per.: March 15th to September15th.

L.term: Inquire with the organisation.

Age: Min.18 - max. 50. Younger with parents' permission.

Qualif.: Volunteers must be fit and good swimmers, motivated to walk on soft sandy beaches all night and interested in conservation and animal welfare. Ocean kayaks may be used for monitoring during day time.

Work: Night beach patrols with trained personnel, monitoring nesting and hatching activities, measuring/tagging the turtle, counting eggs, disguising turtle tracks and nests to prevent poaching, mapping nests.

Lang.: English.

Accom.: Bunk beds in a Pagoda style accommodation; sheets or sleeping bags and bed mosquito net required.

Cost: US$15/day from 1 to 3 months, US$10/day from 3 to 6 months. Minimum cost is US$450.

Applic.: See website.

Klipkop Wildlife Sanctuary, South Africa

PO Box 76, Welbekend
Gauteng 1517 South Africa
Tel.: ++27 (11) 964 1900
E-mail: info@klipkop.co.za
www.klipkop.co.za

Desc.:   Klipkop is a wildlife and environmental conservation initiative which seeks to preserve a high altitude grassland, Bankenveld. The wildlife sanctuary is home to about 12 varieties of buck (antelope), many small mammals, and has nearly 200 varieties of bird on record (including wetland, savannah and grassland species).

Spp.:   Primarily buck (antelope); lesser emphasis on smaller mammals and birds.

Hab.:   Grassland.

Loc.:   Gauteng, South Africa.

Travel: Volunteers are met at Johannesburg International Airport, or Pretoria Bus Station (if travelling overland).

Dur.:   Minimum stay is 4 weeks; there is no maximum.

Per.:   Year round.

L.term: Typical stay is 4-6 weeks; less often 2-3 months.

Age: Min. 18 - max. 70. Work is physical, so volunteers must be fit.

Qualif.:   No qualifications required. Full training provided.

Work: Mainly environmental conservation work and reporting; also birding and game assessment.

Lang.:   English.

Accom.:   Bunk beds in home-style accommodation. Sleeping bags required.

Cost: US$1,400 for the first month, then US$200 per week.

Applic.:   The application form can be downloaded from Volunteer Programme on the website.

Notes: A comprehensive Volunteer Information Pack and FAQs is available from the website.

La Hesperia, Ecuador

La Hesperia Biological Station and Reserve, c/o Fundacion Tangare
Juan Ramirez N 36-10 y German Aleman, Quito Ecuador
Tel.: ++593 (2) 224 1877 /(9) 597 8163
E-mail: contact@lahesperia.org
carmen@fundaciontangare.org
www.lahesperia.org www.fundaciontangare.org

Desc.: The western forests along the main highway between Quito and Santo Domingo, are a biologically rich mix of both Andean highland and coastal lowland species found together in one place. La Hesperia centers around preserving the biodiversity of the cloud forest and protecting local watersheds. The reserve concentrates on developing reforestation work, maintaining the medicinal garden and performing sustainable activities.

Spp.: 320 bird species have been identified in La Hesperia, of which 19 are endemic and 7 are vulnerable or in danger of extinction.

Hab.: Tropical Cloud forest.

Loc.: Ecuador, Pichincha Province, Tropical Western Andes.

Travel: 2 hours by bus from Quito.

Dur.: Minimum volunteer commitment of 2 weeks.

Per.: Year round.

L.term: All volunteers are welcome to extend their stay.

Age: Min.18.

Qualif.: A college degree is not required to participate as a volunteer.

Work: Programs: cloud forest conservation, sustainability and social development.

Lang.: English and Spanish are spoken by the station staff.

Accom.: Volunteer house, sleeping up to 25 volunteers, with bathroom and shower, social areas and great views of the cloud forest.

Cost: US$475 for the first month. US$855 for the second month and on. One time application fee: US$47.

Applic.: Contact form on website: www.lahesperia.org.

Leatherback Seaturtle Tagging Programme, Grenada

Ocean Spirits Inc.
PO Box 1373, Grand Anse, St.George's
Grenada, West Indies Eastern Caribbean
Tel.: ++ (473) 403 4266
E-mail: volunteer@oceanspirits.org   www.oceanspirits.org

Desc.:	Ocean Spirits Inc. is a non-profit organisation dedicated to the conservation of marine life and the marine environment through 3 programmes: education, research and conservation, community development. The NGO is working to change attitudes towards the sustainable use of resources in Grenada.
Spp.:	Leatherback sea turtle (*Dermochelys coriacea*); Hawksbill sea turtle (*Eretmochelys imbricata*).
Hab.:	Tropical beaches.
Loc.:	Grenada, Caribbean.
Travel:	Flight to Grenada, volunteers are met at the airport.
Dur.:	Volunteers must commit for a minimum period of 3 weeks.
Per.:	March to August.
L.term:	Volunteers may stay for more than1 period at lower cost.
Age:	Min. 18.
Qualif.:	Previous experience of field work and data collection is an advantage. Good physical condition as the work involves long hours and in variable weather conditions.
Work:	Night patrols for nesting turtles, tagging and collecting other data. Morning beach surveys to determine other turtle nesting activity. Conducting educational field trips and school summer camps.
Lang.:	English.
Accom.:	Dormitory style accommodation, sheets and towels needed.
Cost:	From GB£895 for 3 weeks. Accommodation, food and airport transfers are included.
Applic.:	On www.workingabroad.com/page/24/ocean-spirits-grenada.htm application form available.

Leatherback Turtle Conservation, Panama

Endangered Wildlife Trust and Rainforest Concern
Avenida 10 (entre calle 27 y29) N.2550
San José Costa Rica
Tel.: ++ (506) 224 8568
E-mail: c.fernandez@turtleprotection.org
www.turtleprotection.org

Desc.: Volunteers are needed in Panama to help protect endangered Leatherback turtles. Volunteers participate in every aspect of the projects. Soropta is a prime leatherback beach on a narrow strip of land between the sea and a canal. Playa Larga is a golden sand beach on the island of Bastimentos.

Spp.: Leatherback turtles, green turtles, hawksbill turtles.

Hab.: Tropical coasts.

Loc.: Soropta or Playa Larga, Panama.

Travel: Flight to San Josè, Costa Rica or Panama City, then buses and boat to Soropta or Playa Larga. Detailed directions provided on application.

Dur.: Minimum 1 week, but short term visits from Bocas are possible.

Per.: Mid March to mid July.

Age: Min. 18. Children under 18 must be accompanied by a responsible adult.

Qualif.: No particular skills needed, but a keen interest in conservation required.

Work: Volunteers assist with tagging, beach patrols, nest protection and monitoring of hatching success. All training is provided.

Lang.: English and Spanish useful but not required.

Accom.: Shared accommodation in simple cabins with mosquito screens. Showers and flush toilets. No electricity.

Cost: US$30/day, including meals and accommodation. Volunteers are responsible for transportation to site (scheduled ferries past the project site).

Applic.: The Green Volunteers Standard Application Form is welcome.

Leatherback Turtle Project, Costa Rica

Estaciòn Las Tortugas
Matina, Region Mondonguillo Costa Rica
Tel.: ++ (506) 8846 7591 (Costa Rica, March-June)
E-mail: estacionlastortugas@yahoo.co.uk
www.estacionlastortugas.org

Desc.: Each year the leatherback turtle visits the Caribbean coast of Costa Rica to nest. The biological station, Estaciòn Las Tortugas is one of their most important nesting beaches. Since 2000, the project has been focusing on the conservation and protection of this now critically endangered species as well as education.

Spp.: Leatherback turtle (*Dermochelys coriacea*).

Hab.: Secondary coastal rainforest.

Loc.: Caribbean coast of Costa Rica (40 km from Puerto Limon).

Travel: Flight to San José, Costa Rica. Volunteers will be picked up at the airport and taken to Matina.

Dur.: 1-4 months.

Per.: March to July.

L.term: Long term opportunities might be available for research.

Age: Min. 18.

Qualif.: No specific skills required, just enthusiasm, willingness to work and ability to live in basic conditions and high humidity levels.

Work: Volunteers will assist researchers. Long distance walking without assistance is required, as 4-hour beach patrols will be carried out each night. Leatherback nests will be collected and relocated.

Lang.: English or Spanish.

Accom.: Basic accommodation with rooms of 4-6 people and shared showers. Basic food of rice and beans provided 3 times a day.

Cost: Up to US$750/month, including accommodation, 3 meals/day, transport from airport and accommodation in San Jose.

Applic.: Contact Stamie at the above address for further information and application forms.

Madagascar Fauna Group Station
BP 442
Toamasina (Tamatave) 501 Madagascar
Tel.: ++261 20 533 0842
E-mail: mfgmad@moov.mg
www.savethelemur.org

Desc.: Madagascar Fauna Group (MFG) has been running a wide range of projects near Tamatave for 20 years with focus on the Lemur Rescue Center in Ivoloina. MFG offers volunteers the possibility to really contribute while working in a beautiful environment as part of a motivated team. This opportunity is about real work and serious contribution, it is not a holiday.

Spp.: Lemurs, Amphibiae, Frogs.

Hab.: Lowland forest.

Loc.: Madacascar East Coast.

Travel: Flight to Antananarivo then national flight to Tamatave, or flight to La Reunion and onwards to Tamatave.

Dur.: Min. stay of 2-3 months.

Per.: Year round.

L.term: Long term welcome.

Age: Min. 20.

Qualif.: Ability to work independently and to adapt into different cultural settings, previous experience in developing countries.

Work: Several positions available: responsible volunteer program, reception officer, marketing officer, ecotourism trainer, mechanics or electronics expert, creative artist, GIS/remote sensing expert.

Lang.: Knowledge of French necessary, English.

Accom.: Accommodation on site in Ivoloina (dormitory, double room with bunk bed, small kitchen, showers, filtered water for drinking).

Cost: Volunteers must provide for own transport to Tamatave. Accommodation is provided by MFG.

Applic.: Email CV, motivation letter (in French) and names of 3 references.

Marine Conservation and Diving, Tanzania

50-52 Rivington Street
London EC2A 3QP UK
Tel.: ++44 (020) 7613 2422
E-mail: info@frontier.ac.uk
www.frontier.ac.uk

Desc.:   This marine research and conservation programme, run in association with the University of Dar es Salaam, aims to provide the local stakeholders and government bodies with the information they need to design and implement management plans for the future protection of this marine ecosystem.

Spp.:   Turtles, manta rays, sea cucumbers, feathery starfish, spiny urchins, octopus, dolphins, whale sharks, sharks etc.

Hab.:   Tropical Indian Ocean island.

Loc.:   Mafia Island, Tanzania

Travel: Flight to Dar Es Salaam, pickup at the airport.

Dur.:   Min. 3, Max. 10 weeks

Per.:   January to November, exact dates on website.

L.term: Max. 10 weeks.

Age: No min. age but parental consent required if under 18.

Qualif.:   High level of fitness and stamina needed: conditions can be arduous and trekking strenuous. PADI dive qualification provided.

Work: To gather the data needed volunteers dive, locate and map the extensive coral reefs and study the various communities existing on them. Volunteers will also explore and record the living organisms that inhabit the mangrove forests and sea grass beds.

Lang.:   English and Swahili.

Accom.:   Volunteers will be staying in communal huts made from woven palm leaves, poles and mud, and cook over an open campfire.

Cost: 3 weeks £1495, 4 weeks £1695, 5 weeks £1895, 6 weeks £2095, 8 weeks £2295, 10 weeks £2595. Includes dive qualification.

Applic.:   www.frontier.ac.uk and then click the "Apply Now" button.

The Marine Mammal Center (TMMC), California USA

2000 Bunker Road, Fort Cronkhite, Sausalito, California 94965 USA
Tel.: ++1 (415) 289 7325 /979 4357 (volunteer inquiries)
Fax: ++1 (415) 289 7333
E-mail: volunteer@tmmc.org
www.tmmc.org; www.marinemammalcenter.org

Desc.: The Marine Mammal Center is a nonprofit veterinary research hospital and educational center with a mission to expand knowledge about marine mammals – their health and that of their ocean environment – and inspire their global conservation. The Marine Mammal Center is dedicated to the rescue and rehabilitation of ill and injured marine mammals – primarily elephant seals, harbor seals, and California sea lions. Since 1975, we've been headquartered in Sausalito, CA in the Marin Headlands within the Golden Gate National Parks, and have rescued and treated more than 15,000 marine mammals.

Spp.: Marine mammals, primarily pinnipeds like California sea lions, northern elephant seals, harbor seals, sea otters, whales, dolphins, porpoises, and even sea turtles.

Hab.: Pacific coast.

Loc.: Northern California (San Francisco).

Travel: Flight to San Francisco, then by car.

Dur.: Not less than 1 month.

Per.: Year round, but preferably during high season (March to August).

L.term: Volunteers can remain as long as they like.

Age: Min. 18.

Qualif.: Ability to work as part of a team and with wild animals, which can be physically demanding.

Work: Volunteers prepare food, feed animals, help rescuing stranded mammals, restrain animals for tube feeds and physical exams, clean pens, wash dishes, do laundry, administer medication, weigh animals and chart all observations. Shifts of 6–12hrs depending on the season. Training is provided. Volunteering opportunities are available in many fields within TMMC.

169

Lang.:   English.

Accom.:   Volunteers provide for their own accommodation.

Cost: No cost. Room, board and transportation are volunteer's responsibility. There is no public transportation to the site, so a bike is useful.

Applic.:   After admission volunteers must attend an orientation upon arrival and complete a liability waiver. All info on the TMMC website.

Notes: This work requires good health and a current tetanus shot is recommended.

Marine Turtles Adriatic Arché Project, Italy

A.R.C.H.E'. Research and Educational Activities for Chelonian Conservation
Via Mulinetto, 40/A-I, 44100 Ferrara Italy
Tel.: ++39 (0532) 767 852 - Fax: ++39 (1782) 253 279
Mob.: ++39 (349) 393 7924
E-mail: archeturtle@tiscali.it
www.archeturtle.org

Desc.:	The research project focuses on interactions between marine turtles and fishing methods, tagging and recapture, migrations, rescue of injured animals, education program for fishermen and for tourists.
Spp.:	Loggerhead sea turtles (*Caretta caretta*).
Hab.:	Mediterranean coast, north-western Adriatic Sea.
Loc.:	Porto Garibaldi (Italy).
Travel:	Train from Bologna to Ferrara or Ostellato, bus to Porto Garibaldi.
Dur.:	Min. 1 week.
Per.:	June to July.
L.term:	There is no limit for long-term stays.
Age:	Min. 24.
Qualif.:	No special qualifications, other than to be able to work in a team, enthusiasm, adaptability, love for animals and willingness to work long hours. Respect for other people.
Work:	Volunteers carry on educational activities for tourists on the beach in the morning; in the afternoon when the fishing boat comes back to the harbour, they start the work on the marine turtles accidentally captured by fishing nets and collect data. Depending on fishing boats' availability, volunteers and researchers will go on board to experience a fishing day (12/14hrs).
Lang.:	English, basic Italian useful.
Accom.:	Shared rooms in a house with cooking and washing facilities.
Cost:	EUR220/week in June, EUR250/week in July, including food and accommodation. Travel and personal expenses are not included.
Applic.:	Via e-mail or by completing the online application form.

Marine Turtle & Youth Environmental Education, Mexico

Grupo Ecologico de La Costa Verde
2163 Lime Loop, Laredo, Texas 78045 USA
Tel.: ++52 (311) 258 4100
E-mail: grupo-eco@project-tortuga.org
www.project-tortuga.org

Desc.:	This group is a Mexican non-profit environmental Civil Association, with special interest in the protection of the marine turtles and in youth environmental education.
Spp.:	Olive Ridley (*Lepidochelys olivacea*); leatherback (*Dermochelys coriacea*); eastern Pacific green turtle (*Chelonia agassizi*).
Hab.:	Marine, tropical, coastal.
Loc.:	Central Pacific coast of Mexico.
Travel:	Flight to Puerto Vallarta, where volunteers are met, or bus from Puerto Vallarta, to San Francisco or San Pancho.
Dur.:	Min. 2 months, although 5 would be ideal.
Per.:	July 1st to November 15th.
L.term:	Inquire with the organisation.
Age:	Min. 18.
Qualif.:	No special skills required, other than enthusiasm, efficiency, sense of humour, ability to work in team and to deal with the public.
Work:	Collect and relocating nests, maintain records, release hatchlings, teaching. Work is 5 to 7 nights a week in occasional heavy rain, and implies operating a Volkswagen dune-buggy.
Lang.:	English (with some Spanish) is needed for Marine Turtle Project. Spanish (with some English) for teaching.
Accom.:	Houses for volunteers.
Cost:	Volunteers pay for their own accommodation and living expenses. In some cases free lodging is available, rooms rent (US$40/week), or single home (US$400/month). Food: approx. US$35-40/week.
Applic.:	By e-mail only on www.project-tortuga.org/volunteers.htm.

Mediterranean Marine Research Program, Spain

Kenna Eco Diving
Passatge Clavell 9, No 8
L'Escala 17130 Girona Spain
Tel.: +34 (9) 7277 2746
E-mail: gaynor@kennaecodiving.net www.kennaecodiving.net

Desc.:	Mediterranean ecosystem conservation research project in Catalonia, Spain, providing volunteer opportunities for marine biology students and eco-minded divers. Also for anyone interested in marine life wishing to learn to dive. Project involves mapping coastal habitats and recording key species present within the ecosystems.
Spp.:	Seahorse, Pipefish, Wrasse, Octopus, Blenny, Grouper, Coral, Sponges, Posidonia oceanica seagrass, algae, etc.
Hab.:	Mediterranean coastal ecosystems.
Loc.:	Catalonia, Spain.
Travel:	Fly to Girona (Barcelona Girona airport) or by train to Girona or Figueres.
Dur.:	Minimum 2 weeks.
Per.:	May to October.
L.term:	Up to 6 months.
Age:	Min. 18. Must be fit enough to dive.
Qualif.:	Volunteers can learn to dive via the Eco Dive program if not already qualified to PADI Open Water or equivalent level.
Work:	Volunteers map and record data from underwater coastal habitats, learning how to correctly identify the key species that reveal the health of the ecosystem.
Lang.:	English.
Accom.:	Volunteer shared bunkhouse with subsidised food option.
Cost:	From EUR486 for two weeks, including accommodation, all transport, research training and unlimited eco diving.
Applic.:	Apply via email to gaynor@kennaecodiving.net.

Mission Rhino 2020, Nepal

Team for Nature and Wildlife
PO Box 7403,
Kathmandu, Nepal
Tel.: ++977 (98) 4132 0785
E-mail: info@tnwnepal.org greenvolunteersnepal@gmail.com
www.greenvolunteernepal.blogspot.com

Desc.:	In Nepal, rhinoceros population was estimated at 1000 individuals until 1950 in the Chitwan valley; currently, rhino population size is estimated at 403 individuals in three Terai protected areas of Nepal. In order to control rhino poaching on a sustainable way, Team for Nature and Wildlife (TNW), a youth's environmental organization has launched a campaign titled "Mission Rhino 2020". The campaign includes lobbying activities, led and run by youths at local and central level to influence the government to revise existing policies and practices.
Spp.:	Indian rhino (*Rhinoceros unicornis*).
Hab.:	Chitwan National Park.
Loc.:	Chitwan National Park, Nepal.
Travel:	Flight to Kathmandu, then flight or bus to Chitwan.
Dur.:	Min. 1 week.
Per.:	Year round.
L.term:	Up to 6 months.
Age:	Min.18.
Qualif.:	No specific qualifications required.
Work:	Education in local schools, monitoring and keeping record of wildlife crime, survey of animals behaviour.
Lang.:	English.
Accom.:	Lodging provided by local families during the program period.
Cost:	US$ 300 for 2 weeks, US$150 for every additional week, US$300 for every additional month.
Applic.:	Via e-mail.

The Monkey Sanctuary Trust, England
Looe
Cornwall PL13 1NZ UK
Tel./Fax: ++44 (1503) 262 532
E-mail: info@monkeysanctuary.org
www.monkeysanctuary.org

Desc.: The Monkey Sanctuary is home to a colony of woolly monkeys, rescued capuchins and Old World monkeys. It was founded in 1964 as a reaction against the pet trade in primates. The Sanctuary is open to the public during the summer and the main emphasis is to encourage an attitude of caring and respect toward primates and the environment. The Sanctuary gardens and meadows contain many native species of plants and animals.

Spp.: Woolly monkeys, capuchins and Old World monkeys.

Hab.: N/A.

Loc.: Looe, Cornwall, UK.

Dur.: 2-5 weeks.

Per.: Year round.

L.term: Invitation to stay long term if the initial visit proves successful.

Age: Min. 18.

Qualif.: No specific skills required, although applicants should have an interest in the field and practical skills are always welcome.

Work: Maintaining and cleaning the enclosures, preparing food for the animals, providing information to the public.

Lang.: English.

Cost: A voluntary donation for room and board is requested. Volunteers must provide transportation to the Sanctuary.

Applic.: Write or email for further details (please enclose international postage coupon or stamped SAE for UK residents), then fill out an application form. Owing to the large number of applicants, please apply at least 6 months in advance.

Monte Adone Wildlife Protection Centre, Italy

Via Brento, 9
40037 Sasso Marconi (Bologna) Italy
Tel./Fax: ++39 (051) 847 600
E-mail: info@centrotutelafauna.org
www.centrotutelafauna.org

Desc.: A voluntary non-profit institution working in the rescue and rehabilitation of wild animals found injured. Emergency service is active 24hrs/day. It also takes care of different exotic animals found abandoned or confiscated from Government authorities. Guided visits for schools and families available.

Spp.: Local wildlife (ungulates, mammals, raptors) and exotic fauna (primates, felines, reptiles, etc.).

Hab.: Temperate mountain woodland.

Loc.: Monte Adone, Sasso Marconi, near Bologna, Italy.

Travel: From Bologna by train to Pianoro or to Sasso Marconi.

Dur.: Min. 20 days, after a 1 week trial period.

Per.: Year round, busiest months during the spring.

L.term: Inquire with Centre's Director after initial period.

Age: Min. 20.

Qualif.: True love for animals, attitude to live and work in community, goodwill and spirit of adaptation, sense of responsibility.

Work: Work (8-10hrs/day) depends on the season: feeding, cleaning and caring of animals; day/night rescuing operations of wounded fauna; maintenance/building activities; help in the housekeeping.

Lang.: Italian; English is also spoken by centre coordinators.

Accom.: In shared rooms in the Centre.

Cost: EUR80/first week, with food and insurance. Thereafter free full board.

Applic.: Contact the Centre to have the application form and more details.

Notes: Anti-tetanus is required and B hepatitis is advised.

Munda Wanga Wildlife Park and Sanctuary, Zambia

PO Box 350068, Kafue Rd,
Chilanga Zambia
Tel.: ++260 (1) 278 614 Fax: ++260 (1) 278 529
E-mail: mundawanga@iconnect.zm
www.mundawanga.com

Desc.: Most animals are confiscated from poachers or the illegal pet trade. Some animals are kept as ambassadors for their species, however the majority of the animals is released back to the wild in Munda Wanga Wildlife Park. The volunteers' tasks is to assist the keepers in taking care of the new arrivals, prepare and feed animals, prepare enrichment among other duties.

Spp.: African birds and mammals: wild dogs, lions, antelope and primates. Exotic species: camels and African Grey Parrots.

Hab.: Wetland, woodland and grassland.

Loc.: Approx. 15km outside of Lusaka, the capital of Zambia.

Travel: Flight to Lusaka, overland from southern/eastern Africa.

Dur.: 3 weeks. Volunteers can stay for longer or shorter periods

Per.: Year round.

L.term: Possible after approval from the project manager.

Age: Min. 18; no maximum age, but volunteers need to be physically fit.

Qualif.: Ability to work hard; those with relevant experience are preferred.

Work: Designing enrichment and educational materials, monitoring animals, fundraising, hand-rearing orphaned animals, cleaning enclosures, construction, etc. Work is 6 days/week, 8hrs/day.

Lang.: English.

Accom.: Basic dorm style room, with bathroom and cooking area.

Cost: US$750 per 3 weeks, including accommodation.

Applic.: Request for a form via e-mail or fax.

Notes: Volunteers' contributions help continual development of the park and staff capacity building.

Naucrates Conservation Project, Thailand

Naucrates 'Conservation Biology'
Colle Tenne, snc
04010 Giulianello di Cori (LT) Italy
Tel.: ++39 (333) 430 6643 - Fax: ++39 (031) 716 315
E-mail: info@naucrates.org
www.naucrates.org

Desc.: The Conservation project focuses on sea turtles' nest monitoring and protection, mangrove forest rehabilitation, environmental education, and community development.

Spp.: Olive ridley (*Lepidochelys olivacea*), leatherback (*Dermochelys coriacea*), green (*Chelonia mydas*) and hawksbill (*Eretmochelys imbricata*) turtles, reefs and mangroves.

Hab.: Tropical coast.

Loc.: Phra Thong Island, Phang-Nga province, Thailand.

Travel: Flight to Phuket Island or to Ranong (via Bangkok), then bus or car to Kura Buri pier and boat to Phra Thong Island.

Dur.: Min. 10 days.

Per.: January to April.

L.term: Inquire with the organisation.

Age: Min. 18.

Qualif.: Volunteers must be prepared for long walks in hot and humid conditions on the beach and able to work in group.

Work: Beach patrols; environmental education activities for children; natural resources conservation and management with villagers; collaboration with local fishermen; English teaching.

Lang.: English, Italian and Thai.

Accom.: Home-stay with Thai families. One house is used as office and common area.

Cost: EUR650/2 weeks with 3 meals/day, training, information materials and 1 year membership. Travel expenses and insurance excluded.

Applic.: Contact the organisation for more information and availability.

Nkombi Research and Volunteer Programme, South Africa

PO Box 20784
Protea Park, North West Province, 0305 South Africa
Tel.: ++27 (14) 558 3300
E-mail: mankwe@telkomsa.net
www.mankwewildlifereserve.net

Desc.: Researching on a Wildlife Reserve in South Africa is an occasion to develop research and life skills by getting involved with conservation projects and to learn about local environment and cultures.

Spp.: Brown hyena, caracal, serval, white rhino, raptors, small mammals, large herbivores.

Hab.: Bushveld, savannah, grassland.

Loc.: Mankwe Wildlife Reserve, north-west Province, South Africa.

Travel: Flight to Johannesburg, where volunteers are met.

Dur.: Project runs for 2 or 4 weeks with option to extend further.

Per.: Monthly, year round.

L.term: Option to extend after first month period with approval.

Age: Min. 17 - max. 50. Volunteers must be fit as a lot is spent on foot.

Qualif.: No skills required as all training is given.

Work: Fire management, game capture, rhino monitoring, nocturnal surveys, scavenger and predator monitoring, camera trapping, game counts on foot, African drumming.

Lang.: English.

Accom.: In 2 sleeper log cabins with beds, hot showers and flush toilets on site. Sleeping bag required.

Cost: GB£650 for 2 weeks, GB£1,200 for 4 weeks, including accommodation, food, local transport.

Applic.: The Standard Green Volunteers Form is welcome.

Notes: This is a research based project, with a lot of time in the field. Certificates and references are awarded at the end of the stay.

Noah's Ark, Greece
Supporters' Association for Animal Welfare on Crete Noah's Ark
Gierkezeile 29
D 10585 Berlin Germany
Tel.: ++49 (172) 741 3900 (Germany) /++30 (694) 294 1443 (Greece)
E-mail: rschmid@archenoah-kreta.com
www.an-kreta.de

Desc.:	Noah's Ark is the supporters' association for animal welfare on Crete, based in Germany, operating on donations and membership subscriptions only. The project is aimed at supporting the local animal welfare activists in offering island-wide castration actions and re-homing of animals.
Spp.:	Domestic cats and dogs.
Hab.:	Mediterranean.
Loc.:	Crete, Greece.
Travel:	Flight to Chania airport, Heraklion, or Athens (then night boat to Chania or Heraklion).
Dur.:	2 weeks to 1 year.
Per.:	Year round.
L.term:	Long-term encouraged, inquire with organisation.
Age:	Min.18 - max. 60.
Qualif.:	Volunteers should love animals and be strong enough to handle the sight of animal cruelty, starvation, illness.
Work:	Nursing, cleaning, feeding, diet control, treating small animals under supervision.
Lang.:	English, German, Greek.
Accom.:	Local accommodation at reasonable rates.
Cost:	Volunteers pay for accommodation. Noah's Ark's partners will assist in obtaining accommodation.
Applic.:	No official form needed, send letter of inquire.
Notes:	High summer is very hot; winter months are wet and muddy.

The Oceania Research Project, Australia

The Oceania Project
PO Box 646
Byron Bay NSW 2481 Australia
Tel.: ++61 (2) 668 58128 - Fax: ++61 (2) 9225 9176
E-mail: traineeship@oceania.org.au
www.oceania.org.au

Desc.: The Oceania Project is a non-profit research and education organisation dedicated to raising awareness about cetaceans and the Ocean Environment. The Oceania Project is in the twentieth year of a long-term study of the social organisation and behaviour of humpback whales in the Whale Management and Monitoring Area of the Hervey Bay Marine Park, off the northeast coast of Queensland, Australia. The Hervey Bay research is conducted during the annual humpback migration from July to November. Each year there is a limited opportunity to participate in the Whale Research Expedition as a Research Trainee.

Spp.: Humpback whale (*Megaptera novaeangliae*), brydes tropical whale (*Balaenoptera edeni*), minke-piked whale (*Balaenoptera acutorostrata*), common dolphin (*Delphinus delphis*), bottlenose dolphin (*Tursiops truncatus*), Indo-pacific humpback dolphin (*Sousa chinensis*).

Hab.: Tropical coast/ocean bay/ancient sand island.

Loc.: Hervey Bay/Fraser Island, northeast coast of Queensland, Australia.

Travel: Flightg to Brisbane (capital of Queensland). The expedition departure point is Urangan Boat Harbour, Hervey Bay (approx. 400km north of Brisbane, with access by car or daily bus, train or intrastate airline).

Dur.: Minimum a week, preferably 3 weeks.

Per.: August to October.

L.term: Not applicable.

Age: Min. 14.

Qualif.: Previous field experience in marine mammal research useful. Common sense, a committed interest in whales and dolphins and willingness to work long hours and learn as part of a small, highly motivated and focused field research team.

Work: Assist with research including humpback whale observations, collection and collation of photo-identification, genetic, spatial and environmental data. General duties associated with daily operation aboard the research vessel.

Lang.: English.

Accom.: Ship-style bunk. The present expedition vessel is a 12-metre catamaran. Information about what to bring, etc., will be provided to successful applicants.

Cost: US$1,800 per week (US$1,350 for under-18). Transportation or accommodation to and from the departure point or personal insurance is not included.

Applic.: Application by e-mail. See website for more information about The Oceania Project and the Whale Research Expedition.

Notes: The research programme is conducted and supervised by the expedition leaders, Trish and Wally Franklin. They are PhD Candidates at the Southern Cross University Whale Research Centre, see: http://www.scu.edu.au/research/whales/index.php/2/.

Orangutan Foundation, Indonesia

7 Kent Terrace
London, NW1 4RP UK
Tel.: ++44 (20) 7724 2912
Fax: ++44 (20) 7706 2613
E-mail: elly@orangutan.org.uk
www.orangutan.org.uk

Desc.: The Orangutan Foundation is the world's foremost orangutan conservation organisation. It protects Asia's endangered great apes by preserving their tropical forest habitat, working with local communities and promoting research and education.

Spp.: Bornean Orangutan (*Pongo pygmaeus*).

Hab.: Tropical rainforest.

Loc.: Lamandau Wildlife Reserve and Tanjung Puting National Park, Central and West Kalimantan, Indonesian Borneo.

Travel: Flight to Jakarta, then direct flight to Pangkalan Bun, Kalimantan.

Dur.: 6 weeks.

Per.: 3 teams of 12 people, May to November.

L.term: Max. 6 weeks.

Age: Min. 18.

Qualif.: Previous experience in the field is desirable but not necessary. Good health, physical fitness, team spirit and a willingness to do manual work. Enthusiasm and a commitment to conservation.

Work: Help is needed to build guard posts, mark out borders and assist with reforestation. The project operates in extremely remote conditions. There may be some lines of work around the original release site at Camp Leakey.

Lang.: English or Indonesian.

Accom.: Very basic. In huts on the floor or hammocks in the forest.

Cost: GB£775 for room and board, travel expenses not included.

Applic.: Application form at www.orangutan.org.uk.

Orangutan Health, Indonesia

Dr Ivona Foitova – Principal Investigator
c/o Leuser International Foundation
Jl. Bioteknologi, Kampus USU, Medan 20155 Indonesia
Tel.: ++62 (813) 6214 6476
E-mail: orangutanhealth@nusa.net.id
www.orangutan-health.org

Desc.:	This unique project is investigating the special behaviours and ecological conditions necessary for the maintenance of health in wild orangutans. Volunteers perform various research tasks for the project and have the chance to visit and experience a living, breathing rainforest in one of the most beautiful areas of the world.
Spp.:	Orangutan (*Pongo abelii*).
Hab:	Tropical rainforest.
Loc.:	Bukit Lawang, Sumatra, Indonesia.
Travel:	Flight to Medan via Jakarta, Kuala Lumpur, Singapore or Penang. Volunteers are met at the airport.
Dur.:	Min. 13 days.
Per.:	Year round.
L.term:	Possible, inquire with the organisation.
Age:	Min. 18, with a good level of fitness (able to hike 10km per day in difficult terrain), without health problems, allergies or phobias.
Qualif.:	Volunteers are required to be patient and attentive.
Work:	Work is split between 3-4 day treks in the jungle, and rotating computer/lab work at base camp, depending on people's strength.
Lang:	English.
Accom.:	Accommodation is very basic: a bed, a mosquito net and a basic Asian toilet. No shower, but a supply of water to wash.
Cost:	US$1,289, excluding travel.
Applic.:	Request an application form via e-mail.
Notes:	There is no physical contact whatsoever with orangutans. A medical certificate of good health is mandatory.

Orangutan Tropical Peatland Progect (OuTrop), Indonesia

Kampus UNPAR, Jl. Yos Sudarso, Tunjung Nyaho, Palangka Raya,
C. Kalimantan 73112 Indonesia
Tel.: ++62 (536) 36 880
E-mail: info@orangutantrop.com
www.orangutantrop.com; www.indonesiangibbons.blogspot.com

Desc.: The research focuses on biodiversity monitoring, habitat assessments and primate population surveys based on a pioneering orangutan and gibbon research, in the Sebangau National Park, Borneo.

Spp.: Orangutan, gibbon, langur, sun bear, birds, seed dispersal research.

Hab.: Tropical peat-swamp forest.

Loc.: Central Kalimantan, Indonesia (Island of Borneo).

Travel: Base camp is 1 hour from Palangka Raya. Travel is by car, boat.

Dur.: 7 week expeditions.

Per.: June to November.

L.term: If carrying out research for a B.Sc or MSc 10 weeks min.

Age: Min. 18 – max. 40. Be physically and mentally fit.

Qualif.: Applicants should be undertaking or have completed a bachelor's degree in a relevant subject or have relevant experience.

Work: Biodiversity research, ape density surveys and habitat monitoring. Full training in field methods and survey techniques will be given.

Lang.: English.

Accom.: At base camp: shared accommodation in style of traditional Dayak longhouse, mossie net and sleeping bags required. During the expedition: camping at remote sites in the jungle.

Cost: GB£1,475 with airport transfers, local transport, room, board and supplies, visas, visits to National Park and Reintroduction Centre.

Applic.: Download application pack from website or contact by e-mail. Please return applications at least 3 months before start date.

Notes: Contact the organisation for dissertation/thesis research.

Orchid Conservation, Ecuador

Jardin Botanico las Orquideas
Casilla 16-01-710
Puyo, Pastaza
Tel.: ++593 (9) 532 2635
E-mail: jblorquideas@gmail.com
ww.jardinbotanicolasorquideas.com

Desc.: Volunteers have a chance to aid in the restoration of the Ecuadorian Amazon, with a particular focus on orchids restoration. Volunteers can also help direct environmental education activities in the new interpretive center.

Spp.: Orchids, palms, moths, butterflies, spiders.

Hab.: Rainforest.

Loc.: Amazon region, Ecuador.

Travel: 5 hours by bus from capital city, Quito.

Dur.: Volunteers who can stay for at least two months are preferred.

Per.: Year round.

L.term: Long term volunteers are encouraged.

Age: Min. 20. No max age but fitness and good health are required.

Qualif.: Intermediate - advanced spanish skills are needed; however, volunteers with specific skills, such as biology, botany, video or fundraising, are welcome.

Work: Plant restoration, photography, and classification; environmental education; outreach and networking.

Lang.: Spanish.

Accom.: In a bunk house, sleeping bag required. Lodging is located at the Orchid Reserve.

Cost: US $70/week, room and board included, plus a one time admin fee.

Applic.: See the volunteer page of the website.

Notes: Staff is composed by an Ecuadorian family and one American.

Pandrillus Foundation, Nigeria

Drill Rehabilitation & Breeding Center ("Drill Ranch")
H.E. PO Box 826, Calabar Nigeria
Tel.: ++234 (803) 592 1262
E-mail: info@pandrillus.org
www.pandrillus.org
(see www.limbewildlife.org for Limbe Wildlife Centre)

Desc.: The centre recovers captive drill orphans and rehabs them into breeding groups, in enclosures of natural habitat of up to 9ha. The project also maintains 25 non-breeding chimpanzees and is involved in conservation of Afi Mountain Wildlife Sanctuary where wild drills, gorillas and chimps survive and are released. Pandrillus also runs the Limbe Wildlife Center (Cameroon) where volunteers may apply.

Spp.: Drill (*Mandrillus leucophaeus*), chimpanzee (*Pan troglodytes*).

Hab.: Tropical rainforest.

Loc.: South-east Nigeria.

Travel: Flight to Lagos, then to Calabar.

Dur.: Min. 1 year.

Per.: Year round.

L.term: Highly encouraged.

Age: Min. 25.

Qualif.: Mature persons with: 1) animal/veterinary/medical experience or practical skills (carpentry, electrical, etc.); 2) appropriate educational background; 3) developing country and administrative/management experience; 4) interest in conservation; 5) team-work ability.

Work: Staff management and training, animal management and record-keeping, administration, public relations, education, construction and maintenance. Versatility is a must.

Lang.: English.

Accom.: House at urban site, open-walled cabins at field site.

Cost: Room and board provided. Travel to the project is not provided.

Applic.: Send CV with references, a photograph and a letter of intentions. Interview with an appointed person will follow.

Peace River Refuge & Ranch, Florida USA

PO Box 1127
2545 Stoner Lane
Zolfo Springs, Florida 33890 USA
Tel.: ++1 (863) 735 0804 - Fax: ++1 (863) 735 0805
E-mail: volunteer@PeaceRiverRefuge.org
www.PeaceRiverRefuge.org

Desc.: A non-profit wild animal sanctuary, fully licensed and accredited by the American Sanctuary Association, dedicated to the lifetime care of abused, neglected or confiscated wild animals to prevent them from being destroyed. The volunteers and staff ensure that their medical, nutritional, and emotional needs are well met.

Spp.: Tigers, leopards, cougars, bears, lynx, capuchin and spider monkies, tamarins, wolves, lemurs, bats and more.

Hab.: As natural as possible.

Loc.: Florida, USA.

Travel: Flight to Orlando, then by car to project.

Dur.: Minimum 2 weeks, maximum 12 months.

Per.: Year round.

L.term: Only with project leaders approval after the regular period.

Age: Min. 21; maximum age is determined by physical capabilities.

Qualif.: No particular skills needed; must have negative Tuberculosis test or TB vaccine documentation, and proof of health insurance.

Work: Wide range of duties: sorting and cutting fruit for fruit bats and monkeys, feeding animals and providing enrichment, cleaning enclosures, building habitats, maintaining the grounds, etc.

Lang.: English.

Accom.: Shared living quarters with bunk beds, basic but comfortable with water, electricity and air conditioning.

Cost: US$350/week, including room and board. US$100 upon request for pick up and drop off at Orlando Airport. Independent room and board can be arranged, but a car is necessary.

Applic.: Application and procedural forms will be provided upon request.

Penguin Research, Argentina and Chile

Volunteer Latin America
PO Box 585, Rochester
Kent ME1 9EJ UK
Tel.: ++44 (20) 7193 9163
E-mail: info@volunteerlatinamerica.com
www.volunteerlatinamerica.com

Desc.:	A small number of volunteers are needed each year to conduct daily observations of penguin nests from November to February.
Spp.:	Various species of South American penguins.
Hab.:	Ocean.
Loc.:	Argentina/Chile.
Travel:	Independent travel to project site.
Dur.:	Min. 2 months.
Per.:	November - February.
L.term:	Inquire with organisation.
Age:	Min.18, Max. 65.
Qualif.:	Applicants must be at least 21 years of age, have a working knowledge of Spanish, and willing to work for a minimum of eight weeks.
Work:	Daily observation of Penguin nests. The work requires lots of walking.
Lang.:	Spanish.
Accom.:	Accommodation is provided in a lighthouse.
Cost:	There is no charge but volunteers must pay their own food (US$10-30 per week).
Applic.:	Visit VLA website for further details.

Project Kial, Australia

AACE
PO Box 47 Marlborough
Queensland 4705 Australia
Tel.: ++61 (07) 4935 6076
E-mail: info@aace.org.au
www.aace.org.au

Desc.: This is a community based conservation recovery program, focused on the endangered bridled bailtail wallaby.

Spp.: Bridled nailtail wallaby (*Onychogalea fraenata*).

Hab.: Semi-arid bushland.

Loc.: Marlborough, Queensland, Australia.

Travel: By plane or train: travel to Rockhampton. By bus: travel to Marlborough.

Dur.: Minimum stay 2 weeks.

Per.: Year round.

L.term: Only on approval of project coordinator.

Age: Min 18. Younger only with consultation between parent and coordinator.

Qualif.: No particular skills needed.

Work: Being responsible for maintaining a high level of day to day animal husbandry and observation of animals behaviour.

Lang.: English.

Accom.: Bunk beds in rural shed, sleeping bag recomended for winter months.

Cost: AU$20/day, including accommodation, food and pick-up from Rockhampton/Marlborough.

Applic.: Application form is required to be completed on confirmation of stay.

Project «MEER La Gomera», La Gomera, Spain

M.E.E.R. e. V.
Bundesallee 123
12161 Berlin Germany
Tel./Fax: ++49 (30) 6449 7230
E-mail: info@m-e-e-r.de
www.m-e-e-r.de

Desc.: Courses in behavioural biology for students, biologists and interested lay people. Observation of cetaceans off La Gomera. Scientific study aboard small whale-watching vessels. Documentation of the behaviour of cetaceans and the kind of interaction between the vessel and the whales. Long term collection of sighting data.

Spp.: Many different species of dolphins, pilot whales, occasionally large whales, also turtles and large fish.

Hab.: Coastal subtropical waters of the Atlantic Ocean.

Loc.: South-west of La Gomera (Canary Islands, Spain).

Travel: Flight to Tenerife, then ferry to La Gomera.

Dur.: 2 weeks.

Per.: Spring and autumn.

L.term: Not possible.

Age: Min. 18.

Qualif.: No particular skills needed. Previous experience in marine mammal research, photography or ethology is welcome.

Work: Volunteers participate in whale-watching trips, gather and input data. A full training programme, written working materials, scientific supervision and a certificate of attendance are provided.

Lang.: English, German.

Accom.: Tourist apartments (2-4 persons).

Cost: EUR899, including accommodation, a donation to MEER e.V., 6-7 whale-watching trips and all other expenses related to the project.

Applic.: Apply directly through info@m-e-e-r.de.

Proyecto Campanario, Costa Rica

Campanario Biological Reserve
Apdo. 620-1007 San Jose Costa Rica
Tel.: ++(506) 2258 5778
Fax: ++(506) 2256 0374
E-mail: volunteers@campanario.org; info@campanario.org
www.campanario.org

Desc.:	Since 1990 Proyecto Campanario has maintained a tropical rainforest biological reserve in south-west Costa Rica. Through tropical ecology courses and eco-tourism, funds are generated to keep the reserve in its natural state. The programme also offers opportunities for eco-tourists, students and researchers to learn more about the biodiversity and ecology of the Osa Peninsula to promote the cause of rainforest protection in their own communities.
Spp.:	Rainforest and tropical coastal flora and fauna.
Hab.:	Tropical rainforest; mangrove forest, coastal zone.
Loc.:	Osa Peninsula (Corcovado National Park), south-west Costa Rica.
Travel:	Flight to San José, bus to Palmar, then boat to Campanario.
Dur.:	Min. 3 months.
Per.:	Year round.
L.term:	Possible with project leader's approval.
Qualif.:	No particular skills are needed, only enthusiasm and a positive attitude. Every effort is made to utilize skills of volunteers, who should be able to swim, to work without supervision and be in good physical and emotional health.
Work:	Manual labour restoring trails, species inventories, building observation points (sometimes under hot or wet conditions), etc.
Lang.:	English, Spanish helpful but not essential.
Accom.:	In a rustic field station (no hot water) or in a tent cabin close to the beach. Shared room or tent with at least 1 other volunteer.
Cost:	A non-refundable US$25/day contribution for food, prior to arrival.
Applic.:	Request application form via e-mail or fax.
Notes:	A medical, accident and evacuation insurance is compulsory.

Rainsong Wildlife Sanctuary, Costa Rica

Apdo. 182-5361
Cobano de Puntarenas Costa Rica
Tel.: ++ (506) 8387 3607 (voice-mail)
E-mail: rainsongwildlifesanctuary@gmail.com
www.rainsongsanctuary.com

Desc.: Wildlife rescue centre and community wildlife refuge on the edge of Reserva Cabo Blanco, Cabuya: conservation education; reforestation (rare tropical hardwoods, native fruits); reintroduction of endangered animals and birds; biodynamic gardening, farming and landscaping; butterfly gardens; native medicinals and edibles.

Spp.: All native species of animals and birds accepted in the rescue centre.

Hab.: Primary jungle, secondary jungle, tropical dry jungle.

Loc.: Southern tip of Nicoya Peninsula, Costa Rica.

Travel: San José; Puntarenas; ferry to Paquera; Montezuma; Cabuya. Direct shuttle available from San José Airport.

Dur.: Minimum stay: 1 week; no maximum.

Per.: Year round.

L.term: Long term desired.

Age: Min. 18. Children with parents are welcome.

Qualif.: No skills required. Volunteers must be able to work in harmony within a group of people from diverse cultures.

Work: Animal and bird care in the sanctuary; reforestation; assist in Conservation Education events; garden tasks.

Lang.: No language requirements. Everyone helps with Spanish.

Accom.: Lodging options: sharing house, loft rooms, homestay, camphuts, local hotel (with big discount), or tent (during dry season).

Cost: US$5/day per person for lodging. Volunteers prepare their own meals.

Applic.: E-mail to be sent 1 month before intended stay, with foreseen dates of stay and lodging choice. Travel info on website.

Rathlin Island Seabird Centre, Northern Ireland

RSPB - The Royal Society for the Protection of Birds
The Lodge, Sandy
Bedfordshire SG19 2DL UK
Tel.: ++44 (1767) 680 551 Fax: ++44 (1767) 692 365
www.rspb.org.uk volunteers@rspb.org.uk

Desc.: Within its Residential Volunteering Scheme, the RSPB (see Organisation list) offers projects, such as Rathlin Island Seabird Centre, based at a Cliffside lighthouse within a National Nature Reserve on Northern Ireland's only inhabited island.

Spp.: Puffins (*Fratercula arctica*), guillemots (*Uria aalge*), gannets (*Morus bassanus*).

Hab.: Cliffs and off-shore stacks.

Loc.: Rathlin Island, off shore from county Antrim, Northern Ireland.

Travel: Full travel details are given to selected applicants.

Dur.: Min. 2 weeks (Saturday to Saturday).

Per.: Late March to early September.

L.term: By arrangement with the organisation.

Age: Min. 18.

Qualif.: Good spoken English and willingness to engage with visitors.

Work: Meeting/greeting visitors and showing them the seabirds from an outdoor viewing platform; enthusing, educating and recruiting new members; taking part in community activities; looking after facilities.

Lang.: English.

Accom.: Accommodation is provided free. Food and travel expenses are not included.

Cost: Shared room in cottage hostel.

Applic.: Application form at www.rspb.org.uk/residentialvolunteering or email volunteers@rspb.org.uk.

Reef Check Global Coral Reef Monitoring

PO Box 1057
17575 Pacific Coast Highway
Pacific Palisades, California 90272-1057 USA
Tel.: ++1 (310) 230 2371 - Fax: ++1 (310) 230 2376
E-mail: rcinfo@reefcheck.org
www.ReefCheck.org

Desc.:	Reef Check works with communities, governments and businesses to scientifically monitor, restore and maintain coral reef health. Its objectives are to educate the public about the coral reef crisis and create a global network of volunteer teams trained in Reef Check's scientific methods who regularly monitor and report on reef health.
Spp.:	Coral reef organisms, including fish, invertebrates and coral.
Hab.:	Tropical and subtropical coral reefs.
Loc.:	Volunteers are needed in all coral reef countries.
Travel:	Travel arrangements are the responsibility of the participant.
Dur.:	Min.1 week.
Per.:	Year round.
L.term:	To be arranged with Headquarters.
Age:	Min. 18
Qualif.:	Participants must be confident swimmers and comfortable with snorkeling for long periods of time. SCUBA may be used, in which good buoyancy skills are a must.
Work:	Volunteers will be trained in RC methods and carry out coral reef surveys in water no deeper than 12m.
Lang.:	Language used in country of choice.
Accom.:	Accommodations vary with location.
Cost:	Cost varies with location.
Applic.:	See website or contact e-mail address above for information.

Reserva Pacuare, Costa Rica

Avenida 10 (entre calle 27 y29) N.2550
San José Costa Rica
Tel.: ++ (506) 224 85 68
E-mail: c.fernandez@turtleprotection.org
www.turtleprotection.org

Desc.:	Reserva Pacuare is a 800ha tropical rainforest area where conservation, education and research projects are carried out. It is the most important beach in Costa Rica for leatherbacks, and is owned by the NGO Endangered Wildlife Trust.
Spp.:	Leatherback (March-July), green and hawksbill turtles (July-Sept.), howler, whitefaced and spider monkeys, birds (211 spp.), amphibians (17 spp.), butterflies (70 spp.). Occasionally: peccary, anteater, paca, jaguarundy, crocodile, iguana, basilisk, caiman.
Hab.:	Lowland rainforest, coastal and freshwater lagoons and canals.
Loc.:	Province of Limon, south of Pacuare River, Costa Rica.
Travel:	Flight to San José, bus to Matina (2hrs 1/2), taxi to the canal dock (30min.), where boat transportation is provided to the Reserve.
Dur.:	Min. 1 week.
Per.:	March to end September.
L.term:	There is no limit of time for long-term stays.
Age:	Min. 18.
Qualif.:	No qualifications needed except for research assistants, just good physical condition to be able to walk the soft sandy beach.
Work:	Assistance on all conservation and research projects. Monitoring turtles and nests at night, and nest excavations during the day.
Lang.:	Spanish and English are spoken.
Accom.:	Cabins for 2/3, shower block and flush toilets.
Cost:	US$150/week, including boat transportation, room and board.
Applic.:	Via e-mail, preferred dates must be indicated.
Notes:	Positions for long term Research Assistants available. See website.

Rhino Rescue Project, Swaziland

The Ecovolunteer Network
Meyersweg 29, 7553 AX Hengelo The Netherlands
Tel.: ++31 (74) 250 8250
Fax: ++31 (74) 250 6572
E-mail: info@ecovolunteer.org
www.ecovolunteer.org

Desc.:   Hands-on participation in various activities in order to preserve the wildlife and its habitat, assisting also with anti-poaching activities.

Spp.:   White (*Ceratotherium simum*) and black rhinos (*Diceros bicornis*); many other spp. such as elephants, buffaloes, antelopes, crocodiles, hyppopotamus, zebra, giraffes, monkeys, leopards, can be observed.

Hab.:   African savannah.

Loc.:   Swaziland, Africa.

Travel: Flight to Mbabane; a visa and a passport valid for at least 6 months after leaving Swaziland are necessary.

Dur.:   Min. 2, max. 5 weeks.

Per.:   Year round.

L.term: Max. 5 weeks.

Age: Min. 18.

Qualif.:   Volunteers must be able to walk long distances and tolerate heat. Some knowledge of wildlife and birds is helpful.

Work: Daily monitoring of endangered species, nightly detecting of poachers from watchtowers, animal surveys, maintenance work. Most work starts before sunrise. Cooking and cleaning tasks are rotated.

Lang.:   English.

Cost: US$1,400/2 weeks; US$300/3rd week; US$175/4th week, 5th week free. Flights, visa, local taxes and insurance not included.

Accom.:   Simple huts or tents close to the working area. Overnight camping is very primitive with cold-water shower and pit latrine.

Applic.:   The Ecovolunteer Network (see Organisation list).

Notes: Volunteers can visit nearby parks. Malaria treatment is required.

Rolda Rescue Center, Romania

Feroviarilor 16 Bl.C2 ap.18
Galati 800563
Tel.: +40 (748) 903 612
E-mail: rolda@care2.com
www.rolda.org

Desc.: ROLDA offers free spay/neuter services and runs two private dogs shelters (500 dogs). ROLDA is planning to build a veterinary clinic for strays, a shelter for cats and a sanctuary for horses and donkeys.

Spp.: Dogs, cats.

Hab.: Dogs and cats shelter.

Loc.: Galati, Romania.

Travel: Plane to Bucharest, car/train to Galati (approx 300 km from Bucharest).

Dur.: Min. 1 month; 2-3 months is ideal.

Per.: Year round.

L.term: Inquire with the organisation.

Age: Min.18.

Qualif.: Volunteers with previous experience in the field or in a similar shelter are preferred.

Work: Taking the dogs out, teach them the basics like going in the leash, play with them, grooming, cleaning the kennels and the running spaces. Maintenance work, or any other activity at the shelter.

Lang.: English.

Accom.: House with two bedrooms, one kitchen and a bathroom.

Cost: EUR20/day. Accommodation free of charge; transport and food provided by the volunteers.

Applic.: Applications on website.

The Rumi Wilco Nature Reserve and Ecolodge, Ecuador

Vilcabamba, Loja, Ecuador
E-mail: rumiwilco@yahoo.com
www.rumiwilco.com

Desc.:	A self-sustainable conservation reserve at low income level in Vilcabamba. Tourism, volunteer work and research are combined to accomplish a model suitable to many modest property owners with environmental values.
Spp.:	125 species of birds recorded, 500 of plants, 78 of butterflies.
Hab.:	Wilco-dominated forest remnants.
Loc.:	Vilcabamba, Ecuador.
Travel:	Flight to Quito; then flight or bus to Loja; then 1 hour by bus to Vilcabamba; then 15 minutes walking to the reserve.
Dur.:	From 1 week to several months.
Per.:	Year round.
L.term:	Up to 3 months.
Age:	Min. 18 - max. 50 or older if fit.
Qualif.:	No specific skills required for volunteers in general. Scientists or students interested in tropical ecology or other topics may perform their activities (under the pertinent norms) on the Reserve's lands.
Work:	Most work is in open air: trail/ecolodge maintenance, reforestation, riverbank repair, organic gardening, minor construction, shade-grown coffee picking/processing, making marmalades, etc.
Lang.:	English, Spanish, French and Italian are spoken. Spanish lessons are available in town.
Accom.:	In the Ecolodge with other guests, in shared rooms (sometimes private) with 2 well-furnished kitchens used also by travellers.
Cost:	US$5.60/day, but food and transportation are not included. Foods/ingredients are easy to find in Vilcabamba village.
Applic.:	The Green Volunteers Standard Application Form is welcome.

Saving Kenya's Black Rhinos

Earthwatch Institute (Europe)
256 Banbury Road
Oxford OX2 7DE UK
Tel.: ++44 (1865) 318 831 - Fax: ++44 (1865) 311 383
E-mail: projects@earthwatch.org.uk
www.earthwatch.org/europe

Desc.:	In 30 years, poaching has reduced Kenya's black rhinos population from 20,000 to 400. Sanctuaries like this have kept rhinos on the map, bringing them back to about 500. But new concerns have arisen: competition with giraffes and elephants, calf predation by hyenas and lions, having too many rhinos in enclosed reserves. Only a close examination of interactions between these competing large mammals and the sanctuary's carrying capacity will preserve them.
Spp.:	Black rhino (*Diceros bicornis*), zebra, impala, kudu, lion, leopard, hyena, wild dog, giraffe, elephant, wildebeest, buffalo.
Hab.:	Savannah with acacias.
Loc.:	Sweetwaters Black Rhino Reserve, Nanyuki, Kenya.
Travel:	Flight to Nairobi then bus to Nanyuki.
Dur.:	15 days.
Per.:	January, February, July, August, September, October.
L.term:	No long-term volunteer opportunities available.
Age:	Min. 18.
Qualif.:	No special skills required.
Work:	Observing rhinos and other large mammals, gathering data on vegetation and feeding preferences of the competing species.
Lang.:	English.
Accom.:	Comfortable rooms in the Sweetwaters Research Centre.
Cost:	GB£1,595.
Applic.:	Apply on www.earthwatch.org/europe or call ++44 (1865) 318 831.
Notes:	Earthwatch Headquarters are in USA: 3 Clock Tower Place, Suite 100, Box 75, Maynard, MA 01754. See website for national offices.

Scottish Wildlife Rescue, Scotland UK

Hessilhead Wildlife Rescue Trust
Hessilhead, Gateside, Beith Ayrshire
Scotland KA15 1HT UK
Tel.: ++44 (1505) 502 415
E-mail: info@hessilhead.org.uk
www.hessilhead.org.uk

Desc.: Rescue, care, rehabilitate and release all native species of wild birds and mammals. Hand rearing, cleaning and feeding animals; maintenance and construction work and monitoring the casualties after release. Some groups of birds will be ringed, and hopefully some species will be radio-tracked.

Spp.: All Scottish wild birds and mammals.

Hab.: Urban, woodland, farmland, coast, moorland.

Loc.: West central Scotland.

Travel: The Centre is within easy travelling distance from Glasgow.

Dur.: Min. 2-3 weeks.

Per.: March to October.

L.term: Suitable volunteers may be able to stay for 6 months or more.

Age: Min. 18.

Qualif.: Ability to work as part of a team. Training will be given. Experience of radio tracking could be useful. Veterinary experience useful.

Work: Volunteers may help with all aspects of the Trust's work: rescue, treatment, feeding, cleaning, preparing of birds and animals for release and post-release monitoring. Educational work with the public may be possible.

Lang.: English.

Accom.: Log cabins.

Cost: GB£15/week for cabins, food excluded. Volunteers must arrange their own transport, though can be collected from local train or bus stations.

Applic.: Apply directly to HWRT with relevant details and a contact number or address. More information on website.

Sea Turtle Conservation Program, Costa Rica

Asociaciòn WIDECAST

PO Box 2164-3000, Heredia Costa Rica

Tel.: ++(506) 2241 7431 / 8818 2543

Fax: ++(506) 2241 7149

E-mail: volunteers@latinamericanseaturtles.org

www.latinamericanseaturtles.org

Desc.:   Asociación WIDECAST has been working since 1997 as volunteer structure for the conservation and sustainable development of the coastal regions of Costa Rica, such as north and south Pacific and south Caribbean. This last region represents around 5% of the national territory and it is one of the biologically richest areas of the planet with over 2% of the entire world's biodiversity. With Costa Rica's largest native Indian population, English speaking Caribbean Blacks, and campesinos, its cultural heritage is equally rich.

Spp.:   Leatherback (*Dermochelys coriacea*), Hawksbill (*Eretmochelys imbricata*), Loggerhead (*Caretta caretta*) and Green (*Chelonia mydas*) sea turtles.

Hab.:   Southern Caribbean, Southern Pacific, Northern Pacific.

Loc.:   Southern Carribean: Gandoca (Gandoca Manzanillo Wildlife Refuge) and Cahuita (Cahuita National Park).

Southern Pacific: Osa Peninsula (Project in Playa Carate, Pejeperro and Río Oro).

Northern Pacific: Ostional Refuge.

Travel: Flight to San José, then bus to the different programs.

Dur.:   Min. 1 week, max. 6 months.

Per.:   Cahuita: February 15th to October 31st.

Gandoca: February 15th to August 15th.

Osa: July 15th to December 15th.

Age: Min. 18; between 16 and 18 with permission letter from parents; under 16 with family or group leaders.

Work: The main work of the volunteers involves night patrols and hatchery shifts. Other daytime work at the project may involve beach clean-up and small projects, including initial construction of the hatcheries. Main duties: measuring nest dimensions; collecting eggs; tagging the rear flipper of the turtle; relocating the eggs either on the beach or in the hatchery; recording information about number of eggs, nest location and turtle identification, including the hatchling survival rate; checking of nests during the incubation time; counting and releasing the hatchlings, watching them until they reach the sea. Sometimes volunteers are asked to work longer than normal.

Lang.:   English, Spanish useful but not necessary.

Accom.:   Cahuita: WIDECAST Sea Turtle Field Station.

Gandoca: choose between accommodation with local families, camping or stay at Biology Field Station.

Osa: Locally run cabins.

Cost: US$45 per night, with a minimum stay of 6 nights. Training and food included. US$10 per night in Gandoca, but food is not included.

Agents: Contact Asociaciòn Widecast directly.

Applic.:   Use online application form, or by email.

Sea Turtle Conservation Project, Greece

Katelios Group for the Research and Protection of Marine and Terrestrial Life
28086 Kefalonia Greece
Tel.: ++30 (26) 7108 1161
E-mail: info@kateliosgroup.org
www.kateliosgroup.org

Desc.:	Local project for the conservation of the Loggerhead sea turtle (*Caretta caretta*) in Greece. Main volunteer activities: nesting beach patrols, turtle monitoring, data collection, environmental education and awareness raising.
Spp.:	Loggerhead sea turtle (*Caretta caretta*).
Hab.:	Mediterranean sea, coast and beach sand dunes.
Loc.:	Kefalonia, Greece
Travel:	Flight to Athens, then bus or ferry boat; otherwise, direct charter flight to Kefalonia.
Dur.:	Minimum stay 4 weeks, longer stay (up to whole summer) welcome.
Per.:	May to October (turtle nesting season).
L.term:	Long term volunteers welcome.
Age:	Min. 18; no upper age limit.
Qualif.:	No specific skills or background required. For beach patrols good fitness is essential.
Work:	Nesting beach patrols, turtle monitoring, data collection, environmental education and awareness raising.
Lang.:	English. Greek and any other European language welcome.
Accom.:	Provided in shared rented rooms.
Cost:	Contribution ranges between EUR200-300, accommodation is included. Travel, food and insurance covered by volunteer.
Applic.:	Apply by e-mail; applications are accepted from January every year.
Notes:	Volunteers need to show strong motivation and committment.

Sea Turtle Conservation Projects, Costa Rica

Apdo. 1203-1100 Tibàs
San José Costa Rica
Tel.: ++ (506) 241 5227
Fax: ++ (506) 236 6017
E-mail: voluntarios@pretoma.org
http://www.pretoma.org

Desc.:	PRETOMA is a Costa Rican NGO, whose aim is to protect, conserve, and restore the populations of sea turtles, sharks and other marine species through scientific research, hands-on conservation, public awareness, litigation, and collaboration with communities and fisheries. It has 2 turtle projects, Punta Banco and San Miguel.
Spp.:	Olive ridley (*Lepidochelys olivacea*). Sometimes green (*Chelonia mydas*) and leatherback turtles (*Dermochelys coriacea*).
Hab.:	Tropical and subtropical coast.
Loc.:	Punta Banco: south Pacific coast of Costa Rica, 65km south of Golfito. San Miguel: north-central Pacific coast of Costa Rica .
Travel:	Flight to San José, then bus to site.
Dur.:	Min. 1 week. 2 weeks are preferred.
Per.:	Punta Banco: July 15th to December 15th; San Miguel: July 7th to December 20th.
L.term:	Up to the entire project period.
Age:	No age restrictions. Inquire for younger than 18.
Qualif.:	The project is open to everyone interested in marine conservation.
Work:	Patrolling beach, tagging, measuring, relocating eggs; environmental education programmes with the community.
Lang.:	Spanish helpful but not necessary.
Accom.:	At the Research Station, with shared bedrooms and bathrooms, or in rustic cabins. Bedding is provided. Meals are provided at the local community restaurant. Home-stay is also available.
Cost:	US$350-790 for 1 to 3 weeks; US$220 for each additional week.
Applic.:	Via e-mail.

Sea Turtle Rescue Centre, Greece

ARCHELON, The Sea Turtle Protection Society of Greece
Solomou 57
GR-10432 Athens Greece
Tel./Fax: ++30 (210) 523 1342
E-mail: volunteers@archelon.gr
www.archelon.gr

Desc.:	Archelon is running sea turtle conservation projects in Greece with the support of international volunteers. The Sea Turtle Rescue Centre focuses on the treatment and rehabilitation of injured or sick turtles found through the National Stranding Network. Activities include raising of public and schoolchildren's awareness.
Spp.:	Loggerhead (*Caretta caretta*) and green (*Chelonia mydas*) turtles.
Hab.:	Mediterranean coast.
Loc.:	Glyfada, about 20km from Athens, Greece.
Travel:	Flight to Athens. Ask the organisation for further instructions.
Dur.:	Min. 4 weeks. 6 weeks or more are recommended.
Per.:	Year round.
L.term:	Long term volunteers are accepted.
Age:	Min. 18.
Qualif.:	Enthusiasm and commitment for the natural environment. Work is physically demanding and outdoors (very hot summer or cold winter).
Work:	Treatment and rehabilitation of injured turtles (applying medications, feeding, etc.), cleaning tanks, maintainance work, providing information to visitors.
Lang.:	English. German and Greek are useful.
Accom.:	Within the Centre, in train wagons converted to host volunteers.
Cost:	Participation fee: approx. EUR200. Volunteers must cover their own travel expenses and food costs (min. EUR9/day).
Applic.:	Prospective volunteers must fill out Archelon's application form.
Notes:	Participation fee includes a 1-year subscription to the newsletter *Turtle Tracks* as an Archelon supporter.

Sea Turtle Summer Field Work, Greece

Archelon - Sea Turtle Protection Society of Greece
57 Solomou Street, GR-10432 Athens Greece
Tel./Fax: ++30 (210) 523 1342
E-mail: volunteers@archelon.gr
www.archelon.gr

Desc.: Archelon is an environmental NGO running sea turtle conservation projects in Greece with the support of international volunteers. Summer field work includes monitoring turtle nesting activities on the beaches, tagging nesting females, nest protection and raising public (visitor and local) awareness.

Spp.: Loggerhead sea turtle *(Caretta caretta)*.

Hab.: Mediterranean coast.

Loc.: Peloponnesus and the islands of Zakynthos and Crete, Greece.

Travel: Flight to Athens, then bus or ferry boat to the allocated area.

Dur.: Min. 4 weeks. 6 weeks or more are recommended.

Per.: May to October.

L.term: Volunteers applying for long-term are welcome.

Age: Min. 18.

Qualif.: Enthusiasm and commitment for the natural environment. Work is physically demanding because of hot weather. Training is provided.

Work: Beach surveys, nest protection, tagging nesting females at night, raising public awareness through information stations and slide shows.

Lang.: English. German, Italian, French and Swedish useful.

Accom.: Designated free campsites in tents. Basic sanitary and cooking facilities. Some areas have limited water supply.

Cost: Participation fee: EUR200-300, depending on arrival date. Volunteers must cover travel expenses and food costs (min. EUR10/day).

Applic.: Prospective volunteers must fill out Archelon's application form.

Notes: Participants receive a 1-year subscription to *Turtle Tracks* newsletter. International health insurance is required.

Shisong, Kumbo, Cameroon

BTCV
Sedum House
Mallard Way, Potteric Carr, Doncaster, DN4 8DB UK
Tel.: ++44 (1302) 388 883 - Fax: ++44 (1302) 311 531
E-mail: information@btcv.org.uk; International@btcv.org.uk
www.btcv.org.uk

Desc.:	This area of Cameroon is dominated by gentle rolling hills and beautiful grasslands, near the Bamenda highlands and the impressive Mt. Oku with its crater lake. Working in partnership with Green Care Shisong this project brings volunteers into daily contact with local communities. As BTCV work alongside them, volunteers will be doing more than just planting trees, they will be helping to preserve precious water supplies.
Spp.:	Native flora and fauna.
Hab.:	Bamenda Highlands.
Loc.:	Shisong, Kumbo, Cameroon.
Travel:	Flight to Douala International Airport.
Dur.:	2 weeks.
Per.:	Spring and summer.
L.term:	Contact organisation for details.
Age:	Min. 18.
Qualif.:	No specific skills required.
Work:	Tree planting, preserving water supplies.
Lang.:	English.
Accom.:	Hotel.
Cost:	From GB£690, excluding flight.
Applic.:	Contact BTCV at www.btcv.org.uk or ++44 (1302) 388 883. GB£100 deposit is required.
Notes:	Conservation Holidays brochure available on request or visit the online shop.

Siberian/East Russian Volunteer Program, Russia

Building the Great Baikal Trail - Earth Island Institute
2150 Allston Way, Suite 460, Berkeley,
California 94704 USA
Tel.: ++1 (510) 717 1805 - Fax: ++1 (510) 859 9091
E-mail: baikal@earthisland.org   www.earthisland.org

Desc.:	Earth Island and Great Baikal Trail Association are building the first national hiking trail in Russia. The Great Baikal Trail will lead some 1,600km around Lake Baikal, through 3 national parks and 3 nature reserves. Every year multiple teams of volunteers are organised to help build the trail. Teams are international, with many local Siberians mixing with foreign participants. Some 15-25 project sites are planned each year. Examples would be: 1) in Pribaikalski National Park, where the final stretches of shoreline trail are to be constructed between the mouth of the Angara River and Olkhon Island, located some 150 miles to the north; 2) in Baikalski Nature Reserve, which already has built 30 miles of an eco-educational trail that now needs to be extended further; and 3) along the northern shores of Baikal, where trails will be extended to reach across from Bright and Sandy Islands all the way to the remote Frolikha River Valley. For more information on all the volunteer work sites, for both the summer and early spring, please see www.greatbaikaltrail.org.
Spp.:	Varies greatly: along the trail one might see Baikal seal, bears, eagles, sable or red deer. Divers may see many exotic species of fish and even coral.
Hab.:	Lakeshore habitat, temperate forests, wetlands and meadowlands.
Loc.:	Lake Baikal region, south central Russia, near the Mongolian border.
Travel:	Flight to Irkutsk (via Moscow or the Far East) or by the Trans-Siberian train, which takes 3 days of travel from Moscow.
Dur.:	2-4 weeks.
Per.:	Mostly in Summer, May to September, but some projects in early spring
L.term.:	Opportunities for volunteering for several projects around Baikal

are available for those who wish to stay on longer.

Age: Min.18.

Qualif.: Helpful (but not required) trail-building experience. Good health and ability to do hard work are a must, since some heavy tools will be used, with training provided.

Work: Mostly physical, all outdoors, with opportunities to assist the design teams as they choose the best sites and methods for building each trail. Also some projects involve helping local Siberians on various environmental education and English-language teaching programs.

Lang.: Some knowledge of Russian would be helpful but not required. At least one English-language interpreter will be working on every team.

Accom.: Field work involves sleeping on boats or in tents; sleeping bag required.

Cost: Earth Island charges no fees for referring to the trail-building crews. However, the Association is a non-profit group and will depend on international volunteers to pay for their own travel and all food costs at Baikal: US$450 for each 2-week project. Volunteers should also bear the cost of insurance and accommodations in Russia before and after the work period.

Agents: Prospective volunteers can communicate directly with Earth Island's staff (at baikal@earthisland.org) or with the Russian partners at the national parks and nature reserves, through their English-speaking colleagues with the Association at gbt.volunteers@gmail.com.

Applic.: See http://www.greatbaikaltral.org/volunteer_gbt/anketa_en.html for an application form.

Notes: There are many other volunteer and internship opportunities with Siberian environmental groups available, where knowledge of Russian is preferred. For more information on these programmes, contact Earth Island Institute.

Skaftafell National Park, Iceland

BTCV
Sedum House
Mallard Way, Potteric Carr, Doncaster, DN4 8DB UK
Tel.: ++44 (1302) 388 883 - Fax: ++44 (1302) 311 531
E-mail: information@btcv.org.uk; International@btcv.org.uk
www.btcv.org.uk

Desc.:	Skaftafell Vatnajökull National Park in southeast Iceland has been described as a green oasis surrounded by a landscape of snow-capped mountains, glaciers and vast black sand plains. This amazing scenery makes it one of the most beautiful and most visited places in the country. Work may include building stone drains, resurfacing paths with gravel and the construction of timber bridges and boardwalks. This vital work allows visitors to enjoy the beautiful national park and helps to conserve its unique landscape and wildlife.
Spp.:	Subarctic species of flora and fauna (ptarmigan, arctic fox).
Hab.:	Glacier area, subarctic tundra.
Loc.:	Skaftafell National Park, south-east Iceland.
Travel:	Pick-up at Skaftafell Visitors Centre.
Dur.:	1-2 weeks.
Per.:	Summer.
L.term:	Contact organisation for details.
Age:	Min. 18.
Qualif.:	Strenuous work: a reasonable level of fitness required.
Work:	Footpath, drainage, bridge construction and repair.
Lang.:	English.
Cost:	From GB£345, excluding flights.
Agents:	Contact BTCV at International@btcv.org.uk or ++44 (1302) 388 883.
Applic.:	Deposit of GB£100 required.
Notes:	Conservation Holiday brochure available on request or visit the online shop.

SOS Tartarugas (Turtle SOS), Cabo Verde

Turtle SOS Cabo Verde
Cultural Cafe, Santa Maria, Ilha do Sal, Cabo Verde
Tel.: ++238 745 020
E-mail: info@turtlesos.org
www.turtlesos.org

Desc.: Work with nesting loggerhead turtles. Patrol beaches, collect data, work with tourists, hatchery and working with community. Long and short term opportunities June to December. Beautiful accommodation in a surf hotel provided and some positions have a small salary. For some positions no experience is necessary.

Spp.: Loggerhead Turtles.

Hab.: Atlantic beach.

Loc.: Sal island, Cabo Verde, Africa.

Travel: Direct flights from Europe and USA to Sal. Short bus ride to Santa Maria where project is based.

Dur.: Duration depends on position applied for.

Per.: June to December.

L.term: Inquire with organisation.

Age: Min. 18. Must be very fit.

Qualif.: Qualifications depends on position applied for. Everyone must be fit, committed, hardworking and flexible.

Work: Protection of nesting beaches and turtles through night and morning patrols. Tagging, relocation of nests, hatchery duties, tourism duties, community work.

Lang.: English. German is spoken in the island.

Accom.: Shared accommodation in surf hotel with communal areas in beach resort.

Cost: Accommodation and food allowance paid for long term volunteers. No travel to project paid. Short term volunteers (less than one month) pay own expenses.

Applic.: http://turtleconservationjobs.blogspot.com/ or contact by e-mail.

Southwestern Research Station, Arizona USA

American Museum of Natural History
PO Box 16553 Portal
Arizona 85632 USA
Tel./Fax: ++1 (520) 558 2396
E-mail: tglore@amnh.org
http://research.amnh.org/swrs/

Desc.: The intern programme offers students in biological sciences outstanding opportunities to observe and become involved with scientists doing field research. Food and lodging are provided to volunteers in exchange for 24hrs/week of routine chores, with the remaining time available for research activities.

Spp.: Birds, reptiles, amphibians, mammals, insects, plants.

Hab.: 5 life-zones are encountered, from desert to alpine.

Loc.: Portal, south-eastern Arizona.

Travel: Flight to Tucson, then shuttle to Douglas (meeting place).

Dur.: Generally 6-week commitment.

Per.: Mid-March to the end of October.

L.term.: Possible with the Station director's approval, after initial period.

Age: Min. 18. The station is remote, 3 hours by car from a medical facility.

Qualif.: Some biological background is helpful, but not necessary.

Work: Volunteers work 24 hours on routine Station chores, e.g., housekeeping, grounds keeping, assisting in the kitchen/dining room, in exchange for room and board. Remaining time is available for research activities.

Lang.: English.

Accom.: Shared rooms are provided. All linens are provided. Meals are in a common dining room.

Cost: There is no cost to volunteers, other than transportation.

Applic.: Contact Volunteer Coordinator, Tresa Glore: tglore@amnh.org. An application must be submitted with letter(s) of reference.

Sri Lanka Elephant Conservation Experience

Frontier
50-52 Rivington Street
London EC2A 3QP. United Kingdom
Tel.: +44 (020) 7613 2422
E-mail: info@frontier.ac.uk
www.frontier.ac.uk

Desc.:   Elephants hold a special and sacred role in the culture and heritage of Sri Lanka. With supervision by an expert research team from the Sri Lankan Wildlife Conservation Society, volunteers will be participating in activities that aim to resolve human-elephant conflict with a view to producing sustainable conservation strategies capable of saving elephants and their habitat in the long term.

Spp.:   Elephants.

Hab.:   Indian Ocean.

Loc.:   Sri Lanka.

Travel: Volunteers must make their own way to project site.

Dur.:   2-3 weeks.

Per.:   Year round (April excluded).

L.term: Inquire with organisation.

Age: Minimum age of 18.

Qualif.:   No skills required.

Work: Monitoring elephant populations, conducting a survey of elephant numbers, associations, family demographics, distribution and behaviour; recording their abundance and habitat utilisation; assessing disturbance levels and undertake surveys within local communities to record accurately the levels of crop raiding and damage attributable to elephant herds.

Lang.:   English and Sri Lankan.

Accom.:   Simple but comfortable field lodge which accommodates large groups of people.

Cost: GB£895 for 2 weeks, GB£299 per extra week.

Applic.:   www.frontier.ac.uk and then click the Apply Now! Button.

Sustainable Livelihood Development Association, Sri Lanka

Native Forest Foundation
No 258, Moragoda Road, Mudungoda,
Gampaha Sri Lanka
Tel.: ++94 (33) 222 4023
E-mail: damilda@sltnet.lk

Desc.:	This ONG is a grassroot plant conservation group involved in building up an arboretum with fast disappearing native wild fruits, medicinal and food plants in order to propagate them through the selected churchyards and buddhist monasteries, getting Sunday schools actively involved in plant conservation and creation care. Volunteers' posts are mainly community based and provide a unique opportunity to understand the local culture and values, as well as the genuine hospitality of a Sri Lanka family.
Spp.:	Low impact sustainable crops.
Hab.:	Hilly tropical farmland.
Loc.:	Western province of Sri Lanka.
Travel:	Flight to Colombo, then bus to project area.
Dur.:	Min. 3 weeks.
Per.:	Year round, but rainy season (April-June) is preferable.
L.term:	Volunteers can stay as long as they want.
Age:	Min. 25. Elderly people are welcome.
Qualif.:	No particular skills required; initiative, adaptability, compassion for nature and traditional knowledge are important requisites.
Work:	Soil preparation, planting, manuaring, watering, weeding, assistance in photography of plants, collecting info (ethno botanical surveys) from rural villages, teaching plant conservation in Sunday schools.
Lang.:	English.
Accom.:	With local families: basic, but clean and comfortable.
Cost:	Free contribution for room and board (about US$15/day).
Applic.:	Send a detailed CV via e-mail. Confirm 30 days before arrival.

Tambopata Macaw Project, Peru

Department of Veterinary Pathobiology, Texas A&M University
TAMU 4467, College Station, TX 77843 USA
Tel.: ++1 (979) 458 0563
E-mail: proyectoguacamayo@gmail.com;
dbrightsmith@cvm.tamu.edu
www.macawproject.org

Desc.: Tambopata's work with parrots and wildlife in the rainforest of Perú has been published and useful for conservation worldwide since 1989. This ongoing research project uses long term local and international volunteers to understand parrot behaviour, especially at mineral licks.

Spp.: Parrots (including endangered Blue-headed Macaw), harpy eagles, bamboo birds, otters, jaguars, tapirs, monkeys.

Hab.: Rainforest.

Loc.: South-eastern Perú.

Travel: Flight to Lima, then local flight to Puerto Maldonado. Otherwise, it's 3 days by road.

Dur.: Min. 2 months.

Per.: Year round.

L.term: Long-term volunteers are preferred.

Age: Min. 18 – max. 50; younger with parents' consent or project discretion.

Qualif.: Interest in the outdoors and wildlife is important; sense of humour, patience and team skills are advantageous.

Work: Monitoring food availability, nest sites, foraging behaviour and family groups in clay licks-sites.

Lang.: English or Spanish.

Accom.: Shared accommodation in bungalows with running water and warm meals. Bedding provided.

Cost: US$15/day, including food, local transport, accommodation, internet, unlimited tea and coffee provided by the lodges.

Applic.: Send CV and cover letter to: proyectoguacamayo@gmail.com

Tambopata Resident Naturalist Program, Peru

Explorer's Inn Amazon Lodge
Alcanfores 459 Miraflores
Lima 1 Peru
Tel.: ++51 (14) 478 888 - Fax: ++51 (12) 418 427
E-mail: mgunther@explorersinn.com; jygberg@gmail.com
www.explorersinn.com

Desc.:	The Explorer's Inn, a tourist lodge and research station along the Tambopata River, offers a Resident Naturalist (RN) and a Volunteer programme. RNs have the opportunity to spend an extended period of quality time in the richest and greenest corner of the Amazon rainforest, collaborating on long-term field research projects and learning first-hand about the biodiversity of this area. Volunteers take part in short-term research projects and assist the Resident Naturalists with their duties.
Spp.:	Tropical rainforest species.
Hab.:	Sub-tropical moist forest.
Loc.:	Tambopata region, Peru south-east province of Madre de Dios.
Travel:	Flight to Lima, then to Puerto Maldonado, then river boat.
Dur.:	Volunteers: min. 2 weeks; RNs: min. 3 months.
Per.:	Year round. Applicants should arrive 1 week earlier for training.
L.term:	RNs who wish to stay at least 6 months are preferred.
Age:	Min. 22.
Qualif.:	RNs: graduates in natural sciences, biology or related disciplines.
Work:	RN duties include: training Peruvian staff in languages and natural history; maintaining wildlife sightings logs; helping maintain the trail system; giving natural history lectures to guests. Volunteers assist the RNs.
Lang.:	Spanish.
Accom.:	Shared room in one of the lodge bungalows.
Cost:	RNs receive free room and board, while volunteers pay US$25/day. Travel to Puerto Maldonado is excluded.
Applic.:	Contact the Explorer's Inn via e-mail.

Tiny Island Turtles Project, Maldives

Tiny Island Conservation
Woodlands End Cottage, Mells,
Somerset. BA11 3PG UK
Tel.: +44 (0) 560 248 8085 (UK) - +960 (7) 791 169 (Maldives)
E-mail: info@tinyislandvolunteers.com
www.tinyislandvolunteers.com

Desc.:	TIC aims to protect and effectively increase numbers of both endangered species of Hawksbill and Greens turtles that nest in islands through the country. At any one time there are up to 100 baby Hawksbill turtles cared for in the nursery in preparation for their safe release; volunteers are needed to assist in looking after turtles on a day to day basis. A reef planting program that volunteers can assist with has recently started.
Spp.:	All species of sea turtles, Manta Rays, Sting Rays, Whale Sharks.
Hab.:	Tropical beaches, atolls.
Loc.:	Naifaru Island, Maldives.
Travel:	Flight to Maldives, then speedboat or seaplane to Naifaru Island.
Dur.:	Min. 1 month; 2-3 months is ideal.
Per.:	Year round.
L.term:	Volunteers may stay for a longer period if they wish.
Age:	Min.18. No max age but fitness and good health are required.
Qualif.:	No particular skills needed; enthusiasm and interest in marine life. Basic swimming skills required.
Work:	Caring for turtles including hand feeding, cleaning, monitoring and release, database maintenance, relocating endangered nests, assisted hatching, caring for sick turtles and turtles that have been kept as house pets in preparation for their release. Working directly with Atoll schools encouraging students to volunteer.
Lang.:	English.
Accom.:	Marine Centre room,Volunteer house or family homestay.
Cost:	GB£850/month including room, board, local transfers and visa.
Applic.:	Form on website.

Tolga Bat Hospital, Australia

Tolga Bat Rescue & Research, Inc.
PO Box 685 Atherton 4883 Australia
Tel.: ++61 (7) 4091 2683
Fax: ++61 (7) 4091 2683
E-mail: jenny@tolgabathospital.org
www.tolgabathospital.org

Desc.:	We are a community group that works for the conservation of bats and their habitat through rescue and landcare work, education and research.
Spp.:	Spectacled flying fox (*Pteropus conspicillatus*), Little Red flying fox (*Pteropus scapulatus.*), several species of microbat.
Hab.:	Tropical rainforest.
Loc.:	Atherton, near Cairns, Australia.
Travel:	Flight to Cairns, then bus to Atherton.
Dur.:	Minimum 4 weeks in busy season; 1 week for the rest of the year.
Per.:	Year round; especially October to February.
L.term:	A stay of 2-3 months in the busy season is welcome.
Age:	Min. 21 years.
Qualif.:	Ability to work well in teams and sometimes for long hours. Experience with bats not necessary, though experience with wildlife, veterinary or zoo work is a plus.
Work:	Busy season: searching the colony daily for tick paralysis bats, hospital treatments, feeding babies, preparing food for adults and babies, cleaning, washing, cooking, weighing bats. Low season: may include work in the vegetable and bush gardens.
Lang.:	English necessary.
Accom.:	Single, twin or triple room available. Some form of 'soft volunteering' is possible if people can pay more and work less.
Cost:	AUS$25-50/day for food and board, depends on length of stay.
Applic.:	Application form online.
Notes:	Vaccination for rabies is mandatory from October to February.

Tree Planters Farm, Australia

100 Deserio Rd., Cedar Pocket, Gympie
Queensland 4570 Australia
Tel.: ++61 (7) 5486 6147
E-mail: forest@spiderweb.com.au
www.forest.spiderweb.com.au

Desc.:	This privately owned organic working farm aims to establish rainforest tree species through regeneration and tree planting on former rainforest sites. Special interest is in rare rainforest tree species. Adjoining the state forest, the farm has large rainforest trees, walking trails, swimming holes, a creek, a camping cave, an isolated visitors hut and a small orchard of tropical fruit trees.
Spp.:	Rainforest trees.
Hab:	Rainforest.
Loc.:	South-east Queensland, Australia.
Travel:	Train or bus to Gympie, about 160km north of Brisbane, the meeting point.
Dur.:	2 nights to make sure that both parties are happy and after that by negotiation.
Per.:	Year round.
L.term:	Longer terms can perhaps be arranged.
Age:	Min. 18.
Qualif.:	No specific qualifications required, just enthusiasm.
Work:	To assist with the establishment of the forests and perhaps some other farm jobs.
Lang:	Only English is spoken but the project manager will assist those that wish to improve their English.
Accom.:	Either in a spare bedroom in the house or a self-contained old converted dairy behind the house. Sleeping bags required.
Cost:	No cost. Work is done in return for keep.
Applic.:	Contact Bob Whitworth, owner, directly either by telephone or writing to the above address.

Trees for Life, Scotland UK

The Park, Findhorn Bay, Forres
Scotland IV36 3TZ UK
Tel.: ++44 (1309) 691 292
Fax: ++44 (1309) 691 155
E-mail: trees@findhorn.org
www.treesforlife.org.uk

Desc.:	Trees for Life is a conservation charity working to restore the Caledonian Forest in the Scottish Highlands. Volunteers are invited to join us on our Conservation Holidays and spend a week in the hills and glens, planting trees, carrying out nursery work and more.
Spp.:	Scots pine, silver birch downy birch, hazel, willow, juniper, deer, red squirrel, black grouse, wild boar and more.
Hab.:	Caledonian Forest.
Loc.:	Highlands of Scotland, west of Inverness.
Travel:	Transport is provided from Inverness station.
Dur.:	Holidays run for 1 week, Saturday to Saturday.
Per.:	March to May, September to November.
L.term:	Long-term opportunities are possible.
Age:	Minimum 18 years.
Qualif.:	None required, although volunteers would need to be reasonably fit to take part. An interest in conservation is useful but not essential.
Work:	Tree planting, removing redundant fences, small scale stock fencing and tree tubing, wetland restoration, felling non-native trees, seed collection, nursery work.
Lang.:	English.
Accom.:	Simple but comfortable, ranging from a renovated croft house to well appointed bunkhouse with all facilities.
Cost:	GB£140 (GB£80 unwaged: students, unemployed, retired). Includes accommodation, food and transport from Inverness.
Applic.:	Via e-mail, online form, or by phone.

Turtle Conservation Project (TCP), Sri Lanka

11, Perera Mawatha
Madakumbura, Panadura Sri Lanka
Tel.: ++94 (777) 810 508-9 /(38) 567 0168,
Fax: ++94 (38) 223 3106
E-mail: turtle@sltnet.lk
www.tcpsrilanka.org

Desc.: TCP is an NGO devoted to the conservation of marine and coastal resources in Sri Lanka through community participation.

Spp.: Green (*Chelonia mydas*), hawksbill (*Eretmochelys imbricata*), loggerhead (*Caretta caretta*), olive ridley (*Lepidochelys olivacea*) and leatherback turtles (*Dermochelys coriacea*).

Hab.: Tropical marine and coastal.

Loc.: Marine and coastal areas of Sri Lanka.

Travel: Flight to Colombo. Transportation to project site can be provided.

Dur.: Min. 2 weeks; a minimum of 3 months is preferred.

Per.: Year round.

L.term: There is no limit of time for long-term stays.

Age: Min. 18. A degree of stamina is required for the long shifts and occasional variations in climate.

Qualif.: Enthusiasm, efficiency, adaptability and ability to work in team.

Work: Measuring turtles, beach patrols and mapping, education programmes, environmental hotel presentations, English teaching in monasteries and schools, office administration, fundraising, IT development work, promotion of responsible nature tourism.

Lang.: English.

Accom.: The type of accommodation will vary and may include basic standards of living compared to western standards.

Cost: US$600/month for room and board (meals provided by a local family). Visa: free for the first month; US$150 for 2-3 months; over 3 months, contact TCP head office. Transport to/from the airport: from US$20 by public aircon bus up to USD$250 for private van.

Applic.: Contact the organization by e-mail for an application form.

Turtles and Birds of Tortuguero, Costa Rica

Sea Turtle Conservancy (STC)
4424 NW 13th Street, Suite B-11
Gainesville, Florida 32609 USA
Tel.: ++1 (352) 373 6441 - Fax: ++1 (352) 375 2449
E-mail: stc@conserveturtles.org
www.conserveturtles.org

Desc.: STC has been tagging and monitoring the green turtles of Tortuguero for 50 years. It also gathers information on leatherback turtles, which nest at Tortuguero Beach in impressive numbers.

Spp.: Green turtles (*Chelonia mydas*).

Hab.: Tropical coast.

Loc.: Tortuguero, Costa Rica.

Travel: Flight to San José, Costa Rica.

Dur.: 1-3 weeks.

Per.: June to October.

L.term: Volunteers can stay longer than 3 weeks with prior approval.

Age: Min. 18.

Qualif.: Volunteers must be in good physical condition, be able to live in rustic setting and tolerate harsh weather.

Work: Volunteers assist researchers with tagging turtles and collecting data on size, tag numbers, nest location, etc.

Lang.: English. Spanish may be useful.

Accom.: Volunteers stay at STC's research Station in Tortuguero.

Cost: US$1,599/1 week; US$2,149/2 weeks. Cost includes 2 nights in San José, all room, meals and training. A deposit is required.

Agents: Holbrook Travel, tel. ++1 (800) 451 7111 in North America.

Applic.: Contact Daniel Evans at STC or agent to confirm dates.

Notes: Tortuguero is the most important site in Costa Rica for resident and migratory neotropical birds. CCC's project aims to gather information on the status of bird populations and the number of species residing or migrating here. See website for details.

The University of Georgia Campus, Costa Rica

Apdo.108, Santa Elena de Monteverde, Puntarenas Costa Rica
Tel.: ++ (506) 2645 8049
Fax: ++ (506) 2645 8050
E-mail: progcr@uga.edu
www.ugacostarica.com
www.uga.edu/costarica

Desc.: The University of Georgia operates a satellite campus in San Luis de Monteverde, dedicated to research, education, eco-tourism, conservation and the community. Volunteer opportunities include Administrative Interns, English instructors, and Resident Naturalists.

Spp.: Flora and fauna from cloud forest, montane,premontane and dry forest converge in this area as well as crop species.

Hab.: Tropical cloud forest, tropical agricultural landscape.

Loc.: San Luis de Monteverde, north-western Costa Rica.

Travel: Bus from San José to Monteverde; then taxi to the campus.

Dur.: Interns and Resident Naturalists: min. 6 months.

Per.: Year round.

L.term: Preferred for Resident Naturalists (6 months or longer).

Age: Min. 20.

Qualif.: Interns: excellent physical condition, able to interact with scientists, students and the public. Resident Naturalists: bachelors' degree in Environmental Sciences or similar.

Work: Working as part of a team in: leading hikes, horseback tours, birdwalks, slide shows, community service; helping with logistics; participating in research, education and conservation missions.

Lang.: English; strong conversational Spanish.

Accom.: Bunkhouse or rustic one-room casitas. Bedding provided.

Cost: All volunteers receive room and board for the duration of their internship or volunteer position.

Applic.: Via e-mail or visit website for application form and further details.

Notes: Intensive training in flora and fauna provided for Resident Naturalists.

Vervet Monkey Rescue Project, South Africa

Darwin Primate Group
PO Box 203
The Crags, 6602 Western Cape South Africa
Tel.: +27 (72) 843 4653
E-mail: karinsaks@gmail.com
www.darwinprimategroup.blogspot.com

Desc.:	Volunteers will help with the daily routine at a rescue centre for vervet monkeys, do research into the behaviour of wild baboon troops and participate in all the activities of a South African tourist area.
Spp.:	Vervet Monkeys and Chacma Baboons.
Hab.:	Coastal forest, oceans, fynbos, mountains.
Loc.:	Garden Route, Western Cape, South Africa.
Travel:	Volunteers will need to fly to Johannesburg or Capetown and then fly to George where they will be picked up.
Dur.:	Min. 2 weeks.
Per.:	September to May are preferable.
L.term:	Volunteers may stay for a longer period if they wish.
Age:	21 to 70. Volunteers need to be relatively fit.
Qualif.:	No particular skills necessary other than a passion for animals.
Work:	Chopping food, cleaning enclosures, observing behaviour, researching behaviour, researching natural food sources, socialising rescued monkeys, nursing and mothering if needed.
Lang.:	English.
Accom.:	Our Accommodation: 2 rooms in a rustic farmhouse (shared with us) with one bathroom, kitchen, workshops etc. Limited solar power use. Internet.
Cost:	GB£150 per week. One meal included per day, accommodation, transport from airport included, other petrol costs are extra.
Applic.:	Please email us to apply for details.

Volunteer Peten, Guatemala

Parque Nueva Juventud
San Andres, Peten Guatemala
Tel.: ++ (502) 5711 0040
E-mail: volunteerpeten@hotmail.com
www.volunteerpeten.org

Desc.: Volunteer Peten is a small independent non-profit organization dedicated to: 1) protect and manage a 150-acre ecological reserve in San Andres, Peten; 2) provide environmental education programs to all the schools in the San Andres area; 3) assist and develop small sustainable community projects.

Spp.: Over 160 bird species, 120 medicinal plant species, 95 tree species, and countless insect and reptile species.

Hab.: Semi-humid, deciduous tropical rain forest.

Loc.: San Andres, Peten, northern Guatemala.

Travel: San Andres is 30 min. by bus from Santa Elena/Flores.

Dur.: Volunteers can stay for 1 month to 1 year.

Per.: Year round.

L.term: Volunteers can stay for as long as they want.

Age: Min. 18.

Qualif.: No specific skills required.

Work: Volunteers work Monday through Friday from 8 to 12. Most work is outside and includes trail management, reforestation, gardening, minor construction, environmental education, and making arts and crafts.

Lang.: English, basic Spanish is highly desirable.

Accom.: With local families, which provide food and accommodations.

Cost: US$450/800/1,150 for 4, 8 or 12 weeks respectively; includes all food, housing (with local family), training, activities, and resources for projects.

Applic.: Via e-mail by confirming date of arrival at least 1 week in advance.

Wakuluzu: Friends of the Colobus Trust, Kenya

Colobus Trust
PO Box 5380, Diani Beach 80401 Kenya
Tel./Fax: ++ 254 (07) 1147 9453
E-mail: info@colobustrust.org
www.colobustrust.org

Desc.: The Colobus Trust is a Kenyan ONG that is committed to saving the endemic Angolan colobus monkey and preserving its threatened coastal forest habitat.

Spp.: Primates: Angolan black-and-white colobus (*Colobus angolensis palliatus*), yellow baboons, sykes, vervets, bush babies.

Hab.: Tropical coral rag forest.

Loc.: Diani Beach, south of Mombasa, Kenya.

Travel: Flight to Mombasa via Nairobi or direct.

Dur.: Preferably 3 months.

Per.: Year round.

L.term: Subject to prior approval.

Age: Preferably over 22.

Qualif.: Preferably undergraduates or graduates with experience in conservation, education, zoology, journalism, ecology, veterinary medicine, marketing, fundraising, but everyone will be considered.

Work: Primate rescue and rehabilitation, practical conservation activities (construction and repair of monkey road-crossing bridges, tree planting, invasive scrub clearance, removal of snares from forests, etc.), assisting with education workshops, ecological and primate surveys, maintenance work, office work.

Lang.: English. Swahili, German, Dutch, Italian, French are useful.

Accom.: Basic but clean and comfortable accommodation in shared rooms at the Trust headquarters.

Cost: EUR940/month or 1750 for 3 months. Food, accommodation, laundry and housekeeping are included.

Applic.: There is a standard form to be completed on the website.

Wild Chinchilla Conservation, Chile

Save the Wild Chinchillas
El Balcon, Parcela 65
Illapel, IV Coquimbo Region Chile
E-mail: amy_deane@yahoo.com
www.wildchinchillas.org

Desc.: Save the Wild Chinchillas is a conservation organisation, aiming to restore essential habitat for endangered Chilean chinchillas while deterring further habitat degradation.

Spp.: Short and long-tailed chinchillas.

Hab.: Chilean drylands.

Loc.: Aucò field station, Ilian, Chile.

Travel: Flight to Santiago, then bus to Ilapel.

Dur.: Min. 2 weeks.

Per.: Year round.

L.term: Inquire with organisation.

Age: Min. 18.

Qualif.: No particular skills are needed.

Work: Seeds collecting from mountains, follow germination in the basic nursery, and seedlings transplanting into restoration areas; surveying wild chinchillas behaviour; local community education.

Lang.: English and Spanish.

Accom.: In a wooden cabin in the Aucò field station. Food is not provided.

Cost: No charge for volunteers.

Applic.: By email. The Green Volunteers form is welcome.

Wild Ones WILD Center, Wisconsin USA

PO Box 1274
Appleton, Wisconsin 54912-8755
Tel.: 1-877-394-9453 (877-for-wild)
E-mail: wildcenter@for-wild.org; execdirector@for-wild.org
www.for-wild.org
www.wildones.org

Desc.: A not-for-profit environmental education organisation promoting the benefits of using native plants in sustainable landscaping to preserve our environmental biodiversity. Volunteers can help develop the WILD Center site to showcase preservation of pollinators and potable water by using native plant species.

Spp.: Trees and shrubs. Wetland, oak savanna and prairie, wet mesic, and ephemerals and shade flower and grass species.

Hab.: Marsh, riparian woodland, prairie, raingarden.

Loc.: Neenah, Wisconsin, USA.

Travel: Flight to Appleton, Wisconsin (Outagamie Airport).

Dur.: Min. 3 days. 1 week to 1 month ideal.

Per.: Primarily warm season months, but cool season also acceptable.

L.term: Volunteers may stay for a longer period if they wish.

Age: Min.18. No max age but fitness and good health are required.

Qualif.: No particular skills needed; enthusiasm and interest in plant life.

Work: Develop and maintain native plant demonstration areas and eradicate invasive plant species. Construct trails and boardwalks. Create educational signage and written materials. Environmentally educate local residents and visitors. Survey plant and wildlife, including birdwatching. Catalog library materials.

Lang.: English.

Accom.: Bunk bedrooms with access to dining/kitchen area, showers, toilets and computers. Outside deck overlooks Stroebe Marsh.

Cost: US$75 per week, including accommodation and transport to/from the airport. Motel accommodations within hiking distance.

Applic.: The Green Volunteers Standard Application form is welcome.

Whale Research in the St. Lawrence Estuary, Canada

Mériscope
1 rue de la Marina, Portneuf-sur-Mer, Québec Canada
Tel.: ++1 (418) 231 2033 (summer) /++41 (76) 530 9192 (winter)
E-mail: info@meriscope.com; dany@meriscope.com
www.meriscope.com

Desc.:	The 'Mériscope' is a non-profit research base on the North shore of the St. Lawrence estuary. Its projects include bioacoustics of minke, finback and blue whales, and habitat utilisation, social behaviour and feeding behaviour of baleen whales. Work is conducted with 2 rigid-hulled inflatable boats; day trips typically last 5–9hrs. Talks, lab work and land excursions complete the courses in marine biology.
Spp.:	Baleen whales: blue, finback, minke, and humpback whales. Toothed whales: belugas, sperm whales, harbour porpoises.
Hab.:	Subarctic estuary (coastal waters).
Loc.:	St. Lawrence estuary, about 350km north-east of Québec City.
Travel:	Flight to Montreal or Québec, then bus to Portneuf-sur-Mer.
Dur.:	Courses last 2 weeks, 3 courses per summer, 12 people max.
Per.:	July to October.
L.term:	Students may join for 2-4 months.
Age:	Min.18 (younger participants only accompanied by parents).
Qualif.:	No particular skills needed; reasonably good physical condition; manual and computer skills welcome.
Work:	All work is under supervision of staff biologists: data collection at sea; observation/identification of marine mammals; behavioural sampling; navigation (GPS); sound recording; photo-ID, video. Data entry, photo matching and sound analysis in the lab.
Lang.:	English, German and French.
Accom.:	4 prospector tents by the sea, with a big kitchen tent. B&B available.
Cost:	US$1,750; students US$1,590. Includes room and board (except for B&B), lectures and boat trips.
Applic.:	Standard form online or contact Dany Zbinden, project coordinator.

Whales and Dolphins Monitoring, Comoros

Moidjio Centre for Research, Conservation And Development
19 Rue Notre Dame 59670 Cassel France
Marine Park of Moheli, Nioumachoua Comoros Islands
Tel.: ++44 (789) 646 3419
E-mail: moidjio@hotmail.com
http://sites.google.com/site/moidjio

Desc.:	This organisation is recruiting volunteers to help out with ongoing research on the Comoros islands. Positions are available for people interested in research and conservation of cetacean species. Substantial training will be provided.
Spp.:	Humpback whales, spotted dolphins, spinner dolphins, Electra dolphins, bottlenose dolphins, false killer whale, Fraser's dolphins.
Hab.:	Tropical remote island of Africa.
Loc.:	Marine national park of Moheli Comoros.
Travel:	Flight to Moroni via Nairobi, and then ferry to Moheli.
Dur.:	Min. 1 month; 2-3 months is ideal.
Per.:	August to November.
L.term:	Inquire with the organisation.
Age:	15 – 70. Under 18, must be accompanied by an adult. Families are welcome.
Qualif.:	Commitment and motivation for the cause. University research projects and research training are welcome.
Work:	Volunteers help in many aspects of cetacean's conservation and research: spotting, data collection, data entry but also site and material maintenance. Use of photo-id and behavioral analyses techniques at standard level.
Lang.:	English or French.
Accom.:	Under a tent on the beach or in a local mud hut.
Cost:	GB£400/week including accommodation, food, transport from airport to the field, boat hiring, local guides and cook.
Applic.:	Before July 15th, by email.

World Bird Sanctuary, Missouri USA

125 Bald Eagle Ridge Road
Valley Park, MO 63088 USA
Tel.: ++1 (636) 225 4390
E-mail: volunteer@worldbirdsanctuary.org
www.worldbirdsanctuary.org

Desc.: World Bird Sanctuary is a non-profit organisation, whose aim is to preserve the earth and its biodiversity and habitats, working mainly with birds of prey and doing wildlife rehabilitation, education, field studies and endangered species propagation.

Spp.: Various species of native birds, such as: peregrine falcons, American kestrels, bald eagles, hawks and owls.

Hab.: Sanctuary situated in forested valley near St. Louis.

Loc.: St. Louis, Missouri, USA.

Travel: 20 minutes from International airport. Transport can be arranged.

Dur.: Typically at least 3 months. Less may be considered.

Per.: Year round.

L.term: Volunteers may stay on long term subject to approval.

Age: Min. 18.

Qualif.: Volunteers must have interest in working with animals and passion for conservation. No experience is necessary. Training provided.

Work: Work throughout the organisation, including: administration, animal husbandry, rehabilitation, handling education animals, delivering education programmes. Specialising in one area is possible with prior approval.

Lang.: English.

Accom.: Communal accommodation is provided on site, maybe shared rooms, with fully equipped kitchen. Bedding and towels required.

Cost: Accommodation and transport while on WBS business is provided. Volunteers must cover their own cost of living.

Applic.: Send e-mail with prospective dates to start application process.

INDICES

TABLE OF ORGANISATIONS AND PROJECTS BY GEOGRAPHIC LOCATION AND COST

(cost is intended approximately per week, with or without food, travel to project site is always not included)

Organisation	Africa	Asia	Europe	Mediterranean	Centr. America	South America	North America	Oceania	US$ 0–100	US$100–500	US$ 500–1500	Over US$ 1500
A' Pas de Loup	X		X			X			X			
ARCAS – Asociación de Rescate y Conservación de Vida Silvestre					X				X			
ASVO – Asociacion de Voluntarios para el Servicio en las Area Protegidas					X				X			
Bergwaldprojekt (Mountain Forest Project)			X						X			
Biosphere Expeditions	X	X	X	X	X	X	X	X			X	
Les Blongios			X						X			
Blue Ventures	X	X									X	
Brathay Exploration Group	X	X	X					X			X	
BTCV	X	X	X	X			X			X	X	
Centre for Alternative Technology			X						X			
Chantiers de Jeunes Provence Cote d'Azur			X							X		
Concordia	X	X	X	X	X	X	X	X	X			
Coral Cay Conservation		X	X		X			X			X	
Cotravaux									X			
CTS – Centro Turistico Studentesco e Giovanile			X	X					X			
CVA - Conservation Volunteers Australia/Conservation Volunteer New Zealand								X	X	X		
Earthwatch	X	X	X	X	X	X	X	X				X
Ecovolunteer Network	X	X	X	X	X	X	X	X		X	X	
EDGE of AFRICA	X								X	X		
ELIX – Conservation Volunteers Greece			X	X					X			
EUROPARC Deutschland			X						X			
Frontier	X	X			X	X		X			X	
Gapforce	X	X	X		X	X	X	X	X	X	X	
Geography Outdoors	X	X	X	X	X	X		X		X	X	X
Global Service Corps	X	X						X			X	X
Global Vision International	X				X					X	X	
Hellenic Ornithological Society			X	X					X			
Iceland Conservation Volunteers			X						X			
International Otter Survival Fund			X							X		

TABLE OF ORGANISATIONS AND PROJECTS BY GEOGRAPHIC LOCATION AND COST

(cost is intended approximately per week, with or without food, travel to project site is always not included)

	Africa	Asia	Europe	Mediterranean	Centr. America	South America	North America	Oceania	US $0–100	US$100–500	US$ 500–1500	Over US$ 1500
Involvement Volunteers Association	X	X	X	X	X	X	X	X			X	
IUCN – The World Conservation Union	X	X	X	X	X	X	X	X	X			
Legambiente			X	X						X		
LIPU Italian League for Protection of Birds			X	X						X		
Mingan Island Cetacean Research Expeditions					X		X				X	
The National Trust			X						X			
The Nature Corps							X			X		
NZTCV - The New Zealand Trust for Conservation Volunteers								X	X			X
Oceanic Society Expeditions					X	X	X	X			X	
Operation Wallacea	X	X			X	X					X	
Raleigh International		X			X						X	
RSPB – The Royal Society for the Protection of Birds			X						X			
SANCCOB – South African Foundation for the Conservation of Coastal Birds	X								X			
SCA – Student Conservation Association							X		X			
SCI – Service Civil International			X				X	X	X			
Tethys			X	X							X	
United Nations Volunteer (UNV)	X	X			X	X			X			
USDA Forest Service							X		X			
US Fish and Wildlife Service							X		X			
US National Park Service							X		X			
Volunteer Latin America					X	X			X			
Volunteers for Outdoor Colorado							X		X			
Wilderness Foundation, the	X		X		X	X	X			X		
WWF Italy	X	X	X	X	X	X	X	X		X		
YCI - Youth Challenge International	X			X	X	X	X	X			X	

PROJECTS	Africa	Asia	Europe	Mediterranean	Centr. America	South America	North America	Oceania	US $0–100	US$100–500	US$ 500–1500	Over US$ 1500
ACE - American Conservation Experience, Arizona USA							X		X			
Adriatic Dolphin Project, Croatia				X								X

TABLE OF ORGANISATIONS AND PROJECTS BY GEOGRAPHIC LOCATION AND COST

(cost is intended approximately per week, with or without food, travel to project site is always not included)

	Africa	Asia	Europe	Mediterranean	Centr. America	South America	North America	Oceania	US$ 0-100	US$100-500	US$ 500-1500	Over US$ 1500
African Impact Lion Rehabilitation Programmes, Zambia	X										X	
Altai Snow Leopards Survey Expedition, Russia		X									X	
American Bear Association, USA							X		X			
Andean Bear Research Project, Ecuador						X			X			
Andean Condor and Puma Surveys, Peru						X					X	
Animal Aid Unlimited, India		X							X			
Antigua Nesting Turtles Arché Project, West Indies					X					X		
APES - Umpalazi Community and Wildlife Project, South Africa	X									X		
The Ara Project, Costa Rica					X				X			
Azafady, Madagascar	X									X		
BDRI - Bottlenose Dolphin Research Institute, Italy				X						X		
Bimini Lemon Shark, Bahamas					X					X		
BioMindo, Ecuador									X			
Black Howler Monkey Project, Argentina						X				X		
Black Sheep Inn, Ecuador						X			X			
Blue Mountains Conservation, Iceland			X							X		
Bohorok Environmental Center, Indonesia		X								X		
Brown Bear Project, Russia			X							X		
California Wildlife Center, California USA							X		X			
Cambodian Marine Biodiversity Monitoring and Conservation										X		
Cano Palma Biological Station, Costa Rica					X					X		
Cape Tribulation Tropical Research Station, Australia								X		X		
Cardigan Bay Marine Wildlife Centre, Wales UK			X						X			
Caretta Research Project, Georgia USA							X				X	
Cats of Rome, Italy			X							X		
Cats Unlimited Wildlife Foundation, Namibia	X										X	
Centre for Dolphin Studies (CDS), South Africa	X									X		
Centre for Wolf Studies, Russia		X								X		
CERCOPAN, Nigeria	X								X			

236

TABLE OF ORGANISATIONS AND PROJECTS BY GEOGRAPHIC LOCATION AND COST

(cost is intended approximately per week, with or without food, travel to project site is always not included)

Organisation	Africa	Asia	Europe	Mediterranean	Centr. America	South America	North America	Oceania	US$ 0–100	US$100–500	US$ 500–1500	Over US$ 1500
Cetacean Research & Rescue Unit (CRRU), Scotland UK			X							X		
Cetacean Research Project, Scotland UK			X								X	
Cetacean Sanctuary Research, Italy and France				X							X	
Charles Darwin Foundation, Galapagos						X						X
Cheetah Conservation Fund, Namibia	X								X			
Cheetah Conservation, Botswana	X									X		
Chiloé Silvestre Wildlife Rehabilitation Centre, Chile						X			X			
Cochrane Ecological Institute (CEI), Canada							X		X			
Comunidad Inti Wara Yassi, Bolivia						X			X			
Conservation of Gialova Lagoon, Greece				X					X			
Conservation Volunteering in St. Lucia, Caribbean					X					X		
CREES Volunteers Programme, Peru						X			X			
Crocodile Conservation, India		X							X			
Dolphin Research Center, Florida USA							X			X		
Dolphins and Sea Life around the Maltese Islands, Malta				X					X			
Donkey Sanctuary, the Netherlands Antilles					X				X			
Earthwise Valley Sustainable Living Programme, New Zealand								X				
East African Whale Shark Trust, Kenya	X								X			
Eco-City in Bahia de Caraquez, Ecuador						X			X	X		
El Eden Flora y Fauna: Animal Rescue and Rehabilitation, Argentina						X			X	X		
Elephant Nature Park, Thailand		X								X		
Endangered Species Conservation, South Africa	X								X		X	
Everything Elephants, South Africa	X								X		X	
Faia Brava Reserve, Portugal			X						X			
Fauna Forever Tambopata, Peru						X				X		
Flat Holm Island, Wales UK			X						X			
Fundación Proyecto Ecologico Chiriboga, Ecuador						X			X			
Giant Panda Reserve, China		X								X		
Gibbon Rehabilitation Project, Thailand		X								X		

TABLE OF ORGANISATIONS AND PROJECTS BY GEOGRAPHIC LOCATION AND COST

(cost is intended approximately per week, with or without food, travel to project site is always not included)

	Africa	Asia	Europe	Mediterranean	Centr. America	South America	North America	Oceania	US$ 0–100	US$100–500	US$ 500–1500	Over US$ 1500
GoEco, Israel				X						X		
La Gran Vista Agroecological Farm, Costa Rica					X					X		
Great Whales in their Natural Environment, Canada							X				X	
Grey Wolf Recovery & Sanctuary, Oregon and Idaho USA							X		X			
Griffon Vulture Conservation Project, Croatia			X							X		
Grupo Lobo, Portugal			X									
Hawaiian Forest Restoration Project, Hawaii USA							X		X			
Hellenic Wildlife Hospital, Greece				X					X			
Hoedspruit Endangered Species Centre, South Africa	X									X		
Iguana Research and Breeding Station (IBRS), Honduras					X				X			
International Conservation Volunteer Exchange, Nevada USA							X		X			
Ionian Dolphin Project, Greece				X							X	
Iracambi Atlantic Rainforest Research and Conservation Center, Brazil						X			X			
Irish Seal Sanctuary, Ireland			X						X			
Ischia Dolphin Project, Italy				X							X	
Jaguar Conservation, Brazil						X			X			
Jatun Sacha, Ecuador						X			X			
Karumbé Sea Turtles Project, Uruguay						X				X		
Kido - WIDECAST Sea Turtles Nesting Monitoring, Grenada					X					X		
Klipkop Wildlife Sanctuary, South Africa	X									X		
La Hesperia, Ecuador						X			X			
Leatherback Seaturtle Tagging Programme, Grenada					X					X		
Leatherback Turtle Conservation, Costa Rica and Panama					X					X		
Leatherback Turtle Project, Costa Rica					X					X		
Madagascar Fauna Group Station	X											
Marine Conservation and Diving, Tanzania	X								X			
The Marine Mammal Center, (TMMC), California USA							X				X	
Marine Turtles Adriatic ARCHE' Project, Italy				X					X			
Marine Turtle & Youth Environmental Education, Mexico					X				X			

238

	Africa	Asia	Europe	Mediterranean	Centr. America	South America	North America	Oceania	US $0–100	US$100–500	US$ 500–1500	Over US$ 1500
Mediterranean Marine Research Project, Spain			×							×		
Mission Rhino 2020, Nepal		×								×		
The Monkey Sanctuary, England			×						×			
Monte Adone Wildlife Protection Centre, Italy			×						×			
Munda Wanga Wildlife Park and Sanctuary, Zambia	×									×		
Naucrates Conservation Project, Thailand		×								×		
Nkombi Research and Volunteer Programme, South Africa	×									×		
Noah's Arc, Greece				×					×			
The Oceania Research Project, Australia								×			×	
Orangutan Foundation, Indonesia		×								×		
Orangutan Health, Indonesia		×									×	
Orangutan Tropical Peatland Project (OuTrop), Indonesia		×								×		
Orchid Conservation, Ecuador						×			×			
Pandrillus Foundation, Nigeria	×								×			
Peace River Refuge & Ranch, Florida USA							×			×		
Penguin Research, Argentina and Chile						×			×			
Project Kial, Australia								×	×			
Project «MEER» La Gomera, Spain			×							×		
Proyecto Campanario, Costa Rica					×					×		
Rainsong Wildlife Sanctuary, Costa Rica					×				×			
Rathlin Island Seabird Centre, Northern Ireland			×						×	×		
Reef Check Global Coral Reef Monitoring					×	×	×	×	×	×		
Reserva Pacuare, Costa Rica					×				×	×		
Rhino Rescue Project, Swaziland	×									×	×	
Rolda Rescue Center, Romania			×						×			
The Rumi Wilco Nature Reserve and Ecolodge, Ecuador						×			×		×	
Saving Kenya's Black Rhinos, Kenya	×								×			
Scottish Wildlife Rescue, Scotland UK			×						×			
Sea Turtle Conservation Program, Costa Rica					×				×	×		

TABLE OF ORGANISATIONS AND PROJECTS BY GEOGRAPHIC LOCATION AND COST

(cost is intended approximately per week, with or without food, travel to project site is always not included)

Organisation	Over US$ 1500	US$ 500–1500	US$100–500	US$ 0–100	Oceania	North America	South America	Centr. America	Mediterranean	Europe	Asia	Africa
Sea Turtle Conservation Project, Greece				X					X			
Sea Turtle Conservation Projects, Costa Rica			X					X				
Sea Turtle Rescue Centre, Greece				X					X			
Sea Turtle Summer Field Work, Greece				X					X			
Shisong, Kumbo, Cameroon				X								X
Siberian-East Russian Volunteer Program, Russia			X								X	
Skaftafell National Park, Iceland			X							X		
SOS Tartarugas (Turtle SOS), Cabo Verde			X									X
Southwestern Research Station, Arizona USA				X		X						
Sri Lanka Elephant Conservation Experience		X									X	
Sustainable Livelihood Development Association, Sri Lanka				X							X	
Tambopata Macaw Project, Peru				X			X					
Tambopata Resident Naturalist Program, Peru				X			X					
Tiny Island Turtles Project, Maldives			X								X	
Tolga Bat Hospital, Australia				X	X							
Tree Planters Farm, Australia				X	X							
Trees For Life, Scotland UK				X						X		
Turtle Conservation Project (TCP), Sri Lanka				X							X	
Turtles and Birds of Tortuguero, Costa Rica			X					X				
University of Georgia San Luis Research Station, the, Costa Rica	X							X				
Vervet Monkey Rescue Project, South Africa			X									X
Volunteer Peten, Guatemala				X				X				
Wakuluzu: Friends of the Colobus Trust, Kenya				X								X
Wild Chinchilla Conservation, Chile				X			X					
Wild Ones WILD Center, Wisconsin USA				X		X						
Whale Research in the Saint Lawrence Estuary, Canada		X				X						
Whales and Dolphins Monitoring, Comoros		X										X
World Bird Sanctuary, Missouri USA				X		X						

TABLE OF ORGANISATIONS AND PROJECTS BY SPECIES OR GROUP OF SPECIES

(species or group of species are indicated with common names)

Organisation / Project	Various Spp.	Trees/Vegetat.	Birds	Sea Turtles	Amph./Reptile	Corals	Sharks	Seals	Whales/dolph.	Oth. Mammals	Wolves/Canids	Felines	Primates	Bears	Bats	Africa Herbiv.
A' Pas de Loup				X				X			X					X
ARCAS – Asociación de Rescate y Conservación de Vida Silvestre			X	X	X					X		X	X	X		
ASVO - Asociacion de Voluntarios para el Servicio en las Area Protegidas	X	X	X	X	X					X			X	X		
Bergwaldprojekt (Mountain Forest Project)		X														
Biosphere Expeditions	X		X							X	X	X	X	X		X
Les Blongios	X	X														
Blue Ventures	X					X										
Brathay Exploration Group	X		X													
BTCV	X	X	X		X								X			
Centre for Alternative Technology	X															
Chantiers de Jeunes Provence Cote d'Azur	X															
Concordia	X															
Coral Cay Conservation	X					X										
Cotravaux	X															
CTS - Centro Turistico Studentesco e Giovanile	X			X	X				X	X	X			X		
CVA – Conservation Volunteers Australia/ Conservation Volunteer New Zealand	X		X	X	X				X	X						
Earthwatch	X		X	X					X	X		X	X	X		X
Ecovolunteer Network	X		X	X					X	X	X	X	X	X		X
EDGE of AFRICA	X		X							X		X				X
ELIX – Conservation Volunteers Greece			X													
EUROPARC Deutschland		X														
Frontier	X	X				X				X						
Gapforce	X		X			X							X			
Geography Outdoors	X		X													
Global Service Corps	X															
Global Vision International	X	X				X				X						X
Hellenic Ornithological Society			X	X												
Iceland Conservation Volunteers	X	X	X	X						X						
International Otter Survival Fund										X						

TABLE OF ORGANISATIONS AND PROJECTS BY SPECIES OR GROUP OF SPECIES

(species or group of species are indicated with common names)

	Africa Herbiv.	Bats	Bears	Primates	Felines	Wolves/Canids	Oth. Mammals	Whales/dolph.	Seals	Sharks	Corals	Amph./Reptile	Sea Turtles	Birds	Trees/Vegetat.	Various Spp.
Involvment Volunteers Association																X
IUCN – The World Conservation Union																X
Legambiente																X
LIPU - Italian League for the Protection of Birds														X		
Mingan Island Cetacean Research Expeditions								X								
The National Trust															X	
The Nature Corps															X	X
NZTCV - The New Zealand Trust for Conservation Volunteers															X	X
Oceanic Society Expeditions							X	X			X		X	X		X
Operation Wallacea		X		X	X		X				X	X	X	X	X	X
Raleigh International					X										X	X
RSPB – The Royal Society for the Protection of Birds														X		X
SANCCOB – South African Foundation for the Conservation of Coastal Birds														X		X
SCA – Student Conservation Association															X	X
SCI – Service Civil International								X							X	X
Tethys Research Institute								X								
United Nations Volunteer (UNV)															X	X
USDA Forest Service							X								X	X
US Fish and Wildlife Service							X							X	X	X
US National Park Service															X	X
Volunteer Latin America				X			X					X		X	X	X
Volunteers for Outdoor Colorado															X	X
Wilderness Foundation, the			X												X	X
WWF Italy								X					X	X	X	X
YCI - Youth Challenge International							X							X	X	X

PROJECTS

	Africa Herbiv.	Bats	Bears	Primates	Felines	Wolves/Canids	Oth. Mammals	Whales/dolph.	Seals	Sharks	Corals	Amph./Reptile	Sea Turtles	Birds	Trees/Vegetat.	Various Spp.
ACE- American Conservation Experience, Arizona USA															X	X
Adriatic Dolphin Project, Croatia								X								

TABLE OF ORGANISATIONS AND PROJECTS BY SPECIES OR GROUP OF SPECIES

(species or group of species are indicated with common names)

Organisation / Project	Africa Herbiv.	Bats	Bears	Primates	Felines	Wolves/Canids	Oth. Mammals	Whales/dolph.	Seals	Sharks	Corals	Amph./Reptile	Sea Turtles	Birds	Trees/Vegetat.	Various Spp.
African Impact Lion Rehabilitation Programmes, Zambia	X				X											
Altai Snow Leopards Survey Expedition, Russia					X		X									
American Bear Association, USA			X													
Andean Bear Research Project, Ecuador			X													
Andean Condor and Puma Surveys, Peru					X		X							X		
Animal Aid Unlimited, India				X		X	X							X		
Antigua Nesting Turtles Arché Project, West Indies													X			
APES - Umpalazi Community and Wildlife Project, South Africa				X												
The Ara Project, Costa Rica														X		
Azafady, Madagascar				X								X		X	X	
BDRI - Bottlenose Dolphin Research Institute, Italy								X								
Bimini Lemon Shark, Bahamas										X						
BioMindo, Ecuador														X	X	
Black Howler Monkey Project, Argentina				X	X	X	X							X	X	
Black Sheep Inn, Ecuador			X												X	
Blue Mountains Conservation, Iceland														X	X	
Bohorok Environmental Center, Indonesia				X											X	
Brown Bear Project, Russia			X													
California Wildlife Center, California USA						X	X							X		
Cambodian Marine Biodiversity Monitoring and Conservation								X	X				X	X		X
Cano Palma Biological Station, Costa Rica				X		X	X					X	X	X		X
Cape Tribulation Tropical Research Station, Australia		X													X	
Cardigan Bay Marine Wildlife Centre, Wales UK								X	X							X
Caretta Research Project, Georgia USA													X			
Cats of Rome, Italy					X											
Cats Unlimited Wildlife Foundation, Namibia	X				X	X										
Centre for Dolphin Studies (CDS), South Africa								X								
Centre for Wolf Studies, Russia						X										
CERCOPAN, Nigeria				X												
Cetacean Research & Rescue Unit (CRRU), Scotland UK								X								

243

TABLE OF ORGANISATIONS AND PROJECTS BY SPECIES OR GROUP OF SPECIES

(species or group of species are indicated with common names)

Organisation / Project	Africa Herbiv.	Bats	Bears	Primates	Felines	Wolves/Canids	Oth. Mammals	Whales/dolph.	Seals	Sharks	Corals	Amph./Reptile	Sea Turtles	Birds	Trees/Vegetat.	Various Spp.
Cetacean Research Project, Scotland UK								X	X	X				X		
Cetacean Sanctuary Research, Italy and France								X	X	X						X
Charles Darwin Foundation, Galapagos								X	X	X		X	X	X	X	X
Cheetah Conservation Fund, Namibia					X											
Cheetah Conservation, Botswana					X									X		X
Chiloé Silvestre Wildlife Rehabilitation Centre, Chile						X	X									
Cochrane Ecological Institute (CEI), Canada				X	X	X	X					X		X	X	X
Comunidad Inti Wara Yassi, Bolivia				X	X									X		X
Conservation of Gialova Lagoon, Greece							X							X	X	
Conservation Volunteering in St. Lucia, Caribbean				X	X		X					X		X	X	X
CREES Volunteer Programme, Peru												X		X	X	X
Crocodile Conservation, India												X				
Dolphin Research Center, Florida USA								X								
Dolphins and Sea Life around the Maltese Islands, Malta								X					X	X		
Donkey Sanctuary, the Netherlands Antilles							X				X					
Earthwise Valley Sustainable Living Programme, New Zealand							X			X						
East African Whale Shark Trust, Kenya										X						
Eco-City in Bahia de Caraquez, Ecuador				X			X					X		X	X	X
El Eden Flora y Fauna: Animal Rescue and Rehabilitation, Argentina				X	X		X							X	X	
Elephant Nature Park, Thailand							X									
Endangered Species Conservation, South Africa	X				X	X										
Everything Elephants, South Africa	X															
Faia Brava Reserve, Portugal				X			X							X		
Fauna Forever Tambopata, Peru							X					X		X	X	
Flat Holm Island, Wales UK														X		
Fundación Cabo San Francisco, Ecuador							X					X		X	X	X
Fundación Proyecto Ecologico Chiriboga, Ecuador					X		X					X		X	X	X
Giant Panda Reserve, China			X	X			X							X	X	
Gibbon Rehabilitation Project, Thailand				X										X		
GoEco, Israel					X	X	X					X	X	X		X

244

TABLE OF ORGANISATIONS AND PROJECTS BY SPECIES OR GROUP OF SPECIES

(species or group of species are indicated with common names)

Organisation / Project	Africa Herbiv.	Bats	Bears	Primates	Felines	Wolves/Canids	Oth. Mammals	Whales/dolph.	Seals	Sharks	Corals	Amph./Reptile	Sea Turtles	Birds	Trees/Vegetat.	Various Spp.
La Gran Vista Agroecological Farm, Costa Rica				X	X		X							X	X	
Great Whales in their Natural Environment, Canada								X								
Grey Whales Research Expeditions, Canada								X								
Grey Wolf Recovery & Sanctuary, Oregon and Idaho USA						X										X
Griffon Vulture Conservation Project, Croatia														X		
Grupo Lobo, Portugal						X										
Hawaiian Forest Restoration Project, Hawaii USA															X	
Hellenic Wildlife Hospital, Greece							X							X		X
Hoedspruit Endangered Species Centre, South Africa	X				X	X								X		X
Iguana Research and Breeding Station (IBRS), Honduras												X				X
International Conservation Volunteer Exchange, Nevada USA															X	X
Ionian Dolphin Project, Greece								X							X	
Iracambi Atlantic Rainforest Research and Conservation Center, Brazil							X					X		X	X	X
Irish Seal Sanctuary, Ireland									X							
Ischia Dolphin Project, Italy								X								
Jaguar Conservation, Brazil					X											
Jatun Sacha, Ecuador							X					X		X	X	X
Karumbé Sea Turtles Project, Uruguay													X			
Kido - WIDECAST Sea Turtles Nesting Monitoring, Grenada													X			
Klipkop Wildlife Sanctuary, South Africa	X															
La Hespería, Ecuador												X		X	X	X
Leatherback Seaturtle Tagging Programme, Grenada													X			
Leatherback Turtle Conservation, Costa Rica and Panama													X			
Leatherback Turtle Project, Costa Rica													X			
Madagascar Fauna Group Station				X			X									
Marine Conservation and Diving, Tanzania												X	X			
Marine Mammal Center (TMMC), California USA								X	X		X	X				
Marine Turtles Adriatic ARCHE' Project, Italy												X	X			
Marine Turtle & Youth Environmental Education, Mexico													X			
Mediterranean Marine Research Project, Spain											X					X

TABLE OF ORGANISATIONS AND PROJECTS BY SPECIES OR GROUP OF SPECIES

(species or group of species are indicated with common names)

	Africa Herbiv.	Bats	Bears	Primates	Felines	Wolves/Canids	Oth. Mammals	Whales/dolph.	Seals	Sharks	Corals	Amph./Reptile	Sea Turtles	Birds	Trees/Vegetat.	Various Spp.
Mission Rhino 2020, Nepal							X									
Monkey Sanctuary, the, England				X												
Monte Adone Wildlife Protection Centre, Italy				X	X		X					X		X		X
Munda Wanga Wildlife Park and Sanctuary, Zambia	X			X	X	X	X							X		X
Naucrates Conservation Project, Thailand											X		X		X	
Nkombi Research and Volunteer Programme, South Africa	X					X	X							X		X
Noah's Arc, Greece					X	X	X									X
Oceania Research Project, the, Australia								X								
Orangutan Foundation, Indonesia				X												
Orangutan Health, Indonesia				X												
Orangutan Tropical Peatland Project (OuTrop), Indonesia				X										X	X	X
Orchid Conservation, Ecuador															X	
Pandrillus Foundation, Nigeria				X												
Peace River Refuge & Ranch, Florida USA		X	X	X	X	X	X									X
Penguin Research, Argentina and Chile														X		
Project Kial, Australia							X						X			
Project «MEER» La Gomera, Spain								X		X						
Proyecto Campanario, Costa Rica				X			X					X		X		X
Rainsong Wildlife Sanctuary, Costa Rica				X			X					X		X		X
Rathlin Island Seabird Centre, Northern Ireland														X		
Reef Check Global Coral Reef Monitoring											X					
Reserva Pacuare, Costa Rica					X		X					X	X	X		X
Rhino Rescue Project, Swaziland	X															
Rolda Rescue Center, Romania					X	X										
The Rumi Wilco Nature Reserve and Ecolodge, Ecuador							X					X		X	X	X
Santa Martha Rescue Centers, Ecuador			X	X	X	X	X							X	X	X
Saving Sweetwaters' Rhinos, Kenya	X			X	X	X	X							X		
Scottish Wildlife Rescue, Scotland UK		X												X		
Sea Turtle Conservation Program, Costa Rica												X	X			
Sea Turtle Conservation Project, Greece												X	X			

TABLE OF ORGANISATIONS AND PROJECTS BY SPECIES OR GROUP OF SPECIES

(species or group of species are indicated with common names)

Organisation or Project	Various Spp.	Trees/Vegetat.	Birds	Sea Turtles	Amph./Reptile	Corals	Sharks	Seals	Whales/dolph.	Oth. Mammals	Wolves/Canids	Felines	Primates	Bears	Bats	Africa Herbiv.
Sea Turtle Conservation Projects, Costa Rica				X												
Sea Turtle Rescue Centre, Greece				X												
Sea Turtle Summer Field Work, Greece				X												
Shisong, Kumbo, Cameroon	X	X	X							X				X		
Siberian-East Russian Volunteer Program, Russia	X	X	X							X	X					
Skaftafell National Park, Iceland		X	X					X								
SOS Tartarugas (Turtle SOS), Cabo Verde				X												
Southwestern Research Station, Arizona USA	X	X	X		X											
Sri Lanka Elephant Conservation Experience										X						
Sustainable Livelihood Development Association, Sri Lanka		X														
Tambopata Macaw Project, Peru	X	X	X		X					X		X	X			
Tambopata Resident Naturalist Program, Peru	X	X	X		X					X		X	X			
Tiny Island Turtles Project, Maldives				X	X	X										
Tilos Park Association, Greece		X	X													
Tolga Bat Hospital, Australia															X	
Tree Planters Farm, Australia		X														
Trees For Life, Scotland UK		X														
Turtle Conservation Project (TCP), Sri Lanka				X												
Turtles and Birds of Tortuguero, Costa Rica			X	X												
University of Georgia San Luis Research Station, the, Costa Rica	X	X	X		X					X			X			
Vervet Monkey Rescue Project, South Africa													X			
Volunteer Peten, Guatemala	X	X	X		X					X			X			
Wakuluzu: Friends of the Colobus Trust, Kenya													X			
Wild Chinchilla Conservation, Chile										X						
Wild Ones WILD Center, Wisconsin USA																
Whale Research in the Saint Lawrence Estuary, Canada									X							
Whales and Dolphins Monitoring, Comoros									X							
World Bird Sanctuary, Missouri USA			X													

ORGANISATION ALPHABETICAL INDEX

PROJECT ALPHABETICAL INDEX

THE *Green Volunteers* PHOTO CONTEST

Good photographs of wildlife and people together are extremely rare, especially those that give the idea of involvement and participation, which is what *Green Volunteers* is all about. *Green Volunteers* is therefore launching a contest among all its readers and active volunteers. We are looking for good pictures of wildlife together with people (possibly volunteers) to be published in our website and to be chosen as the cover picture (such as the picture on the current cover) for future issues of the Guide.

If your pictures get published, you will not be paid by *Green Volunteers* but you will have the opportunity of helping your favourite project by allowing it to receive more exposure and therefore more volunteers, and you will have the satisfaction to see your picture published in our website. *Green Volunteers* will award US$ 100 to the pictures that will be chosen for covers of next issues of the Guide. Please send your pictures exclusively via e-mail (possibly in low density) to: green@greenvolunteers.org. No picture will be used for publication without prior permission of the photographer. If the picture is selected, you will be contacted, and asked if your picture can be added to our website. **Make sure, however, that for taking your pictures of volunteers in action you don't interfere with the work of the project. We look forward to seeing your great pictures. Good luck with your Green Volunteering!**

STANDARD APPLICATION FORM
Green Volunteers © 2011

To be photocopied enlarged, retyped or downloaded from the Green Volunteers Database (ask for a User ID and password to access it, see contacts at www.greenvolunteers.org). This is not an official application form; many organisations have their own, others may accept this.
(Please print)

Last name: .... First name: ....

Nationality: .... Date of birth: .... Passport nø:................................

Occupation:..

Address for correspondence:..

Tel.: .... Fax : .... E-mail: ....

Next of kin (name, address and tel. number): ....
....

If you are a student, write the name and address of the school, College or University:
....

Mother tongue:.. Other languages spoken:
excellent:.......................very good:...................... good:....................... basic:................................

Education:...

Indicate your experience in volunteering (also in other fields) or in participating in environmental projects, wildlife rescue centres, fieldwork, camping, backpacking or other outdoor activities:
....
....
....

Skills which may be useful to the project:
....
....
....

Are you a member of any environmental organization? If yes, specify:
....

Do you have any health problems? If yes, specify:
....

Indicate your preferences for project's dates and location:
....

Any additional relevant information (feel free to add additional pages):
....
....
....

Date: ..... / ..... /...... Signature: ....

255

From the same publisher

(available from your bookstore or from website **www.greenvolunteers.com**)

Green Volunteers – The World Guide to Voluntary Work in Nature Conservation

Over 200 projects worldwide for those who want to experience active conservation work as a volunteer, also without previous experience. Projects are year round, in a variety of habitats, from one week to one year or more. From dolphins to rhinos, from whales to primates, this guide is ideal for a meaningful vacatiion or for finding thesis or research opportunities.

Price: £11.99 €16.00 $ 16.95   Pages: 256

World Volunteers – The World Guide to Humanitarian and Development Volunteering

About 200 projects and organisations worldwide for people who want to work in international humanitarian projects but don't know how to begin. Opportunities are from 2 weeks to 2 years or longer. An ideal resource for a working holiday or a leave of absence. A guide for students, retirees, doctors or accountants, nurses or agronomists, surveyors and teachers, plumbers or builders, electricians or computer operators... For everyone who wants to get involved in helping those who suffer worldwide.

Price: £11.99 €16.00 $ 16.95   Pages: 256

Archaeo-Volunteers – The World Guide to Archaeological and Heritage Volunteering

Over 180 projects and organisations in the 5 continents for those who want to spend a different working vacation helping Archaeologists. Placements are from 2 weeks to a few months. For enthusiastic amateurs, students and those wanting hands-on experience. Cultural and historical heritage maintenance and restoration and museum volunteering opportunities are also listed. The guide also tells how to find hundreds more excavations and workcamps on the Internet.

Price: £11.99 €16.00 $ 16.95   Pages: 240